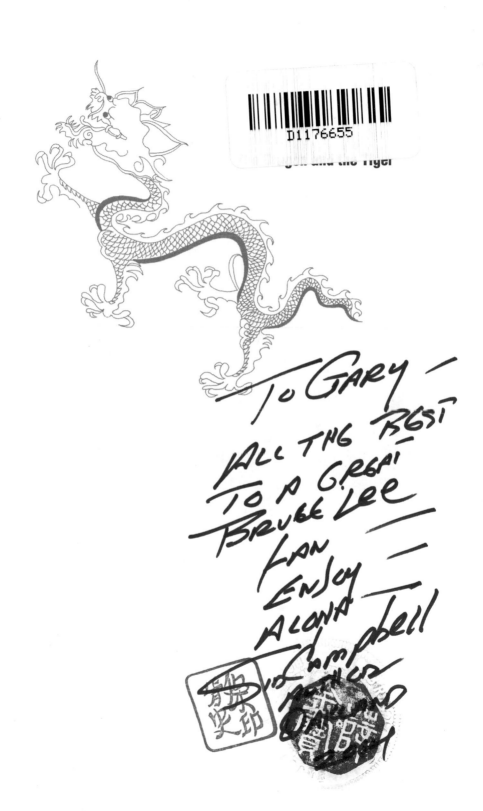

...gon and the Tiger

To GARY —

ALL THE BEST
TO A GREAT
BRUCE LEE
FAN
ENJOY
ALOHA
Campbell

The
Dragon
and

the
Tiger

The Birth of BRUCE LEE's
Jeet Kune Do

The Oakland Years, Volume 1

Sid Campbell and Greglon Yimm Lee

Frog, Ltd.
Berkeley, California

Published by Frog, Ltd.
Frog, Ltd. books are distributed by
North Atlantic Books
P.O. Box 12327
Berkeley, California 94712

Cover design by Paula Morrison
Book design by Brad Greene
Printed in Canada

North Atlantic Books' publications are available through most bookstores. For further information, call 800-337-2665 or visit our website at www.northatlanticbooks.com.

Substantial discounts on bulk quantities are available to corporations, professional associations, and other organizations. For details and discount information, contact our special sales department.

Library of Congress Cataloging-in-Publication Data

Lee, Greglon, 1953-
    The dragon and the tiger : the birth of Bruce Lee's Jeet Kune Do, the Oakland years / by Greglon Lee and Sid Campbell.
        p. cm.
    ISBN 1-58394-089-8 (pbk.)
    1. Lee, Bruce, 1940-1973. 2. Lee, J. Yimm (James Yimm) 3. Martial artists—United States—Biography. 4. Motion picture actors and actresses—United States—Biography. 5. Jeet Kune Do. I. Campbell,
Sid. II. Title.
    GV1113.L44L45 2003
    796.8'092—dc21

                                                            2003012827
                                                            CIP

1 2 3 4 5 6 7 8 9 TRANS 08 07 07 06 05 04 03

To you, the reader

Contents

Preface

Destiny is defined as something that is fated to happen to particular persons or things. For lack of a better word, destiny seems the cause when two great men meet and are instantly attracted by a common interest in a subject. So it was with the late Bruce Lee and James Yimm Lee, who were destined to achieve greatness that exceeded their broadest expectations.

The Dragon and the Tiger is the story of these two martial artists from a historical perspective, true accounts of the formative years of their friendship in Oakland, California. Although Bruce Lee went on to achieve stardom in the world of cinema, little has been documented of these earlier years, when many of his ideas, concepts, techniques, and martial arts talents were gradually becoming a reality. His early exploits were crucial in preparing him for the bigger and better things that were destined to enter his short life. *The Dragon and the Tiger* is a story of creative genius, philosophical enchantment, comradeship, evaluation and development of martial arts principles, determination, and zealous achievements. It is also the story of two men who shared a love for an art that seemingly exceeded the boundaries of sheer physical ability.

Bruce Lee and James Yimm Lee were unique in many distinct ways. Each had a tremendous impact on the other in a way that goes beyond the facade of a passing friendship; they were friends, business associates, and most of all, brothers in the spirit. The accounts in this book will present a side of two men dedicated to the study and perfection of martial arts that few have had the opportunity to witness.

Many of the parallels that existed between Bruce and James are astounding, to say the least, and the Oakland years with the Dragon and the Tiger may quite possibly be the last piece of the puzzle concerning the lives of Bruce and James and the impact that Bruce Lee had on the world. Many facts and little known anecdotes have come to light nearly twenty years after the untimely deaths of these great martial arts pioneers, through the dedicated efforts of those who have known Bruce and James personally. The compilation of this enormous work has required literally thousands of hours of painstaking research. If the result of these thousands of hours of research contributes, in a true and factual manner, the missing details surrounding the lives of these incredible men who literally changed the course of martial arts practice and its development over the past thirty years, then the efforts of the authors will have been considered worthwhile in every sense of the word.

Sid Campbell
Greglon Yimm Lee

Acknowledgments

Bruce Lee Photographs Foundation Digital Transcription

Editing

Negative Scanning

Photo Contributions

Magazine Articles

Photo Credits

Bruce Lee Educational

Bruce Faron

Robin Klassen

Jude Anthony

Richard Baca

Michael Bishop

Jess O'Brien

Wade Fox

Martin Eng

Karena Lee (Oakland Bruce Lee Fan Club)

James Lee Estate

Linda Lee

Black Belt Magazine

Karate International Magazine

George Lee

Leo Fong

Inside Kung Fu magazine

Felix Macias Sr. and Jr.

Black Belt Magazine

Karate International Magazine

Inside Kung Fu magazine

Barry Hay

Todd Mathews (Seattle)

Newspaper Articles	*Oakland Tribune*
Publicity (Article)	*Kickboxx Magazine*
Staff Writer	George Estrada
Freelance Writer	James Carter
Magazine Article	David Cox
Marketing and Promotion	Robert Alsted
Sifu Gin Foon Mark	Dr. Marty Eisen
Maps	MapQuest
Seattle Research	Wing Luke Asian Cultural Museum
Letter Contributors	Al Novak
	Wally Jay
	Ed Parker
	Professor Ralph Castro
	George Lee
	Dan Inosanto
	Bob Baker
	John Lee
	Ed Kim Yee
	Eric Lee
	Robert Garcia Jr.
	Karena Beverly Lee
	Jim Wong
	Hilton Wong
	Ernest Benavidez
	Felix Macias Sr.
	Gary Cagaanan
	Jasper Cummings
	George Tom

	Bryant Wong
	Norman Marks
	Sifu Ming Lum
	Dr. James Durkins
	Sam Allred
	Aloy and Claire Brunk
	Ricky Ramirez
Seattle History	Kyoshi Tom Tanaka
	De Welle F. "Skip" Ellsworth
	Taky Kimura
	James DeMile
	Joe Cowles
	Jesse Glover
	Johnny Williams Jr.
	Seattle Times newspaper
Additional Photos	San Francisco Historical Society
	United States
Additional Photo Credits	New York Tourist Information Bureau
	Chinese Opera Historical Society
	De Welle F. "Skip" Ellsworth
	James DeMile
	Joe Cowles
	Jesse Glover
	Quan Ging Ho
	Taky Kimura

Prologue
The Dragon's Rowdy Beginning

On the morning of November 27, 1940, in the Chinese year of the dragon, Lee Jun Fan was born in San Francisco, California, under the supervision of Dr. Mary Glover. The baby boy's mother, Grace Lee, had not considered an American name for him. At the time of the unexpected birth, his father, Lee Hoi Cheun, was touring as a comedic entertainer with a Chinese opera troupe that was visiting the United States from Hong Kong. Dr. Mary Glover, who delivered the child, thought of the name Bruce. Grace Lee agreed to the name, and from then on, the baby became known as Bruce Lee. Bruce was one of five children born to the Lee family. He had two brothers, Peter and Robert, and two sisters, Agnes and Phoebe.

After the completion of the Chinese opera tour, the Lee family returned to their home in Hong Kong, but not before Bruce, at the age of three months, made his first appearance as a stand-in baby in an American film entitled *Golden Gate Girl*. By the time that Bruce was four, he and several of his siblings had performed as walk-on extras for a Chinese war play produced in Hong Kong. And when Bruce was six, at the request of the director, Bruce was offered a part in his father's latest Chinese film. From this early beginning, Bruce eventually accumulated over twenty roles in Chinese motion pictures produced in Hong Kong. This stage of his career, from age six to his midteens, concluded with his last child role in a film entitled *Orphan*, which was an enormous success. It was probably during these formative years that Bruce developed a love of theatrics and acting that would follow him throughout his career.

During his childhood years, like other children of his age, Bruce developed many interests. Within the Lee family and among many of his childhood friends, he became known for the practical jokes and surprising tricks he would play. When he was very small, his sister Agnes gave him the nickname "the Little Dragon," a name that would follow him into his adult years.

When he was a teenager, much of Bruce Lee's energy began to be negatively channeled into a growing involvement with the street gangs that were becoming increasingly popular in Hong Kong at the time. He began to get in more and more street fights, and through these encounters, he developed an incessant desire to win, becoming furious in situations in which he fared poorly. Many of these gang-style fights occurred while he was attending LaSalle Junior High School in Hong Kong and continued even after he had graduated and begun attending Saint Francis Xavier Catholic High School. In his school years, Bruce became very wild and realized that, out of necessity and in order to back up his verbal challenges, he should begin the study of the sophisticated self-defense system known as Wing Chun. Although Bruce had studied several other styles of self-defense prior to his involvement with Wing Chun, he felt that this style had more to offer in his encounters with Hong Kong gang members. He immediately began training under Wing Chun master Yip Man, the head of a style that had a lineage extending back over four hundred years. As Bruce began his training with Yip Man, many of his fears of humiliation that had evolved from his street fighting episodes began to disappear. By the time that he entered Saint Frances Xavier High School, he had become a proficient martial artist, as well as a rather feared bully and street fighter.

It was during these crisis years that Bruce expressed an avid interest in dancing and excelled in a ballroom dance style known as cha-cha. With his natural grace and a keen sense for picking up complicated movements and step patterns, he had very little difficulty in learning the dances. He spent countless hours practicing and developing the extremely complex dance routines. As a result of this effort, Bruce eventually became the Hong Kong Crown Colony cha-cha champion.

During Bruce Lee's high school years, the street fighting continued, until his mother threatened to tell his father if Bruce did not start behaving. Since Bruce had a great respect for his father and knew that his father abhorred violence of any kind, Grace Lee assumed this threat would put a halt to their child's rowdy and often mischievous behavior. Unfortunately, Bruce continued to engage in street fighting.

One of the brothers at Saint Frances Xavier High School, Brother Edward, decided it was time to give Bruce a lesson in humility and invited him to the boxing room to put on the gloves and go a few rounds in a friendly match. Although Bruce had never boxed before, he held his own quite well, due to his gung fu training in Wing Chun. Brother Edward recognized Bruce's natural talent and invited Bruce to join the boxing team. Bruce reluctantly joined but refused to train or practice the conventional boxing methods. This did not seem to affect his combat skills. Shortly afterward, in the school boxing tournament, Bruce defeated the boy who had been champion three years in a row. This period certainly must have had an effect on Bruce Lee's later techniques, which would evolve from these experiences.

From the time that the Hong Kong motion picture *Orphan* was released, Bruce's popularity as an actor began to rise, and as a result, Run Run Shaw, an extremely powerful Hong Kong producer, asked Bruce to sign an actor's contract. Having never really liked school and the rigid discipline associated with education, Bruce decided that he would quit and accept Shaw's offer, with the hope of becoming a movie star. Although his mother was convinced that Bruce could become a star, she was fearful of what was happening to him. He was heavily involved with street fighting, movie parts, and social life, and she wanted Bruce to complete his education and receive his diploma; so when he was picked up by the police for fighting, she forbade him to accept Run Run Shaw's offer. In addition, to remove him from the society that she felt was causing his downfall, Grace Lee made arrangements to send her son to the United States to finish his high school education. So in 1959, Bruce Lee boarded an American President Lines ship and set sail to America, where, as his mother had hoped, he completed his high school education and then began attending the University of Washington in Seattle.

Before relocating to Seattle from Kowloon (across Hong Kong harbor from Hong Kong), Bruce had the opportunity to travel to San Francisco to visit a family friend, Quan Ging Ho, an administrator of the Hong Kong Cantonese Opera. The Lee family had met him when Bruce's father was performing with the Chinese opera, and Quan Ging Ho had known Bruce since his birth in San Francisco.

During his brief stay, Bruce had the occasion to accompany Ging Ho to a house party sponsored by Brian Lum, a family relative of James Yimm Lee. Bruce had just turned twenty. He was welcomed as an old acquaintance of Quan Ging Ho. At the dinner,

Bruce entertained the guests by performing gung fu, dancing the cha-cha, and telling jokes in both Chinese and English. He was the life of the party. Everyone was very impressed with his natural and relaxed talent and physical abilities. His reputation traveled throughout the Chinese communities in both Oakland and San Francisco.

Two weeks later Bruce attended a dance at Victory Hall in San Francisco. The dance gave him a chance to sharpen his dancing skills while demonstrating his ability to perform the complex steps that had helped him win the cha-cha championships in Hong Kong. His dancing abilities stood out among the rest of the crowd, and it became apparent to many that this was the same person that had made such an impression at Brian Lum's house party a few weeks before.

Bob and Harriet Lee, brother and sister-in-law of James Yimm Lee, were present at the dance and, having heard of this young Chinese dance performer, took the opportunity during an intermission to meet him. Consequently, through this casual encounter an acquaintance became a key to Bruce's destiny and future career development.

Later, Bruce moved on to Seattle to attend school. To subsidize his tuition at the Edison Technical Vocational School and at the University of Washington, Bruce worked as a busboy and a waiter at the popular Chinese restaurant known as Ruby Chow's. For a considerable period of time, he lived in a small room on the third floor of the restaurant in exchange for his services. But Bruce soon tired of the menial task of waiting tables and eventually quit the job and began teaching Wing Chun gung fu professionally. All the while, he attended the University of Washington.

The Tiger's Humble Beginning

At 8:30 A.M. on January 31, 1920, Lee Kein Heir was born at his parent's house at 927 Webster Street in Oakland, California. Although Lee Kein Heir is recorded on James Yimm Lee's birth certificate, shortly after his birth he was given an American name that included the original family surname. His father's real Chinese surname had been Yimm, but he had changed it to Lee for immigration purposes upon entering the United States. Lee Kein Heir would be known as James Yimm Lee, and James would always feel it was proper to include his true surname when his American name was used.

James Yimm Lee 's proud parents were Lee Look On and Ching Shee Lee. Lee Look On was born in San Francisco in 1880. During his adult years, he established himself as a merchant. For a time, Lee Look On was the proprietor of a shrimp company on Harrison Street in Oakland's Chinatown. He later became a tailor and even ran a prosperous gambling house. James's mother, Ching Shee Lee, was born in China in 1880 and later immigrated to the United States and assumed the American name of Alice Lee.

The Lee family was blessed with three sons and five daughters. There was Jon Y. Lee, Robert Lee, James Yimm Lee, Helen (Lee) Lai, Jamie (Lee) Fong, Jennie (Lee) Lew, Mabel (Lee) Chin, and Gladys Lee, who died of polio at a young age. James was quite close to his older brothers Jon and Robert; the oldest, Jon, was like a second father to young James and seemed to be the only person who could control James or offer him the discipline he needed when he stepped out of line or became mischievous.

All of the Lee children attended local elementary schools in the Bay Area and later attended the local high schools near their home. None of James's brothers or sisters showed any particular interest in athletics, being more scholastically oriented. James was the complete opposite. By the age of ten, James was beginning to excel at sports and other physical activities and had already expressed an avid interest in physical development and martial arts.

James had no intentions of going to college; he had never excelled in the scholastic academic programs offered at the grade school and high school he attended. While in his teens, he became very preoccupied with physical fitness and weight lifting and at the age of eighteen, while still attending Oakland Technical High School, James broke the Northern California weight-lifting record in his weight class. At the time, he was a member of the Oakland YMCA weight-lifting team.

By the time that he had graduated from Oakland Technical High School in January of 1939, James had won many awards for his outstanding performances in gymnastics, wrestling, and even ama-teur boxing. His physique had developed quite nicely, and though he was only five feet, six inches tall, with a very slight frame, he was highly defined. For several years after his graduation at the age of nineteen, James was totally engrossed with physical fitness. Many of his friends would call him nicknames, such as "Shoulders" Lee, Lee the "Vee" man, or, because of his bold and confident attitude, "Tiger" Lee. By the time that James was twenty, the confidence and physical abilities that he had acquired through constant training prompted many of the people in Oakland's Chinatown to refer to him as a real roughneck with a reputation for quickly resorting to his fists. His reputation as a rather tough kid often required him to defend himself against individuals that did not see eye to eye with him. James soon realized that, if he was going to survive, he would need a profession that would gain him financial independ-ence. At the age of twenty, he was accepted as an apprentice welder at the Mare Island naval shipyards in Vallejo, California, and began in earnest to acquire a trade that would become the mainstay of his career. He quickly learned the techniques of the welding trade, and after working with naval ships and submarines for about one and a half years, he began feel the urge for travel and excitement. As the result of a request to transfer to Pearl Harbor, Hawaii, James arrived there on December 1, 1941, just six days before the Japanese were to bomb Pearl Harbor. So it was that, at the young age of twenty-one, James was plunged directly into one of the most devastating battles that ever raged in the Pacific. Before the final bombings had subsided, James, along with many other shipbuilders and welders, was immediately put to work.

For the next two and a half years, James and his coworkers worked tirelessly trying to help salvage what was left of the United States naval fleet. During this time, James began seriously studying martial arts. He and several of his fellow workers began to train in the arts of judo and jujitsu with the late Professor Okazaki at his martial arts gym in Honolulu. On occasions when the workers could not attend the classes at the school, Professor Okazaki would form special classes at the bus terminal near the workers' living quarters.

Early in June of 1944, after nearly three years of intermittent martial arts training and continual work to restore the salvaged ships, James Yimm Lee returned to Oakland to visit his family and friends. Two months later, having been involved with the war firsthand in Pearl Harbor, James was inducted into the United States Army. He and both of his brothers joined the army to fight for their country. After a brief stint in basic training, in November 1944, James was stationed at Fort Knox, Kentucky, where he attended radio operator school. Upon completion of the necessary training, he was attached to the 716th Tank Battalion in the Philippine Islands.

During his tour of duty in the Philippines, James Yimm Lee saw plenty of action and was in combat against the Japanese at the Luzon campaign. Although he was primarily a radio operator stationed with the tank battalion, out of necessity he also became a machine gunner. James was also engaged in the Mindanao campaign, for which he received the Asiatic Pacific Theater Ribbon with two bronze stars, the Philippine Liberation Ribbon, and the World War II Victory Medal. James was never wounded in action during the fierce combat, but during the latter part of the Philippine campaign, he contracted malaria. Before the close of the war, he had severe reoccurring bouts of this tropical fever, nearly dying in the intense South Pacific and weakening his physical condition considerably. On January 10, 1946, he departed the Philippines for intense medical supervision and, eight days later, was registered at Letterman General Hospital in San Francisco, California. After three months of treatment and medical attention, James was released from the United States Army with an honorable discharge and 30 percent medical disability pay. Having seen action in the South Pacific for the duration of the war, he was awarded the rank of private first class and assigned to the 801st Military Police Battalion of San Francisco, California.

◎◎

On returning home to Oakland, California, James resided for the next five years with his father at his home on 321 Perkins Street in Oakland. James remained a confirmed bachelor and resumed his weight training and bodybuilding to restore his health. He was determined to get in the best physical shape of his life. To sustain his livelihood, he took a civilian position as an electric welder for a local firm. During those intense five years, he and many of his friends and close associates from before the war began to train regularly at many of the physical fitness clubs in the Oakland area. This was a very formative time in James's life.

While attending a dinner party given by one of his close friends, James Yimm Lee met a very attractive woman by the name of Katherine Margaret Chow; she would become his wife and the mother of his children. Katherine was raised in San Jose, California, and was one of three daughters of Fannie Chow, a widow. Katherine's sisters were Rebecca (Chow) Eastman and Esther (Chow) Louie. The Chow family had grown up on a farm in San Jose, and Katherine had attended San Jose State College for two years but had never graduated. She had worked as a waitress, a Chinese cook, a clerk-typist for the federal government and at the naval air station in Alameda, California. Before meeting James, Katherine had been married twice before and had a son named Richard Jeong. Like James, Kathy, as her close friends knew her, could speak excellent English and Cantonese dialect. They soon discovered that they shared similar interests, in literature and poetry, and life in general. They began dating after their first introduction and fell in love. They were married on October 13, 1951, by the district judge of Washoe County, Nevada. James was thirty-one and Katherine was thirty.

The following year, they were blessed with a beautiful baby girl who they named Karena Beverly Lee. As the Lees established their new home life in the Oakland area, they were soon blessed with a second child, a son, who was born on Halloween day in 1953. They named their son Greglon Yimm Lee, forming his unusual first name by combining the names of their favorite movie stars, Gregory Peck and Marlon Brando. Soon after Greglon's birth, the Lee family moved to 584 Valle Vista Avenue in Oakland. During this time, both James and Katherine developed new interests and hobbies;

Katherine took an interest in knitting, sewing, gardening, and became involved with church activities, and even began taking professional singing lessons, eventually cutting several records. James took a fond interest in his children and spent hours at a time teaching them about nature, spending great amounts of time outdoors. In addition to bodybuilding and a renewed interest in the practice of martial arts, his first love was for his two children and his wife.

By the late 1950s, James had begun training at the Kin Mon Chinese Institute on Waverly Place in San Francisco's Chinatown, under the tutelage of Professor T. Y. Wong, a noted authority in the Sil Lum art of Chinese gung fu. This proved to be a very rewarding experience for James, and he spent more than three years pursuing the ancient methods of self-defense taught by Professor Wong.

By 1957, James Yimm Lee's martial arts sincerity was beginning to blossom through several outlets. He became involved in operating a weight lifting gym and began to demonstrate his skill in traditional martial arts techniques and martial arts weapon practice. He also began writing and publishing martial arts books and incorporated his welding skills to develop and produce unique training equipment for improving the martial arts practitioner's skills and capabilities. Although James considered many of his creative endeavors involving martial arts and physical development to be primarily hobbies, his insight and creativity were those of a true martial arts pioneer. He was never satisfied with the developments or creations that he constructed and was constantly striving to improve their performance in a way that would better suit the serious martial arts practitioner.

During this time, he wrote the books *Fighting Arts of the Orient, Elemental Karate and Kung Fu,* and *Modern Kung Fu Karate, Iron Poison Hand Training.* These books taught how to construct training equipment for developing and strengthening the hands and feet and demonstrated the proper training methods to prepare to break large stacks of solid bricks without causing injury. A layman, with only 100 days of proper training, could perform many of the breaking techniques taught in James's books.

Much of the Sil Lum knowledge that he had learned from Professor T. Y. Wong, which James continued to practice, was beginning to appear in print so that others could benefit from this information. James Lee was one of the first martial arts practitioners to give the non-Asian American people an insight into the rare and ancient methods of self-defense that had previously only been taught to the Asian community. The years he spent in high school learning boxing, gymnastics, and wrestling, coupled with his experiences while learning judo and jujitsu in Hawaii and the years training at the Sil Lum gung fu school in San Francisco's Chinatown, made him a prime candidate to present this knowledge to people outside Asian communities. James Lee's creative talents extended into the mail-order book business, from which he sold many of his publications, as well as those of other popular martial arts authors of the time. He was instrumental in supplying guidance for other aspiring martial artists who wished to publish their creative works. During these creative years, James constantly remained loyal to his family and supported them through his job as a welder but all of his additional spare time was devoted to finding ways that gung fu could be improved.

☯

Chapter One

The Beginning

Bruce Lee Returns to America

The Hong Kong harbor was bustling with the activities of small boats and Chinese junks that were scurrying about between Hong Kong and the coastal mainland city of Kowloon. Nothing was particularly unusual on this humid spring day in 1959 except that another large American President Lines passenger liner was readying for departure to San Francisco. The crew was preparing for the twenty-day voyage; the passengers were all on board and lined the side of the large vessel while family and friends bid them farewell from the dock. The ship's horn sounded, giving a warning for the junks in the nearby vicinity to make way for the liner. On the starboard side of the deck stood a young Chinese man who was filled with excitement as he waved to his family and friends who had come to see him off. A bold journey to a distant land in the Western world would be enough to excite even the most reserved of individuals, and this almost nineteen year old already had visions of prospering in a strange new world, which was also the place of his birth. Indeed, for him San Francisco was going to be a sight to behold. As the final command for cast off was called, the ship began to move slowly away from the pier. The junks and small water taxis made way for the hulking steamship as it gradually moved into the South China Sea.

For Bruce Lee, this was the opportunity of a lifetime. With the ship's small passageways and crowded quarters, Bruce knew he would have many opportunities to make new acquaintances and to share experiences of life in Hong Kong with his fellow passengers during the course of the journey. The diverse lifestyles found upon the huge sailing vessel were familiar in many respects to what Bruce was accustomed, but the constant rolling of the ship across the rough water was a totally new experience for him. Although many different activities were available on board, Bruce found the dance hall was where he had the most fun. There he could express his unique physical abilities in dance, which completely captivated the shipboard passengers. He was extremely creative and had developed new and innovative dance steps, which he blended into his cha-cha routines. This activity made it easy for him to be at ease with his fellow passengers. It was both fun and rewarding, and greatly helped him pass the time while sailing for the distant port of San Francisco.

After what seemed like almost three months of traveling across the vast waters of the Pacific Ocean, the captain finally announced that they would soon be disembarking in the fabled city of San Francisco. Thoughts of a new life, an education, new friends, and a chance for an exciting career, all ran through Bruce's mind as the ship passed under the Golden Gate Bridge and cruised toward the pier. As he collected his thoughts and pondered his future, he was comforted to know that his sister Agnes was awaiting his arrival, as was Mr. Quan Ging Ho. Mr. Quan, an administrator for the Hong Kong Cantonese Chinese Opera, had been a very close friend of the family when his father had been performing in the Chinese opera tour nineteen years ago.

Thoughts of consequence intermittently clashed with his feelings of anxiety and anticipation. Bruce knew that there were very important tasks that he must address when he set foot on solid ground. First and foremost on his list was the necessity to claim his birthright as an American citizen. Becoming adjusted to the American way of life, completing his high school education, and then attending a university were the next most important priorities. Bruce possessed a reasonably confident level of skill in the art of Wing Chun gung fu, and he was a champion cha-cha dancer. He reasoned that maybe these achievements might well serve him in this new environment. It would be a serious test of his skills for him to survive in this Western world. Bruce further surmised that, with his determination, he could become someone important; in this vastly populated nation, he knew he could do anything he set his mind to, and no one would be able to stop him.

As the dock workers finally secured the mooring lines of the huge ship, Bruce stood on the main deck and searched the docks intensely for his sister. Perplexed at not finding her, he disembarked and descended the stairway into the waiting crowd. Instead of Agnes, Mr. Quan Ging Ho spotted Bruce and rushed to greet him. Bruce was elated to recognize a friend of the family who had cared to see that he had arrived safely.

After clearing customs and exiting the terminal, Bruce and Mr. Quan began the drive through the busy streets of San Francisco. Bruce's parents had made the arrangement that he would stay at Mr. Quan's home while he reclaimed his birthright and made plans for the completion of his education. He was relieved to see that things were beginning to fall into place.

The next several months consisted of excursions to many places around the Bay Area. Bruce started to become comfortable in his new setting and began to adapt to American life. He was meeting new people and attending parties and recitals hosted by Mr. Quan. Every day held different adventures and new challenges for a stranger in a new land. Bruce had been in San Francisco for only a short period after his birth, but he still felt something mystical and special about being in his birthplace of which he had only heard his family talk during reminiscences of his father's travels with the Chinese opera. There was nothing like actually experiencing the wonder firsthand to understand the significance.

Mr. Quan was impressed with Bruce's ability as a dancer and thought that it could be an excellent way for Bruce to earn some extra money. It would also give him a chance to meet many people in the Chinese community and possibly make some contacts for future employment. Although Bruce knew that he would not be in San Francisco for long before going to Seattle to attend college, he concurred with Mr. Quan that teaching dance classes would be a quick and easy way to earn additional spending money. Besides, he had to keep his dance routines sharp if he was going to mention that he was the 1958 Hong Kong cha-cha champion.

Mr. Quan arranged for Bruce to begin teaching at a ballroom dance club in San Francisco. The cha-cha seemed to be the dance that everyone wanted to learn, and word of Bruce's dancing skill quickly spread. Bruce was teaching quite a few couples in a very short time. This was quite exciting for Bruce, as he put together a routine in which he would give dance instruction and then afterward perform various Wing Chun gung fu techniques. He started to improvise new dance routines that were both funny and technically difficult. His students really enjoyed these comical yet highly skilled performances. He had a program that included dancing, martial arts, and comedy all rolled into one.

The classes were somewhat grueling, but Bruce was in good physical condition and he enjoyed the way that the students responded to him. Their enthusiasm made him perform better than ever, and the lesson fee of one dollar per session kept him in spending money. Within three months, Bruce had developed dance and martial arts routines in both English and Chinese languages; this helped increase the enrollment in his classes.

On the weekends, he would often attend the dances held at Victory Hall in San Francisco and would give flawless performances, which both impressed and sometimes embarrassed the other dancers. After a dance one Saturday night, Mr. Quan and Bruce were invited to a house party hosted by Brian Lum. Unbeknownst to them, this event would mark the beginning of an era that has never been paralleled in the history of martial arts. Mr. Brian Lum was the brother of Harriet Lee, who in turn was the wife of Robert Lee. James Yimm Lee was Robert Lee's younger brother.

◎◎

On Friday, June 19, 1959, Quan Ging Ho received a telephone call from Bruce's father, Hoi Cheun, who was in New York City. He reported that the twenty-four-member Hong Kong Cantonese Opera Troupe had arrived in Manhattan's Chinatown to begin their three-week performance schedule. Mr. Quan passed the telephone to Bruce, who had a lengthy conversation with his father. Upon concluding the conversation, Bruce informed Quan Ging Ho that his father wanted to fly him to New York for several weeks to be with him while he was performing. The following Monday morning, Quan Ging Ho procured a roundtrip airline ticket in Chinatown for Bruce to fly to New York's LaGuardia Airport. Bruce departed San Francisco by midmorning and had a one-hour layover in Chicago before continuing his flight into New York. His evening arrival was met with a warm greeting from his father and several production management staff members from the troupe.

Bruce was elated that his father had greeted him with such warmth and kindness. He could not remember such a greeting or meeting with his father ever before. His father had welcomed him as a full-grown man and not like the young son that had caused him so much grief and trouble back home. This greeting was entirely different from that which he had expected from his usually stern father. Only a few short months prior, his father had constantly reprimanded him for inappropriate behavior back home in Kowloon.

On the way back to their quarters in Chinatown, Hoi Cheun described the opera and production that was opening that Friday evening. For the next three weeks, he would be performing in the show and meeting with many of his old New York friends, many of whom were old acquaintances that he and Grace only saw when he was performing with the show there in New York. He also praised Mr. Quan Ging Ho for his gracious hospitality and assistance in caring for Bruce while he was temporarily visiting in San Francisco. Bruce also had a chance to update his father on the status of his academic pursuits. He said that he was in the process of officially registering at the Edison Technical Vocational School in Seattle and, if things went as planned, would be starting school there on September 23. His father was happy that things were going so well and that his son was keeping busy doing something productive with his life. Quan Ging Ho had reported in previous telephone conversations that Bruce was adapting very well to life in America and had been teaching cha-cha lessons to various groups in the Oakland and San Francisco areas to earn additional income. Hoi Cheun was very pleased to know that his son Bruce was becoming a responsible citizen and had been doing things that did not get him in trouble with the law. He was also pleased that Bruce had renewed his United States citizenship and that it was now good for another seventeen years.

⊚⊚

Bruce Enters the World of the Praying Mantis

Hoi Cheun was participating in rehearsals and getting familiar with the positioning on the stage. Bruce had seen this preparatory ritual on numerous occasions and was not at all enamored with the details of preshow production planning. Hanging around a theater stage all day while lighting was adjusted, backdrops were fastidiously being arranged, and costume fittings were going on simply did not appeal to Bruce's sense of the adventure of his first trip to New York City. Besides, he had seen so many Chinese opera performances and rehearsals back in Hong Kong that, after a while, they all seemed the same.

Bruce asked his father if he knew of any gung fu kwoons (schools) located in Manhattan's Chinatown. Hoi Cheun told Bruce that his friend Mr. Jiao Juyin, a longtime friend who worked with the opera productions here, and another longtime New York associate, Mr. Tom Bin Yong, the owner of Bo Bo Chinese restaurant further up on Mott Street, would certainly know if any gung fu sifu (teachers) were in the area. Bruce remembered Tom Bin Yong from his visits to their home in Kowloon but did not remember him being from New York or owning a restaurant. When he was much younger, and on the dozen or so times that Tom Bin Yong had visited their home in Kowloon, Bruce remembered always calling him "Uncle Yong."

Later that morning Hoi Cheun contacted both Jiao Juyin and Tom Bin Yong by telephone. Roughly thirty minutes later, Mr. Jiao Juyin was at the theater. Hoi Cheun was happy to see his old friend, and after renewing their comradeship and reminiscing of times past in New York, Hoi Cheun introduced Bruce. The conversation swiftly gravitated toward the subject of martial arts. Bruce was anxious to know if any Chinese sifu taught in Chinatown. Jiao said that he knew a very skillful sifu by the name of Gin Foon Mark that taught the southern style of Praying Mantis gung fu over on East Broadway, about eight blocks away from the theater. Hoi Cheun then added that he'd also heard of a gentleman by that name that taught Hung Gar gung fu, but he had always thought that the sifu only taught privately sponsored members and their families who belonged to the Chinese Benevolent Society Association. He was not 100 percent sure, but as he recollected, most of the Chinese sifu in America were pretty selective in whom they accepted as members and that it was doubtful that Bruce would be accepted in those closed associations. Jiao then stated that Gin Foon Mark had stopped teaching exclusively for private associations there in Chinatown and had decided to open a commercial kwoon to teach anyone that wanted to learn. He was not only teaching Hung Gar but also Praying Mantis gung fu and had been teaching publicly for about two years. This piqued Bruce's interest even more. He asked Mr. Jiao Juyin if he thought it was possible if he could be introduced to this gung fu sifu. Jiao suggested that they discuss it over lunch, while Hoi Cheun continued rehearsing his parts and working with the production crew.

After a short walk of several blocks over to 17 Mott Street, they entered Wo Hop's Chinese restaurant. It was a cliquish two-floor eatery and was very popular with the opera crowd. Literally hundreds of autographed publicity photos of famous opera stars, local Chinatown actors, and celebrity film stars that had visited and eaten at Wo Hops were displayed. Jiao pointed out a photograph of Bruce's father on the wall near the rear of the establishment. As Bruce perused this fluorescent-and-linoleum grotto, he could tell that this old restaurant was a landmark in Chinatown. Over the years, it undoubtedly amassed much nostalgia and fond memories for the many opera performers and movie stars that had gathered there to eat after the final evening performances.

Once seated upstairs, after ordering, Bruce began asking Mr. Jiao many questions. Jiao confided that he had been Hoi Cheun's friend for a number of years and that they always got together when he was in New York performing with the Hong Kong Cantonese Opera Troupe. Mr. Jiao could see that Hoi Cheun's son was a persistent lad. Mr. Jiao wanted to talk about family and generalities, and Bruce kept redirecting the conversation back to the topic of Chinese gung fu and his sifu friend. Jiao said that his friend Sifu Gin Foon Mark, a very skillful gung fu man, had taught there in Chinatown for twelve years and was well respected for his fighting skills and teaching talents. Because of his young age, by sifu standards, he had been challenged to numerous Chinatown backstreet matches and had come up victorious.

Mr. Jiao said that there was a time when almost every gung fu sifu in New York's Chinatown kept their kwoons secret, and unless you were a family member or belonged to one of the benevolent societies or Chinese associations, it was very doubtful that you would even be admitted much less train with a sifu there. Gin Foon Mark had broken away from this old tradition and was teaching students regardless of their ethnicity. He would teach solely based on a student's desire to pursue the art of gung fu. Sifu Gin Foon Mark was the first sifu in New York to do this, and many other Sifu there were not pleased with his decision.

This information inspired Bruce to ask more questions and to want to meet this mysterious gung fu teacher even more. He wanted to know why gung fu was so secret and guarded by the sifu in America when it was practiced openly back in Hong Kong and most of China. Mr. Jiao explained that most Chinese here, especially gung fu sifu, thought that foreigners would not understand the true philosophy and use of gung fu and so it was dangerous to teach them. They felt that non-Asians only wanted to use gung fu for acquiring superior fighting abilities and did not choose to see its health aspects and social benefits. Sifu Gin Foon Mark was one of the progressive Chinese martial artists that believed that all people were the same. He believed the responsibility rested on the teacher for guiding students in the way of righteousness when teaching potentially deadly martial art skills that had been rooted in Chinese culture for almost 1,500 years. Bruce was hanging on every word and was anxiously looking forward to meeting this Praying Mantis sifu, who seemed to be liberal in his way of thinking. Bruce wondered if this master's Praying Mantis gung fu was as good as his Wing Chun.

After eating lunch and stopping along the street at several shops, Bruce found himself and Mr. Jiao walking back in the direction of the Chinese Opera Theater. Upon their return, Hoi Cheun was engaged in a spirited conversation with Mr. Tom Bin Yong, who had finally arrived from his restaurant on Mott Street. Seeing Bruce for the first time in several years brought a broad smile to Yong's face, as he rushed to greet Bruce as they entered the backstage area. Bruce was also elated to see the man he so affably referred to as uncle for so many years when he visited their home in Kowloon. Hoi Cheun introduced Jiao Juyin to Tom Bin Yong, and as they stood around becoming acquainted, Hoi Cheun invited everyone to have tea in his dressing room. Bruce followed the trio as they retired to the small cubicle to chat about the old times in New York. It was here that Bruce learned that his Uncle Yong was also a long-time friend of Gin Foon Mark.

That night at Mr. Tom Bin Yong's Bo Bo restaurant, Hoi Cheun, Bruce, and Jiao Juyin were honored as special guests of the upscale Chinatown establishment. Bruce was still preoccupied with the idea of meeting Gin Foon Mark at his kwoon, but he knew that other matters were going to take precedence over his desire to meet this sifu. However, during breaks in the conversation Bruce artfully steered discussion back in the direction of gung fu. Uncle Yong had confirmed that he knew several good gung fu sifu in Chinatown and that Sifu Gin Foon Mark was one of the most distinguished martial art teachers in the area.

Although Mr. Jiao had earlier agreed to take Bruce the following day to meet the sifu, Uncle Yong insisted that he would take time off from the restaurant and personally make the introduction to Sifu Mark. Mr. Jiao acquiesced graciously, since Uncle Yong insisted so profusely. Besides, Mr. Jiao recognized that it had been such a long time since Uncle Yong had seen his Bruce and that they wanted to catch up on old times. Uncle Yong also promised to show Bruce some of the sights of New York City. Bruce appreciated the kind gesture from his father's longtime friend.

Early the following afternoon Uncle Yong came to Hoi Cheun's apartment to pick Bruce up. Hoi Cheun had already departed to pick up costume alterations for his nightly performance and would be going to rehearsal at the theater after that. Bruce asked Uncle Yong where he had met the gung fu man, Gin Foon Mark. Yong was caught off guard by the direct question, but he saw that Bruce was quite obsessed with learning all there was to know about Mr. Mark. Uncle Yong disclosed that they had met when Sifu Mark taught at the Chinese Benevolent Society there in Chinatown, prior to Sifu Mark's decision to open his own commercial kwoon a couple of years back.

Most of the day that followed, Uncle Yong drove Bruce around Manhattan and some of the other boroughs in New York City, showing him the sights and giving him some of the history of the town. Bruce thought the traffic was almost as congested as the streets of Hong Kong or Kowloon. Uncle Yong thought that was funny, since he could relate to the experience of Hong Kong as well.

As Uncle Yong continued to chauffeur Bruce around, Bruce kept commenting on just how big New York City really was. He was spellbound by the enormous size of the buildings and width of the streets. Even more so than San Francisco, New York was gigantic in every sense of the word. The Statue of Liberty, the Empire State Building, Brooklyn Bridge, Ellis Island, the United Nations Building and the financial district were all notable landmarks that were indelibly etched in his memory.

During their excursion around New York, Uncle Yong had a chance to tell Bruce more about Sifu Gin Foon Mark. He mentioned that Sifu Gin Foon Mark worked as a chef at the Hilton Hotel there in New York and taught gung fu in the evenings. Uncle Yong recalled that Gin Foon Mark had mentioned that he was teaching at his kwoon Mondays through Thursdays, in the evenings after he finished cooking at the hotel. Uncle Yong confided that he had not been to the new kwoon on East Broadway, but he knew exactly where it was from the directions Gin Foon Mark had given. It was just east of West Houston Street on East Broadway. Sifu Mark had said that there were always students there in the day working out, but it was easiest to reach him during the evenings. In any case, he was sure there would be no difficulty finding the kwoon because everyone in the neighborhood knew Sifu Mark quite well.

Bruce was incessant in his pursuit of knowledge about this sifu who had been so highly touted by Uncle Yong and Mr. Jiao. Bruce brought up Mr. Jiao's comment about the Chinese associations not wanting Sifu Mark to teach people outside of their organization. Bruce was curious about the reasoning behind that peculiar position. Uncle Yong said that since Sifu Mark had opened a commercial kwoon and was accepting people outside of the ethnic Chinese nationalities, he had had a few problems with the elderly members of the various benevolent societies and associations in Chinatown. Bruce wanted to know why there had been problems. Uncle Yong enlightened him by simply stating that the Chinese in New York City had always been very secretive about their cultural affairs. They did not like things like the martial arts, which they considered potentially deadly, to be shared with those outside of their associations. As Uncle Yong put it, it was their "ace in the hole" when it came to defending themselves. Bruce said that he thought they were being selfish. Uncle Yong replied that that was exactly how Gin Foon Mark felt about it.

As they drove over the Manhattan Bridge, returning to Chinatown, the vast city looked like it was waking up. The sun was slowly setting, and the New York skyline was coming alive with the glitter of lights. They took the Canal Street exit and made their way toward Broadway. Turning right onto East Broadway, they began searching for a place to park. Several blocks up, on East 3rd Street, Yong found a parking space that had just become available.

Bruce and Uncle Yong then began their trek through the less than glamorous streets of the nontourist area of New York's Manhattan Chinatown, until they reached East Broadway. From there they turned left and started walking toward Bond Street. Uncle Yong then instructed Bruce to keep an eye out for a three-story building with an opaque plate glass window that prevented people from looking inside. After a moment of thought, he added that Sifu Mark had also mentioned that there was a bar in the basement and that his kwoon was the only business on the first floor. He said there was a small sign that read "Gung Fu" on the outside, next to the door. A half block down on the left Uncle Yong spotted the building. They crossed the street through traffic as they approached the building, which was notably in a state of disrepair. Bruce was getting anxious to meet the sifu that he had heard so much about. He hoped to see for himself just how skillful this gung fu master was and how his techniques would compare with what Bruce had seen back in Kowloon.

After several minutes of persistently knocking on the old door of the kwoon's nondescript facade, the door slowly opened.

SIFU GIN FOON MARK

Sifu Gin Foon Mark has been teaching gung fu for more than fifty years. In 1947, he began teaching in Chinatown, New York, when some trade associations requested that he instruct their young members. He has had kwoons in New York, Philadelphia, and Minneapolis. In Philadelphia, he had classes in a YMCA, and at Temple University and taught self-defense to the police. He is one of the few living people who were trained in monasteries when they were strongholds of gung fu.

Gin Foon Mark, came from a family of four generations of gung fu experts. His gung fu studies began at the age of five, under his uncles and grandfather. At the age of nine, he was admitted to the Chun San Shaolin Temple and studied with the famous monk Ki Fut Sai. Gin Foon Mark received instruction in Sil Lum, White Crane, Eagle Claw, Leopard, and Tiger. He also studied Tiger Claw in the Hoi Jung Temple, Praying Mantis in the Jook Lum Monastery and Moo Gai, a martial form of qigong similar to tai chi. In these monasteries, Sifu Gin Foon Mark was schooled in ming kung, self-defense and healing arts; shin gung, spirit gung fu; chi kung, the use of internal power for martial arts and health. This included iron shirt, iron palm, cotton palm, and dim mak. He continued his studies of Praying Mantis in the United States under Lum Wing Fay for ten more years. When Sifu Lum retired, he designated Gin Goon Mark to be his successor in accordance with established tradition. Sifu Mark thought so highly of Praying Mantis that he decided to devote his life to only teaching this system even though he was an expert in other systems.

Sifu Mark was one of the first masters to openly teach gung fu to non-Asians. Since he was famous, he was selected to appear on *You Asked for it*. This television program depicted the reunion of Sifu Gin Foon Mark and his teacher, Master Lum. Sifu Mark has also been featured on Prism television. Sifu Mark's home state, Minnesota, considered him such a noteworthy figure that he was elected to their Living History Museum. In 1982, Sifu Mark was selected for the World Master's Symposium at Temple University.

Bruce Lee was one of Sifu Mark's students while he was visiting his father in New York during the late 1950s. He was so impressed with the effectiveness of Praying Mantis in combat that he adopted many of its principles in creating Jeet Kune Do.

In 1979, Sifu Mark went back to China. During his stay he studied Six Sounds qigong under a famous tai chi and qigong master, simply known as "Old Master," in Beijing.

When Sifu Mark was a small boy in the monasteries, he watched his teachers painting and also received lessons. Since drawing materials were hard to get and expensive, he practiced in the sand with bamboo for a brush, frequently holding a horse stance for a long time. He painted more and more as he grew older and is now an outstanding Chinese painter.

A student drenched in sweat stood in the doorway, glaring inquisitively at the two uninvited visitors. After briefly introducing themselves and stating that they were there to see Sifu Mark, Uncle Yong and Bruce were allowed admittance to a small dimly lit office. The student told them that Sifu Mark was presently teaching class, but if they would wait, he would let the master know that he had visitors. Then the student disappeared through a door leading to the rear of the building. Uncle Yong and Bruce had a few moments to peruse the small cluttered vestibule. To Bruce this cluttered and diminutive office appeared to be more like an old Chinese doctor's office than a gung fu kwoon. Several antiquated parchment paper acupuncture charts were on the wall. Several bookcase shelves were lined with an assortment of jars and plastic bags containing Chinese herbs. Dozens of bottles of murky brown liniment known as *dit da jow* were indiscriminately placed on the shelves among the herb mixtures. Bruce knew that herbalists and Chinese doctors used dit da jow to treat sprains and bruises, but for a gung fu sifu its main purpose, when used correctly in conjunction with training methods found in gung fu, was to harden the bones and condition the sinew.

When Bruce picked up a bottle to inspect it more closely, Uncle Yong remarked that Sifu Mark also treated people in the community for various ailments and medical conditions here in his office. Most of his patients were elderly Chinese that appreciated the value of acupuncture and herbal remedy treatments from the old country. Some of his students also appreciated of having a sifu with training and experience in this rare and little known healing art.

As Bruce continued to inspect the many traditional Chinese mementos and memorabilia in the office, he was especially infatuated with the certificates that adorned the walls. Each diploma signified that sifu Mark was an accredited and certified sifu in some pretty rare styles of gung fu. Most specifically his credentials that indicated his proficiency in Hung Gar (Tiger-Crane), Sil Lum, White

Crane, Eagle Claw, Leopard, and Tiger. He also studied Tiger Claw at the famous Hoi Jung Temple.

Then, almost as stealthily as a ninja in the night, Sifu Mark appeared in the room. His entrance had been so silent that he had to make his presence known by saying, "Mr. Yong, it's been a while. How are you doing?" Uncle Yong and Bruce almost turned toward the door at the same time. Sifu Mark extended a handshake to his friend.

As the sifu of this Praying Mantis kwoon greeted Uncle Yong, Bruce was casually following behind, studying the environment and wondering what lay in store for him. Bruce stood by silently until the sifu turned and greeted him in kind. The moment they shook hands Bruce noticed that Mark's hand was so soft and flexible that it felt like clasping a handful of gelatin. He had no thick calluses, disfigured knuckles, or dense muscle mass along the palm-heel or ridge of the hand. There was just soft and supple flesh with no signs of conditioning. He seemed to possess the hands of a violinist or musician with very delicate features and long slender fingers. This defied Bruce's experience. It was baffling and paradoxical beyond belief, and not at all what Bruce knew to be typical at the kwoons in Kowloon and Hong Kong. He would have thought that someone so skilled in Tiger Claw, Hung Gar, and Eagle Claw would have highly developed hands and fingers, perhaps with some calluses along the fore-knuckles or along the edge of the hand. However, this was not the case, and he thought it was very suspicious for someone that claimed to be a true gung fu master.

Bruce was then formally introduced to Sifu Gin Foon Mark. Both Sifu Mark and Bruce looked at one another in a cautious, yet friendly, manner. Bruce tried to determine how someone who appeared so young could be a master of gung fu, and Gin Foon

Mark, in turn, was trying to determine the real reason for Bruce's unannounced visit.

Bruce blushed a bit in embarrassment as Uncle Yong introduced him, with lavish compliments bestowed on Bruce's father and mother. He explained that Bruce's father was Lee Hoi Cheun, a famous actor with the Hong Kong Cantonese Opera Troupe that was in town for their annual performance. He then added that Bruce was born the second son of Lee Hoi Cheun, and was also the grandnephew, from his mother Grace's family, of Sir Jay Ho Tung, who was dubbed Hong Kong's first knight of the order by King George V. Bruce politely added that he was here from San Francisco to visit his father and wanted to visit a kwoon to see how its style compared to the Wing Chun he had learned in Kowloon. Sifu Mark then took a closer look at Bruce, as if sizing up what he saw and what he was hearing, and to determine if this was a challenge match or confrontation disguised as a friendly introduction.

Bruce, being most courteous and respectful, showed a humility that was normally not evident to those that knew him well. He did not know how to act, since he felt somewhat out of place. He was concerned that he would violate some traditional protocol by saying something foolish or offensive. As someone seeking knowledge in a rather secretive style of gung fu, he did not want to be construed as being too forward by a master he had just met. His words on their initial introduction had to be carefully selected if he did not want to appear as if he wanted to challenge or test this highly respected sifu's abilities.

After Sifu Gin Foon Mark asked about his experience in Wing Chun, Bruce took a bolder step, hopefully not breaking any of the kwoons protocol, by stating that he was interested in fighting and learning techniques from all styles. He also added that he had studied with Wing Chun master Yip Man in Kowloon. Bruce then confided that Uncle Yong had mentioned his status in the community as an excellent fighter with a good reputation here in Chinatown. While Bruce was speaking about fighting, Sifu Mark was assessing Bruce's moral character. He studied Bruce's eyes closely, hoping to look into his soul. His polite demeanor, well-groomed appearance, his family's credibility, and even Bruce's body language were taken into account as the sifu evaluated this young Chinese lad's ulterior motives. Bruce then, in an almost bashful fashion, concluded his short discourse by saying that he felt all of the good gung fu masters were in Hong Kong and that it was doubtful that anyone in the United States could be as good as the sifu there. Then Sifu Mark walked around Bruce in the cramped office, all the while looking him over from head to foot. And then a subtle smile appeared on Sifu Mark's face. He then replied, "You look like a pretty good fighter. Maybe you'd like to watch the conclusion of the class that is in session." Bruce and Uncle Yong both smiled and accepted the invitation to watch Sifu Gin Foon Mark finish teaching his gung fu class.

Sifu Mark then invited them through the door into the inner sanctum of his kwoon. As he relieved the assistant, who had been instructing in his absence, Bruce and Tom Bin Yong stood at the rear of the class and observed the training. Bruce, in a rather muted fashion made numerous comments to Uncle Yong about how various parts of the Praying Mantis forms resembled those of Wing Chun. Uncle Yong could sense that Bruce was not overly impressed with the skill and performance of the students of Sifu Mark and possibly thought Gin Foon Mark was overrated as an authentic Chinese gung fu instructor. Uncle Yong felt a little embarrassed, since he knew Gin Foon Mark to be an excellent sifu and an incredible fighter. He felt it was unfortunate that Bruce, because of his youth, could not fully see, much less appreciate, Sifu Mark's fighting and teaching skills.

Bruce suddenly became very quiet as he began perusing the interior of this most unusual kwoon. He was almost oblivious to the instruction and more interested in all the training equipment and odd conditioning devices that were housed in the training area.

The main gym was dimly lit and large, around 35 feet by 100 feet. Classical Chinese weapons, such as straight swords, broadswords, hook swords, butterfly knives, staffs, three-section staffs, spears, tridents, and *quan do* halberds lined the walls. In a corner was an assortment of about a half dozen old Chinese wax wood and oak staffs used for stick fighting. A rather ornate and colorful traditional altar with lit candles and burning incense proudly adorned the rear wall of this kwoon. Bruce knew that the purpose of the altar was to provide a display of respect and honor to the venerated masters of the past, the great gung fu masters in Sifu Mark's lineage. Moreover, as tradition would usually have it, the students and teachers would normally salute this consecrated shrine before classes started and after they ended. Due to its position at the far end of the back wall, and since the students were facing it as they trained, Bruce surmised that the students would have to back out of the training area as they left.

As Bruce continued to scrutinize the kwoon, he observed various kinds of training devices. Positioned in the area around the central training floor were crude weights, sandbags, buckets of sand, buckets with tiny pellets and larger stones, bamboo rollers, and hanging chains. Some he had not seen before. However, from experience using the *mook yan jong* (wooden dummy) in his Wing Chun kwoon in Kowloon, Bruce knew that these unusual and somewhat crude training devices were used for hardening the arms and hands. He now understood why there were so many bottles of dit da jow in Gin Foon Mark's office. Before or after class, the students probably used the equipment to toughen and condition their hands and arms and would use the liniment to heal and strengthen their muscles and sinew. On the distant wall, Bruce noticed tree branches that were used to represent arms and legs on a wooden man like the Wing Chun dummy he was familiar with. The wooden appendages were not polished or painted but appeared to be unfinished sapling tree branches that still had the bark on them. In the same area were several punching bags hanging from the ceiling.

From his and Uncle Yong's vantage point, Bruce could see a traditional Chinese ceremonial lion, drums, and cymbals. He had seen many of these items at the kwoons in Hong Kong. They were used in celebration of the Chinese Gung Hay Fat Choy Chinese New Year, on special occasions for parties, and grand openings for business. In all likelihood, Sifu Mark used them in his instruction at the kwoon. In addition to all of the training and ceremonial items, there was an array of old mementos and artifacts that Gin Foon Mark must have collected over the years. This kwoon was clearly one of the most diverse that Bruce had ever seen. This was as close as he could imagine being what the fabled Shaolin temple in China looked like, from what he knew from reading martial arts magazines in Hong Kong. Bruce thought the wall nearest him was rather odd and curious. It had several dozen holes the size of a half-dollar indented into it. It looked as if someone had taken a wooden staff and intentionally poked holes into the partition for no apparent reason at all. Perhaps it was an overzealous student who had used the wall for target practice.

After class had concluded, the students paid their respects to their sifu and to the altar shrine. And, as Bruce had correctly presumed, the students backed out of the training area. Sifu Mark then returned to where Bruce and Uncle Yong were standing at the rear of the kwoon. Bruce was now a little more exuberant and verbose, after having seen the interior of the kwoon and witnessing the remaining portion of the class. He stated to Sifu Mark, trying not to appear too blatant, that back in Kowloon his Wing Chun training seemed to be more intense, with greater emphasis on close-range techniques than he had observed in the class that night. Sifu Mark retorted, "Not many people have seen or understand this rare system. The power in the techniques is hidden." Bruce further belabored his point by physically demonstrating several simultaneous mock block and counterattack techniques found in the Wing Chun Sil Lim Tao form. Sifu Mark watched as Bruce executed these simulated fighting tactics, but it was obvious to Uncle Yong, and to the remaining curious students lingering nearby, that the sifu was not impressed.

When Sifu Gin Foon Mark pointed out that Wing Chun was not very effective against the circular attacks used by many Western boxers, it seemed to raise Bruce's ire. Although Bruce's attitude was subdued to some extent, Uncle Yong noticed it because, during their lunch, he had seen his newly reacquainted friend on terms that were more affable. Bruce said that when a fighter was in very close, circular maneuvers were not that effective in the first place.

In order to clarify and prove his point, Bruce asked Sifu Mark if he could spar with one of his students to demonstrate. The Praying Mantis sifu willingly granted his request. Gin Foon Mark immediately called a student out to spar with Bruce Lee. Each assumed a fighting posture from their respective style. In small steps, they inched toward one another until they were within kicking range. When Sifu Mark gave the command to commence, the gung fu combatants exchanged an instantaneous flurry of quick and explosive punches. With equal skill, both fighters parried and countered these assaults. Sifu Mark stood nearby, assessing their strategy, as neither had gained an advantage. Each time Bruce began a kicking attack it was swiftly blocked or evaded before it could reach its target, likewise with Gin Foon Mark's Praying Mantis fighter. After about five minutes of this pugilistic exhibition, Sifu Gin Foon Mark abruptly ended the match, complimenting each on the excellent performance of their styles and on the use of good solid basic gung fu technique. Gin Foon Mark declared, as both fighters had agreed, that it was a draw and no one was the victor. The observing students had learned an important lesson in how to approach someone that was skilled in close-range frontal fighting.

As Bruce recovered emotionally from this intense engagement, he casually asked Sifu Mark how long the student he had just sparred with had been training. Sifu Mark responded by saying, "Almost a year. He's just a beginner." The casual and unimposing manner in which Sifu Mark responded gave Bruce reason to reassess perception of the earlier training session. He instinctively knew that the years he had spent training with Yip Man had not been in vain. He recalled that Yip Man had once said that Praying Mantis was generally considered an inferior system and that there were not any outstanding practitioners or great fighters in Hong Kong. What he had just witnessed and experienced firsthand seemed to defy what he had heard about this style of gung fu.

Gin Foon Mark, sensing that Bruce had received a little lesson in humility and perhaps had his feelings hurt somewhat, asked if he would like to see some of the weapon arts that he taught at the kwoon. Uncle Yong felt the tenseness of the situation ease with Sifu Mark's question.

Gin Foon Mark then retrieved a single Chinese broadsword from a nearby weapons rack. Without a ceremonial salutation or warning, he burst into a flurry of extremely fast and dazzling slicing and cutting maneuvers. The sword traveled at such high speed that the polished chrome blade appeared to be a solid yet diffused wave of light. It looked as if Gin Foon Mark was cutting down dozens of imaginary opponents. Bruce and Uncle Yong stood mesmerized as Sifu Mark's spectacularly lethal gyrations slashed through the air, making a swishing sound with every explosive technique that he performed.

Bruce, with his keen eye for detail, was duly impressed. Each of these deadly slashes traversed the air with such precision that it was difficult to discern the blocking maneuvers from the actual cutting techniques. Sifu Mark's balance was flawless, which added another level of grandeur to this already brilliant display of sword wizardry. There was never a moment during this flashy display at which he had lost control of the weapon or his balance. Then, as quick as he started, he syopped. Sifu Mark had not even broken a sweat.

As Sifu Mark returned the sword to the weapons rack, Bruce reflected on his experiences back in Kowloon. He had witnessed his seniors at the Wing Chun kwoon wield the shorter broad blade Wing Chun butterfly swords, but he had never seen anyone move so fast and so precisely as he had just witnessed. Under his breath, Uncle Yong commented to Bruce that Sifu Mark was one of the best Praying Mantis sifu in the United States. Bruce was inclined to agree. When he returned from the rack, Sifu Mark resumed their conversation as though nothing out of the ordinary had happened. He asked Bruce how long he had been studying Wing Chun with

Sifu Yip Man in Kowloon. Bruce, a little embarrassed, said that he had practiced on and off for almost four years. Sifu Mark sensed that Bruce was perhaps reluctant to talk more about it, since his student had fared pretty well against Bruce for a student who had only studied for about a year. Then, in a pleasant and matter-of-fact manner, Gin Foon Mark returned to discussing Praying Mantis gung fu. From what the sifu had seen of Bruce's sparring, Bruce had exhibited mostly Wing Chun, with a few boxing techniques. Talking to Bruce like a student, rather than a visiting guest, Sifu Mark said that the Praying Mantis system was very subtle. The most powerful and practical techniques are hidden in the relaxed, circular movements of one's hands and feet. He then demonstrated several of these powerful and explosive short-distance maneuvers as he told Bruce it was difficult to explain these techniques until they had been practiced awhile and had been experienced. Bruce listened with the close attention he gave when being lectured by his senior teacher Ah Hing (William Cheung) or Sifu Yip Man back in Kowloon.

Gin Foon Mark explained that the Praying Mantis style is distinguished from other styles in that it is an internal system. It concentrates on developing internal power rather than external muscle strength. It also has more techniques than many other systems and includes both sticking hands and sticking feet (sticking hands is a martial arts drill that expresses interplay between two training partners). To make Praying Mantis even more unique it, like Japanese judo and jujitsu, uses the opponent's strength to his disadvantage.

Bruce and Uncle Yong became engrossed in Sifu Mark's thorough and precise manner of explaining each of the distinctions found in Praying Mantis. Gin Foon Mark knew that Bruce would have some knowledge of *chi sao* and mook jong training and decided to talk about something that Bruce would know more about. He said that the Praying Mantis techniques rely only on feeling and that the hands react as if they had eyes and a mind of their own. He described the hands as being alive and not lifeless. He said that Praying Mantis was a "soft arm" gung fu system. Bruce's eyebrows furrowed as he heard Mark divulge this fascinating martial information. Sifu Mark resumed by stating that each of the Praying Mantis self-defense formulas has a two or more person breakdown and that a student will learn to use each limb independently of any other limb. He explained that what most people did not appreciate was that the practitioner of Praying Mantis was always relaxed and in a continuous flow, never rigid or emotionally tense as he moved. Bruce realized that he had witnessed this firsthand when he sparred with the student. Bruce also learned that Sifu Mark's sifu and the grandmasters of the Praying Mantis style that preceded him taught and practiced the techniques of their style exactly as they are used. There were never any flashy drills for the sake of show, only practical moves for actual fighting. In fact, the Praying Mantis systems, both the northern style and the southern style, are shortcut systems. In other words, just as in Wing Chun, Praying Mantis was developed to be a fast-track method to teach one to defend against real fighters under realistic combat conditions.

Bruce interrupted to ask Sifu Mark about the functions of power and how it related to the long-range techniques in Praying Mantis. Bruce had keenly observed that Gin Foon Mark had demonstrated awesome displays of power at the shorter close-in ranges. Sifu Mark satisfied his curiosity by saying that the Praying Mantis style emphasizes power at all ranges and, in fact, had many techniques to generate and transfer power through the body to the intended target. He then demonstrated several swift and crisp distance punches that came within inches of Bruce's face. Bruce could feel the wind generated by them and could see that each well-placed punch was powerful without appearing jerky or wound up before delivery. Gin Foon Mark then asked Bruce if he would like to try his hand and play with some of the close-range defense techniques. Bruce declined and politely mentioned that he had too much respect for the sifu's skill to try his luck against him. Sifu Mark smiled and resumed his explanation by saying that Praying Mantis practices high kicking when they train, but he favored the low-level kicks for actual combat, qualifying his statement by demonstrating several swift kicks to the knee and shin areas just inches from Bruce's legs.

As Sifu Mark concluded his lecture-demonstration for Bruce, he touched on the rather secretive art of Chinese *dim mak*. It is notorious as the art of purposefully attacking the acupuncture points in order to produce injury or death at a later point in time. Again, Bruce was impressed with the extent of the knowledge that Sifu Gin Foon Mark possessed. Even in Hong Kong, Bruce had yet to meet anyone with as much knowledge of so many aspects of gung fu.

As Sifu Mark began walking back toward the front of the kwoon, Bruce sensed that this meeting was rapidly ending. However, he felt that Gin Foon Mark had something to offer that he was definitely not going to find anywhere else. He suddenly blurted out, "Sifu Mark, will you have me as a student for about three weeks?" Sifu Mark suddenly stopped, turned around, looked sternly at Bruce, and smiled. Then, he said, "You come here tomorrow night. Do not eat before you come to the kwoon. OK?" Uncle Yong patted Bruce on the shoulder as if to congratulate his acceptance into this tight-knit Praying Mantis organization. As they were politely ushered out the front door, Sifu Mark casually remarked that the club dues were fifteen dollars to train. Bruce said he would be there tomorrow evening ready to train. The door suddenly closed, and they were back on the streets in Manhattan's Chinatown.

While walking back toward the Chinese Opera Theater, Bruce continued to talk about Sifu Gin Foon Mark. He asked Uncle Yong how old he thought the sifu was. Uncle Yong told Bruce that according to a brochure that he had one time, the sifu was born in Toyson, a village near Canton, China in 1927. He said, "I guess he would be about thirty-two years of age." Uncle Yong then asked Bruce how old he was. Bruce responded, "I'm eighteen years old, but in about four months I'll be nineteen, on November twenty-seventh to be exact."

෧෧

ABOUT THE CHINESE OPERA

In 1790, theater companies from all over China arrived in Beijing to perform for the Qing Emperor Qianlong's birthday. Four theater companies from Anhui arrived, and their fresh styles of music and theater electrified the capital and eventually came to replace the *Kunqu* opera style that had been preeminent in the capital for the past two hundred years. Characteristics from other forms of opera, such as *Hopeh, Wuhan,* and *Shansi,* were integrated into the Anhui style. After a while, this form of opera became known as *Ching Hsi,* or "Capital Play." Ching Hsi is what we know today as Peking opera. Because of its long history, Peking opera encompasses a wide variety of drama, and a wide variety of styles of acting. It emphasizes historical and military plays and can be quite patriotic, and so quite popular. But, it is not the only style of opera still extant in China—many regional opera styles still exist. Some references list more than

300 regional opera styles in China. Among those still popular are Cantonese opera, Hebei Clapper opera, and Yue opera.

Although there are many different regional styles, they all share many similarities. Each has the same four role types: the female, the male, the painted face, and the clown. Performances consist of singing, poetry, music, dance, and gesture. Emphasis is on costume and makeup rather than props or scenery. The operas often tell the same stories, though with various regional differences, such as alternate endings or additional characters. The information described within this article will, unless otherwise noted, pertain to Peking Opera specifically, and the regional operas more generally.

Toward the end of the Qing dynasty, teahouses began to double as theaters. Originally, the acting troupes used the teahouses as a place to rehearse plays, since their homes were too small. Business in the teahouses carried on as before, except the patrons could now enjoy performances during their drinks and conversations. After a time, patrons began frequenting teahouses specifically to see the theater, and in some of these establishments, the character for the word tea was eliminated from their name. The acting troupes earned their livelihood through performances for the court and not through public performance. At first, actors had to bribe the eunuchs to ensure that word did not get out that they were performing publicly, because the court frowned on such activity. Eventually, their performance in public teahouses became the common and accepted practice.

Chinese opera has many strong female roles, though for most of its history, no females to play them. Women in China, especially of the upper class, had to observe very reserved and controlled conduct, and for the most part confined themselves indoors. A woman who paraded herself on stage would be considered no better than a prostitute. Instead, men would play the female roles. At certain times in opera history, these female impersonators were the greatest stars of the stage. Their peak in popularity occurred in the 1920s, 1930s, and 1940s. The most celebrated among them being Mei Lanfang, whose performances both at home and abroad in Japan, the Soviet Union, and the United States influenced such famous dramatists as Berthold Brecht and Stanislavsky. He also met and performed for famous actors such as Charlie Chaplin and Mary Pickford. In addition to his mastery of over 100 roles, he also advanced Peking opera by making significant changes to the costumes, staging, makeup, and texts, in effect creating a number of new plays, including his most famous, *Farewell My Concubine*.

By the 1930s, it became acceptable for women to perform in the opera. This led to the gradual disappearance of the role of the female impersonator. Women usually now played female parts, even though the roles still possessed the mannerisms, vocalisms, and styles designed to be performed by men.

Chinese opera survived the passing centuries and the rise and fall of dynasties. It survived the end of the Qing dynasty and the warlord era. It survived the Japanese occupation of Shanghai, but not without some famous actors becoming blacklisted and having their careers destroyed for performing for the Japanese. It even survived the Communist revolution—almost.

Jiang Qing, Chairman Mao's wife and a former film actress, denounced the traditional opera for not serving the needs of the masses. No traditional operas were allowed to be performed. Instead, the party promoted what it called the "eight model plays," which featured the common workers, in plain modern dress and naturalistic sets, promoting communism. When the infamous Gang of Four finally fell from power, traditional opera was restored, though it had lost much of its audience. Many opera schools, facing decreasing returns, were forced to close, and the opera stars entered film, to act and do stunt work.

However, even today traditional opera has a place in modern China, Taiwan, and Hong Kong. It tells the stories common to all the Chinese people: the legend of the Monkey King, the epic tales from *The Water Margin* and *Romance of the Three Kingdoms*, the countless fairy tales and ghost stories. These timeless tales still resonate today, and ensure that the traditional opera will continue to have its place in modern life.

The following morning Bruce left his father's apartment early and set off on an excursion around New York's Chinatown, essentially visiting all of the shops, markets, and restaurants in the heart of this exclusively Asian district. Everything was somehow new but vaguely similar to the Chinatown in San Francisco. What struck him most was that both the San Francisco and New York Chinatown shops were open and quite spacious, as opposed to the shops in Hong Kong and Kowloon, which were crowded and cramped. Even the ocean air was fresher and cleaner than that of the Hong Kong harbor. He had a great sense of freedom and wholeness that he had never experienced back home.

As the sun was setting and the lights of Chinatown suddenly illuminated the streets, Bruce decided that it was time to walk back in the direction of Sifu Gin Foon Mark's Praying Mantis kwoon. The kwoon wasn't open yet, and a dozen or so students werewaiting for Sifu Gin Foon Mark to open the school officially. Bruce immediately introduced himself to the members and tried to fit in to the group. He was curious to know more about Sifu Mark. He asked one of the older Chinese students to give him some of the history about their sifu. Bruce soon discovered that Sifu Mark was the fifth generation inheritor of their style in a long line of distinguished gung fu masters. He came from a family of four generations that were renowned on mainland China.

Gin Foon Mark began studying gung fu at five years old, with his uncles and grandfather. At age nine, he began studying with the monk Ki Fut Sai, receiving instruction in a variety of martial arts techniques. He went on to study at Hoi Jung Temple and at Jook Lum Monastery, where he first studied Praying Mantis style. He studied many internal styles of martial arts and traditional arts. In the United States, he continued Praying Mantis studies with Sifu Lum Wing Fay, who he studied with for ten years and eventually succeeded as master. Sifu Mark thought so highly of the Praying Mantis style that he decided to devote his life to teaching only this system, even though he was an expert in other systems.

This account gave Bruce much to ponder, and he was looking forward to learning all he could in the very short period of three weeks that he would be there visiting his father. As the kwoon opened up, and the students entered, the proper bow and formal salutations were accorded Sifu Mark. Bruce understood the ritual and followed the formalities revealed by the other students. Sifu Mark greeted Bruce personally and welcomed him to the kwoon as though he were a regular member of the club, even though he would only be there for a short stay.

Bruce then presented an envelope containing the fifteen dollars that they had agreed upon the previous day. With this kind of cordiality, Bruce hoped that his Praying Mantis sifu would impart some of the deeper and more secretive aspects of this art to him. From his experience with Yip Man, Bruce knew that newcomers at a kwoon were usually set apart to train in the fundaments of the style. Sometimes it would be many months before a sifu would assign a senior to teach the newcomers the more advanced elements or forms of the style. Bruce was unsure how to approach this delicate matter, but he knew that if Sifu Mark assigned him a senior to instruct him primarily on the fundamental stances, blocks, and counterpunching maneuvers, the lessons would probably be a waste of his time and his money. However, Sifu Mark assigned several of the seniors to work with the class, and it appeared that he was going to instruct Bruce personally. Since Bruce was not equipped with the proper workout gear and did not possess a proper *jing mo* (traditional Chinese gung fu uniform), he was unsure if he would appear acceptable to his sifu. Sifu Mark understood his situation and permitted him to train as he was, in his street clothes.

The first thing that Sifu Mark wanted to modify in Bruce's fighting style was his stance. In addition, the footwork that Bruce used while sparring was not conducive to executing the best techniques from the frontal position, so the sifu wanted to modify that as well. Sifu Mark explained to Bruce that he should position his tight horse stance more toward the frontal direction, and not so much angled inward. That way it was possible to use more of a variety of close-range, low-level kicks. After some thought, and a few practice drills, Bruce understood completely what his new sifu was saying.

To enhance Bruce's Wing Chun fighting style even more, Sifu Mark suggested that Bruce should place his hands farther out from his body, with his strongest hand in the leading position. He had noticed that Bruce, because of the years of training in traditional Wing Chun, held his hands and arms too close to his chest. That had a tendency to telegraph, or forewarn, the opponent of his offensive or defensive intentions.

Next, the sifu began showing Bruce how to generate more explosive short-range power. Since Bruce was already adept at punching and using arm muscle compression to generate power, Sifu Mark could easily show Bruce how to integrate his body force into a punch without winding up his body before releasing an attack. Sifu Mark further explained that, if he wanted to maximize the effect, he should start coordinating and timing his body movement through rapid forward shuffling footwork to coincide with the punch release. This way the body's mass would be behind the punch at the instant of impact with the intended target. This made a lot of sense to Bruce, and he felt a bit embarrassed that he had never thought of it before. Now it was beginning to make sense to him how Sifu Gin Foon Mark could make extremely powerful punches at these extremely close ranges.

☺☺

During the late dinners that Bruce, his father, and opera friends had at various restaurants in New York's Chinatown, Bruce told his father about what he had been doing at the Praying Mantis kwoon. Often his accounts became interspersed with other conversations going on at the table. His father, being the famous opera celebrity that he was, was the focal point of most of the attention. Telling stories about his acting experiences, signing occasional autographs for fans that would come to their table, and telling jokes seemed to preoccupy most of his father's time when they dined together. Bruce, most of the time, was content to simply remain quiet and accept being introduced as Lee Hoi Cheun's son, who was here in the United States to get an education. His father proudly boasted that his son Peter was attending the University of Wisconsin, and Bruce, after he completed his high school studies, would be attending the University of Washington in Seattle.

Some nights they dined at the Wo Hops, where Hoi Cheun was also very popular. In most instances, their dinner hours were the same no matter where they went to eat. On some evenings, Bruce never had an opportunity to tell his father what he had done that day. It was as though he were invisible, except for the fact that he was constantly being introduced to his father's friends and fans.

ABOUT THE CHINESE OPERA ACTORS
THE FOUR CHARACTER TYPES

In the Chinese opera, there are generally four main categories of roles: *sheng* (the male roles), *dan* (the female roles), *jing* (the painted face roles), and *chou* (clowns). Each category is further subdivided into distinct types. An actor typically trains for a single type of role within one category. Actors who can play multiple types of roles within a single category are considered especially talented. An actor *never* plays roles outside his or her category.

Sheng

An actor trains for three main male roles. The first is *lao sheng,* a middle-aged or old man. The lao sheng is dignified and refined. They may be high-level scholars or officials, and wear a black hat with fins on either side to denote rank; or maybe, they are a general in a military play, wearing armor. In either case, the lao sheng wears a beard (black or gray, depending on age). The second type of role is *hsiao sheng,* or young man. The hsiao sheng sings in a warbling voice to indicate adolescence, and does not wear a beard.

The third type of role is *wu sheng,* or acrobat, who performs much of the most exciting elements of Chinese opera. A special wu sheng role is that of the Monkey King, featured in a number of operas based on the famous story *A Journey to the West.*

Dan

There are twice as many female role types as there are male. They are divided according to character, status, and age. *Lao dan* is the old woman role. The costume is subdued, no makeup is worn, and the singing voice is natural and therefore lower than that for the other dan roles. The *wu dan* is the female acrobat, and is equivalent to the wu sheng role for the men. A *qing yi* actress is the noblewoman, of good quality and character. She is the model or ideal of the Chinese woman. She is faithful, proper, shy, and graceful. The *hua dan*, however, is of a lower social status than the qing yi, and represents a feistier, flirtatious young woman. A young woman from a wealthy family, set apart from the world in the family mansion, is called the *gui men dan*. This character is still young and will grow up one day to become either a qing yi or a hua dan. Finally, there is the *dao ma dan*, or warrior woman. This character typically wears full armor and great peacock feathers in her hat. The famed military heroines of China are all played as dao ma dan. The story of *Peking Opera Blues*, featuring three extraordinary women heroes, is actually titled *Dao Ma Dan* in Chinese.

Jing

The painted face role is the most recognizable part of Chinese opera. This part is reserved for high-ranking army generals or bandits, warriors or officials. All jing characters have their faces painted elaborately, the colors on the face indicating the personality and temperament of the character. A white face means treachery, black means uprightness, red indicates courage and virtue, and blue denotes cruelty or wild temperament. A mix of multiple colors indicates a more complicated personality.

Chou

The clown is the only role that can break the "fourth wall," so to speak, and reference current or local events and speak in colloquialisms. Male clowns are easily recognizable because they all wear a distinctive white patch of makeup around the nose and eyes. This same makeup is sometimes used for mean-spirited villains as well. Female clowns do not have the white makeup patch but instead have a reddened face with black eyebrows.

COSTUMES AND PROPS

On the Chinese opera stage, scenery and props are sparse. Often, only a table and chairs are set on the stage to signify various thrones, mountains, and so on throughout the story. A character committing suicide by jumping down a well may in performance simply be stepping off a chair and walking off stage. The actors, through their voice, movement, and gestures, must convey the story to the audience. Each character, furthermore, wears a distinctive and traditional costume and makeup that cues the audience about their status and, sometimes, about their personality.

There are very few props save for combat arms such as swords and spears. An umbrella is sometimes carried in an important person's entourage. Another common prop is the horsewhip. Whenever an actor holds out this whip, it symbolically indicates he is riding a horse. The color of the whip sometimes indicates the color of the horse. A duster is often carried by the most exalted of characters, such as gods, priests, and celestial spirits, whose stories are often told on the opera stage.

Armor

High military officials wear the armor, or *k'ao*. It is a very stiff costume, with brilliant colors and often a design such as a tiger's head or dragon across the front. A fully armored actor wears four pennants on their back. Without the pennants, the actor is only partially armored. The jing role often wears armor, and it is seen on wu sheng and dao ma dan actors.

Hats

Many different kinds of hats are worn in Chinese opera. In general, they do not stand out from the costume as a whole but rather compliment it. Sheng actors who are portraying scholars or officials will often wear a simple black crepe hat with two fins coming out from the sides. These fins denote an actors character or rank: Oblong, almost rectangular fins are worn by high officials, round fins are worn by ch'ou or comic actors, and diamond- or oval-shaped fins are worn by treacherous characters (if only it was this easy to tell in real life). Another type of crepe hat has long, thin fins. Prime ministers only wear this type.

Some of the more striking types of headgear include great pheasant plumes, two of them, of sometimes nearly six or seven feet in length, sprouting from the actors head like antennae. Originally, they indicated that the wearer was an insurgent chief or a minority nationality. However, many types of military stage characters because of their beauty soon adopted them.

Sleeves

Water sleeves are long strips of white silk. These sleeves are flicked to emphasize a point, shaken when angry, stretched out in dance. Typically, all of the high officials' costumes have water sleeves.

SUPERSTITION AND THE SUPERNATURAL

Since the opera often concerns itself with the supernatural world, its players must ever be respectful of the laws of that world. Ritual and ceremony must be properly performed and with respect. Tales like the one that begins *Hocus Pocus* are often told about Chinese opera troupes who visit a remote town and give a performance, only to find in the morning that the town did not exist and that they were entertaining ghosts. It is traditional that during some Taoist ceremonies, and especially during the Ghost Festival in the seventh month, an opera troupe would perform in front of the shrine, to entertain the spirits of that place.

The patron saint of Chinese Opera is T'ang Ming Huang. A figure or tablet of T'ang Ming Huang is set up in every theater, and incense was burned to him before every performance. He was believed to have the power to make each actor perform well or badly. Military actors typically honor another tablet, representing the spirit Wu Ch'ang. This spirit was believed to possess special abilities, including the cruelty needed to wage a successful campaign. Four famous generals from the Warring States period were said to have this spirit's ability bestowed upon them.

Opening a new theater is a special occasion for ceremony. To purify the stage, and drive away devils and harmful spirits, the stage must be doused in dog's blood or chicken's blood while actors appear on the stage dressed as spirits, carrying whips, tablets, and masks. This ceremony thus drives away the devils, placates them, and ensures that they do not appear on stage again.

During the following week, Sifu Gin Foon Mark introduced Bruce to the history of Praying Mantis gung fu. Bruce was rapidly discovering that Sifu Mark was remarkably versed in Chinese martial arts history. In some ways he was as much a professor and martial scholar as he was a gung fu teacher. He could cite important dates and tell colorful biographies of famous masters of the styles of Sil Lum, White Crane, Eagle Claw, Leopard, and Tiger, Hung Gar, and Praying Mantis. Bruce had never read about or heard of some of these styles before. After the sifu explained various advantages and disadvantages of a particular style, he would then follow up by doing a demonstration, sometimes using Bruce and other students as attackers in these very realistic mock self-defense scenarios. After listening to his sifu describe and demonstrate the cause and effect of attacking various vital body points through the meridian channels, Bruce was thoroughly convinced that his sifu was as much a doctor as a martial arts master. Sifu Mark was skilled in the ancient healing art of *shin kung*. Now it was clear why the acupuncture charts were in the office. Bruce reasoned, and rightly so, that the advanced students were taught how to attack the vital points of the body to cripple or disable an antagonist. Many of these same meridian and vital points were used to heal many of the elderly that sought Sifu Mark's professional acupuncture treatments for their relief from various medical conditions.

Sifu Mark then began in earnest to show Bruce a lot more about his own Wing Chun style than Bruce had never explored before. He discovered quite quickly that Sifu Mark was very knowledgeable in the use and application of Sil Lim Tao, the Wing Chun set that Bruce knew. Sifu Mark explained that most styles or systems practice techniques in one way and use them in another. For example, in the first Wing Chun form, Sil Lim Tao, the fists are held at the sides of the chest to execute straight punches. However, in fighting, these punches are executed differently, with the hands held in front of the chest. He elaborated that the Praying Mantis styles were created strictly for fighting against someone that was a skill-ful fighter, unlike Wing Chun, which had been developed by a woman to be used to defend against and thwart off assaults of the sort that might be inflicted against women. This confounded Bruce to some degree, since he had been taught to use the techniques to fight against real fighters, not someone that would try to slap, grab, restrain, or otherwise impair someone in the way they would pos-sibly assault a woman. Nevertheless, he had to agree with Sifu Mark that the use of the techniques were somewhat different from the way they had been taught to him. The point was well taken when Sifu Mark demonstrated the differences between the way Sil Lim Tao was taught and how it should be used in a realistic fighting scenario against foes that wanted to harm you. Bruce began to real-ize that a style could be modified and used differently than the way it was taught. This had a strong impact on his way of thinking when it came to realistic fighting against someone that had exceptional skill in the art of empty-hand combat.

Sifu Mark next introduced Bruce to the three-step arrow for-mula and showed him how he could readily adapt the techniques of Wing Chun Sil Lim Tao to this type of footwork pattern. Mov-ing straight in or directly back for defensive or counteroffensive technique application is a part of this formula. One can move straight in and withdraw at a left or right diagonal angle and, mak-ing it even more confusing to an adversary, numerous combina-tions of this footwork can be employed to keep an opponent guessing. By moving in and out, or sideways, while simultaneously blocking and counterattacking, a skilled practitioner of the three-step arrow formula could also gauge appropriate distances of spe-cific targets or vital nerve points to attack at any given instant. Bruce became very enthusiastic after learning this footwork pattern, and Sifu Mark could see that he respected its value as a fighting tool. Sifu Mark explained to Bruce that, mathematically speaking, the patterns numbered in the hundreds of thousands of possible combinations.

As he learned more about the intricacies of the Praying Mantis footwork, Bruce found that the answers to his incessant barrage of questions only evoked more questions about this style of gung fu. He learned that Sifu Mark's specific style of Praying Mantis was the Jook Lum system, and he was the fifth generation master of this lineage. Bruce found the history of both the southern and northern style of Praying Mantis to be as fascinating as the differences in technique.

Bruce learned that the Hakka Chinese, considered outsiders by the other indigenous peoples of Kwangsi province, developed the southern style, of which Sifu Mark was skilled. There is little known surrounding the style's origin, but the style evidences elements of lamaistic training and close adherence to Taoist philosophy. Highly skilled practitioners and masters are knowledgeable in dim mak (death-touch techniques directed to the vital chi points and meridians of the human anatomy), which can also be used to heal if the techniques are properly applied. Sifu Mark said that two schools developed, these being the Chu and Chow, and both share so much in common as to use the same name for the method, "Bamboo Forest."

Sifu Gin Foon Mark methodically unveiled the deeper intrinsic aspects of this art to Bruce. Bruce discovered that the secrecy surrounding Bamboo Forest Praying Mantis was replete with myths and legends, largely initiated and propagated by the practitioners themselves. Sifu Mark told Bruce that, in some parts of China, becoming a student was extremely demanding and involved nothing less than being adopted by the master and pledging one's life to him. Even family ties are second to choosing the disciples.

Unlike the northern schools, southern Praying Mantis rarely emphasizes one type of technique; the mantis hook is employed, in which the fingers are fixed in a hook position, but so are numerous other trapping and controlling maneuvers. The typical closed fist of other styles is absent from the southern sect, which instead favors the mantis fist, which concentrates all of the striking force through a single finger. Stances are low to moderate, but firmly anchored to the ground. There is tremendous use of the knees, elbows, and low powerful kicks. There are few feints or distraction strikes; everything is designed for 100 percent power output, and is, thus, potentially lethal. There is reason to believe that at least some of the southern method was the direct result of dealing with the political oppression during the mid-nineteenth century, after the Opium War with Britain. This is is further evidenced by the secret society nature of the sect. Bamboo Forest employs fighting philosophies common to Wing Chun and White Eyebrow gung fu, and some stylistic evidence supports the idea that a strong exchange of information has occurred between these schools.

Bruce Lee Discovers New Forms of Training Equipment

On the Tuesday of Bruce's second week as a student at Sifu Gin Foon Mark's Praying Mantis kwoon, Bruce was introduced to the many rustic and crude training devices that were randomly located around the kwoon. He had never seen so many common items used for training and conditioning before. There were simple makeshift contrivances like five-gallon buckets filled with various textures and sizes of stones, gravel, and sand; twenty-five-pound sections of steel railroad track; bundles of iron link chain hanging from the ceiling; sapling tree trunks ingeniously mounted in wooden frames; and dozens of short bamboo poles and five-pound cast-iron ingots used for windowframe counterweights. The only training device that resembled anything Bruce had seen before was short sapling tree appendages that were affixed to a post. This resembled a mook jong, but it was far more rudimentary than the one he had used in Hong Kong.

After introducing Bruce to each of these different training devices, Sifu Mark then demonstrated how to use them. He emphasized that each device was specifically intended to strengthen and condition various parts of the hands and arms. Sifu Mark continually stressed the importance of toughening the muscles and bones without building calluses or causing undue damage to the skin and tissue in the process. What impressed Bruce more than anything else was how Sifu Mark's hands and arms seemed to be so soft and supple, yet when he executed a block against Bruce's forearms, Bruce felt like he was impacting against a solid steel shaft. Even Sifu Mark's fingers and knuckles felt like powerful steel claws grasping Bruce when he demonstrated the Praying Mantis–style parrying and grabbing ploys. This was something entirely new to Bruce, and he wanted to learn how to make his hands and arms that way as well.

When Bruce was introduced to the phoenix-eye fist, a type of striking method, he was not overly impressed with this type of punch. Clinching the fist and extending the fore-knuckle on the index finger and reinforcing it with only the thumb didn't seem like a very effective way to strike an opponent to do any real damage. Sifu Mark smiled, and grabbing Bruce by the arm, led him over to a wall. Bruce had seen all of the small puncture holes in this wall before and was not sure what had caused them, but he was sure he was going to find out soon. Sifu Mark then made a phoenix-eye fist and then, with no forewarning, exploded into the wall with this one-knuckle punch. This sudden and swiftly executed maneuver produced a hole the size of a half-dollar. Bruce was dumbfounded that such a seemingly innocuous-looking punch could do such damage. Not only was it a highly destructive punch but also it could be executed at a very close range of only twelve inches or so. Sifu Mark then explained that all of the body's force had been concentrated into a space on the foreknuckle of less than a quarter of an inch, thus producing the penetrating effect that was dozens of times greater than the power that would be produced if it had been executed with the entire face of the fist. Bruce then understood the logic and the mathematical reasoning behind his sifu's explanation. Sifu Mark was careful to emphasize that learning the punch that generated enormous power like that was not the trick. It was in the conditioning and preparation to insure that one did not damage himself while mastering this technique. Therefore, it is necessary to toughen the bone and sinew and use dit da jow to promote this process.

That is when Sifu Mark introduced Bruce to the training methods used with the assorted buckets of rocks and gravel. He gave Bruce a bottle of the dit da jow liniment and instructed him that he was to rub it into the skin of the hands vigorously before and after each session of stabbing and slicing his hands into the buckets of gravel. He also indicated it was necessary to start with several dozen thrusts daily and to build up gradually until he could do 500 repetitions a day. Sifu Mark continued, "Start with the small-grained textures and then progress to the more coarse rocks, being careful all the time not to lacerate the skin. Otherwise, you will only impede the progress you are trying to make."

Bruce was next introduced to bamboo pole training. Sifu Mark explained that this very old Chinese training method dated back to the Shaolin temple. It was perhaps one of the best training methods for developing and conditioning the arms to become like those of the Praying Mantis. Bruce found this hard to comprehend, because they appeared to be nothing more than simple bamboo poles. At best, he thought, these hard bamboo poles were for striking the arms all over and toughening them through constant pounding. When he asked how one uses them in conditioning the arms, Sifu Mark summoned a student and had him positioned in front of Bruce. He had the student extend his arms and form a cradle. Then Sifu Mark placed three of the dried bamboo shafts on top of the forearms near the wrist. He then instructed Bruce to place both of his arms across the top of the three poles, with the bottom side of forearms resting firmly against the dowels. Bruce was then instructed to force pressure downward against the bamboo as his training partner resisted this effort.

Next, Sifu Mark directed Bruce to push both wrists slowly and methodically outward toward his partner as if he were making a double punch. This caused the three bamboo staves to roll along the bottom sides of the arms and create a deep and invigorating massage to his wrist and forearms. Bruce noticed that his partner was getting the exact same type of toughening and conditioning treatment across the tops of his forearms. Sifu Mark could see that Bruce was excited by the way that these bamboo poles were being used so cleverly. He then explained to Bruce that the praying mantis has very jagged forearms and knows how to use them to great advantage for either fighting or for capturing its prey. He referred to the arms as tools, and a Praying Mantis practitioner must always keep those tools sharp and ready for action. Bruce could appreciate the value and wisdom in this. After about five minutes of this intense training, Sifu Mark saw that both Bruce and the otherstudent's arms were becoming very red. He then instructed them to apply some dit da jow and rub it in for about ten minutes.

Before class closed that night, Sifu Mark taught Bruce how to condition his arms with the bundle chain. This seemingly simple suspended training device could be used to strengthen other areas of the forearms that had not been affected by the bamboo staves. Once in front of the suspended bundle of iron chain, Sifu Mark extended his right arm and placed it against the links, all the while lightly pressing the inner forearm into the heap. Bruce watched carefully as his sifu sucked a deep breath of air into his lungs and tightened his stomach. Suddenly his arm lunged forward, as if making a punch. Then just as quickly, he retracted it. Bruce could see that the pressure of the chains against his inner arm, from this rapid movement, was causing the muscles to massage the inside tissue. Sifu Mark then did this several times with both arms and then stepped away and permitted Bruce to move into position. Bruce imitated everything that he had seen his sifu do. Because Bruce had not paid close enough attention to the breathing, Sifu Mark stopped him and demonstrated the action again. He then explained that the breathing was a very important part of this type of arm conditioning if one was going to get the maximum benefit from it. After Bruce had done only three or four of these rapid pistonlike thrusts, Sifu Mark commanded him to do the other arm.

Sifu Gin Foon Mark emphasized that only a few repetitions were needed to toughen the softer tissue areas of the arm. He further elaborated that it was not the purpose of condition training to irritate or inflame the skin or muscle tissue, but to strengthen it through a gradual exposure to these abrasive devices. That way the skin would remain supple, soft, and devoid of calluses. He then told Bruce that a good Praying Mantis gung fu man will always have arms and hands that appear as soft and delicate as a musician's, yet if someone assaulted him, the gung fu man's blocks would feel like solid steel. Sifu Mark demonstrated this against Bruce's arms, and just the sheer force of the impact caused Bruce to grimace each time their arms made contact. Before leaving the kwoon that night, Bruce purchased two more bottles of dit da jow and thanked Sifu Mark for taking the time to teach him about the arm conditioning and strengthening devices.

Later that night, at dinner, at the Bo Bo Restaurant, Hoi Cheun playfully remarked to his guests that Bruce smelled like a Chinese herb factory. Bruce's arms were stained a dark shade of brown from his wrists to his elbows. Everyone in the party laughed and commented how Bruce was the darkest Chinese that they had ever seen. Even Bruce had to laugh even though he was the brunt of the joke. Hoi Cheun was very proud of how well Bruce was handling their ribbing, carrying himself as a gentleman and becoming accepted into the group of his friends and opera associates in New York. He was also glad that Bruce had not been troublesome or caused any embarrassment to him while they were there with the tour.

The next night's class proved to be as interesting and fascinating as all of the others had been. Upon arriving at the kwoon, Sifu Mark immediately assigned a senior to conduct the formal classes so he could spend time teaching Bruce. After inspecting Bruce's arms and seeing that he had been using the dit da jow, the sifu informed Bruce that he was going to show him more of the other conditioning and strengthening methods. They selected a place near the rear of the kwoon where Sifu Mark then told Bruce that he was going to introduce him to iron ring training. He walked to a small table and returned with four cast-iron rings. Each of these solid rings weighed about one and a half pounds. Bruce commented that he had seen them before in Hong Kong but had never worked with them. Sifu Mark gave him a slight smile and said that most people that use the iron rings use them for the wrong purpose. He continued by saying that almost everyone tries to use them for strengthening the muscles by doing repetitions of punches and blocks while wearing them on their arms, but in Praying Mantis training they are used another way, to condition and toughen the inner muscles and sinew. He then commenced to slip the four rings on Bruce's extended arm. Next sifu Mark instructed Bruce to shake his arm vigorously, in and out, moving like a piston thrusting forward then suddenly reversing direction to the position where it started.

This rapid shaking produced an invigorating massagelike sensation deep into the muscles. Bruce could actually feel the bones of his forearm vibrating. Sifu Mark was pleased with the intensity at which Bruce performed this task and explained that every Praying Mantis student should own a set of iron rings for exercising at home. He then told Bruce that this rapid movement would help stimulate the muscles and help in developing quick and highly explosive speed in his punches and blocks. This would happen not because the workout makes the muscles stronger but because of the stimulation and coordination of the "twitch" muscles in the arm. That is the secret for promoting rapid acceleration in a punch or block when initiated from a stationary position. This revelation prompted Bruce to ask further questions regarding this phenomenon. He had recalled one of his mentors and senior Wing Chun classmates, Ah Hing, back in Kowloon telling him one time that some people are naturally fast while others have to work to achieve this ability. He had also divulged that if someone is naturally gifted with incredible speed and then worked to enhance that quality, they would become extremely fast, so fast, in fact, that they could hit someone in an eye blink. Sifu Mark agreed completely. And he said the iron rings were one of the best pieces of training equipment he had ever found for speed conditioning, and anyone that set up a good training routine that incorporated the iron rings as a part of their regimen would definitely become fast beyond their imagination.

Next Sifu Mark introduced Bruce to the sapling-arm training device. Sifu Mark knew that Bruce would be somewhat familiar with it, because he had studied Wing Chun, but the sifu was confident that, after this training session, Bruce would never look at the mook yan jong the same way again. He then instructed Bruce to step up to the sapling arms and demonstrate some of his Wing Chun wooden dummy techniques. Sifu Mark observed Bruce's performance with a very critical eye to determine if he could spot any flaws in his technique. Sifu Mark complimented Bruce on his excellent exhibition, which brought a broad smile to Bruce's face. Sifu Mark then stepped up to the device and grabbed one of the round wooden appendages with his right hand. He placed his other arm on top of the lower extension. Unlike Bruce, who had demonstrated an intricate and exacting series of parrying and punching techniques, Sifu Mark began pulling down on one wooden arm while jerking the other arm outward and away from him. He did this very rapidly, in a systematic series of jerking motions. His maneuvers set up a set of reverberations that created a sound that was unmistakably produced by Sifu Mark. All of the students in the kwoon stopped what they were doing and watched. Bruce was a little perplexed as to what he was supposed to be seeing. It did not resemble any of the wooden dummy techniques that he had performed earlier. He then asked his sifu what the purpose was of this type of training.

Sifu Gin Foon Mark then stopped the pulling-jerking maneuvers and became very serious. He told Bruce that, in Praying Mantis gung fu, one must perfect skills in reading and reacting to the timing of an attack and develop a sense for an opponent's next ploy. You had to anticipate your opponent's every intention, from the first contact with their arm until you gain the advantage through followups and counterattacks. Bruce was still puzzled, because he did not quite understand what pulling and jerking had to do with it. Sifu Mark sensed this and instructed Bruce to stand in front of him and throw a very fast punch toward his face. Bruce responded as instructed. Sifu Mark swiftly blocked the extended punching arm with a force like a powerful vice. As Bruce tried to pull away, his sifu grabbed his other arm and did exactly what he had done on the sapling-arm device. Bruce lost control of his punching arm and could not escape from Sifu Mark's clutches. When Bruce would pull in one direction, Sifu Mark would go with that motion and redirect it to another angle, all the while keeping Bruce off balance and preventing him from maneuvering. Even Bruce's footwork was limited by this artful and swiftly executed manipulation. Bruce was then thoroughly convinced that the sapling-arm device was an incredible piece of equipment, even though it appeared to be crude compared to the mook jong he was accustomed to practicing on back at the kwoon in Kowloon. Sifu Mark concluded that segment of the lesson by telling Bruce that one must always be alert to the possibilities of using the opponent's weight and strength against them, and he had never found a better way to accomplish this than mastering the techniques of the sapling-arm dummy.

By Thursday of the second week, Bruce had become acquainted with most of the regular students at the Praying Mantis kwoon. His persistence, enthusiasm, and unquenchable desire to spar with his classmates was very apparent, but his sifu had not permitted him to engage in pugilism with them until he was satisfied that Bruce understood the tenets and fundamentals of his Jook Lum Gee Tong Long Pai system (Sifu Mark's unique style of southern Praying Mantis). When Bruce had said that he was only going to be in New York for three more weeks, Sifu Mark had decided to give Bruce accelerated training. Because Bruce had proven to be an exceptional student and was quite advanced for his age, his sifu felt justified in teaching him techniques that were usually reserved for more advanced students. Sifu Mark introduced Bruce to several new forms of training that would prepare him to spar the following week. Among these new techniques was the principle of "borrowing energy" from a sparring partner, something that the other student had used against Bruce during their sparring match the first night Bruce entered the Praying Mantis kwoon.

In order to prepare Bruce in to use the new technique when sparring, Sifu Mark wanted him to practice the sapling arm drills he had demonstrated. Through borrowing energy methods, one develops a sense of their sparring partner's timing and energy when contact begins. Through practice, borrowing energy swiftly enables one to make use of one's opponent's strength when counterattacking. However, the practitioner must integrate effective footwork with the technique. The remainder of that evening's workout consisted of Bruce, under the watchful guidance of Sifu Mark, training with a senior student.

The following class again consisted of one-man and two-man practice drills. The short one-man sets consisted of working on timing footwork, with various hand techniques. Sifu Mark complimented Bruce on his footwork, which was truly exceptional for someone that had only been trained in Wing Chun. He added that most Wing Chun gung fu men were only effective at using the rooted stances, where little movement was required from the lower portion of the body. Bruce explained that he had done some boxing in Hong Kong and was somewhat adept at the cha-cha dance, which could account for his surprising footwork. It made perfect sense to Sifu Mark.

The short two-man sets were a series of techniques extracted from the um han form (Sifu Mark's sets for helping students learn distancing) combined with some diagonal and frontal footwork, all of which Bruce performed with relative ease. Sifu Mark then taught Bruce what he referred to as the sliding step, a seemingly simple mobility drill for moving in and out, lateral to diagonal, and the reverse directions of those combinations. Sifu Mark noted that Bruce had a keen sensitivity of the floor surface that most students didn't possess when they attempted to learn this form of footwork. When novice Praying Mantis students attempted to perform this exercise, they tended to bounce more than slide.

Later that night, as Sifu Mark conducted the formal class with all of his students, Bruce got a chance to observe many of the traditional hand and weapon sets. Each group, beginners, semiadvanced, and advanced students, were skilled at various levels of these Jook Lum Gee Tong Long Pai forms. Sifu Mark supervised and conducted formal instruction in the gamut of the empty hand forms and weapon sets representative of his southern Praying Mantis style. The um han, which Bruce was learning; um moy fat; and the 18-, 36-, 72-, and 108-point formulas were all reviewed. For the first, time Bruce got the opportunity to witness Sifu Mark demonstrate and teach some of his classical Chinese weapon arts. It included various weapons, such as the butterfly knives, the staff, the three-section staff, the quan do, the trident, and swords. Before leaving class that night, Sifu Mark gave Bruce an instructional pamphlet that contained the training curriculum of the kwoon. It contained a brief biographical sketch of Sifu Gin Foon Mark, a listing of the forms and sets taught in the southern Praying Mantis Jook Lum Gee Tong Long Pai style, and several pages of pictorial renderings of the training equipment and instructions for using the crude appearing devices.

That weekend Bruce was obligated to attend several functions that his father had planned for him. Hoi Cheun had reserved front row seats at the opera performance in Chinatown for two shows. One of the reserved tickets was for the Saturday night performance and the other for the Sunday evening gala. Afterward, Bruce was obligated to attend the parties and festivities that followed the events. His father was constantly introducing him to his friends and associates of the Chinese opera troupe. Many were socially prominent and well-respected Chinese from Chinatown and the greater surrounding areas of New York. Since Bruce had been raised in a Chinese opera family, he was not overly enthusiastic about joining in these social functions, but out of respect for his father, he attended nevertheless. He looked forward to the following Monday evening, when he would resume his training at the kwoon. Uncle Yong made life a bit more bearable over the weekend by spending some time in the mornings and afternoons showing Bruce more of New York. They visited Coney Island, Staten Island Zoo, Greenwich Village, the Bronx, Central Park, and Union Square. But what impressed Bruce most of all was the size of the financial district. From the time that they parked and had lunch there, Bruce kept commenting to Uncle Yong about the enormity of the massive sky-scrapers. It was difficult for him to fathom how human beings could construct such awesome buildings. Uncle Yong simply said, "Ingenuity Bruce, ingenuity."

Monday night Bruce was the first student to arrive at the kwoon. When Sifu Mark opened the door, he could see that Bruce was even more serious about his lessons than the previous week. Bruce immediately applied some dit da jow liniment to his arms and forearms, and after formally saluting the altar, entered the training area. While Sifu Mark attended to some office business, Bruce commenced working out on the training equipment, adhering to the training regiment that Sifu Mark had set forth the previous week. For the next thirty minutes, and until the formal class started, Bruce worked diligently strengthening and conditioning his arms, all the while focused and ignoring the other students that were arriving for the night's training session.

When Sifu Mark entered the kwoon and called the class to atten-tion, Bruce joined the group. After several minutes of practicing the um han empty-hand set, Sifu Mark again spent a brief moment working exclusively with Bruce before getting to the crux of the ses-sion. He explained to Bruce that this evening's session would be devoted to working on self-defense techniques. Bruce was disap-pointed, since he had his heart set on sparring with a senior stu-dent. Sifu Mark, sensing this, said that there would be plenty of time for sparring later. He felt it would be best, since the students of that class would be working on self-defense techniques, that Bruce should do that as well. Perhaps he would learn something that would be valuable should he ever be assaulted on the street. Sifu Mark was totally unaware of Bruce's experience in street fight-ing back in Kowloon, but Bruce acquiesced and decided to absorb any knowledge that Sifu Mark may have concerning this very diverse subject.

Sifu Mark had all of the students sit on the floor as he began conducting a lecture about the realities of true self-defense. Everyone listened attentively as he began. He started by emphatically stating that the Jook Lum Gee Tong Long Pai southern Praying Mantis system was created specifically for fighting and had not been diluted to a sport. Therefore, it contained many techniques not found in other systems and considered all ranges in fighting. He followed by saying that this art primarily consisted of punching, kicking, striking, and clawing, attacking nerves and vital points of the human anatomy.

For the next thirty minutes, Sifu Mark, with the help of several senior students, demonstrated many of the exacting fighting tactics and the way that Praying Mantis addresses various fighting scenarios. Bruce, more than ever, was convinced that Sifu Mark was a remarkable human being. Not only was he gifted in the traditional techniques of classical Praying Mantis but was highly skilled in applying it to everyday situations in which practicality was more important than methodology. With simple demonstrations using one of the students to grab or punch him in various ways, Sifu Mark would show how a simple touch to a specific point on the body would cause an attacker to grimace in pain as he ceased his aggressive assault.

Sifu Mark had another student remove his shirt and then pointed out the various nerve and pressure points along the meridians of the body. He explained how the body's internal organs, such as the lungs, spleen, kidneys, and heart, are directly related to these points. Striking someone, as opposed to touching them, on these precise specific meridian points could result in serious injury, or even later death. Bruce, perhaps more than the other students, indicated a real fascination for this very secretive self-defense and fighting knowledge. Again, Sifu Mark was proving to be much more than what he appeared when demonstrating his knowledge and abilities in the deeper meanings of the movements found in the Praying Mantis techniques. In concluding this session, Sifu Mark expressed a serious concern for the dangers of using, or misusing, the acupuncture points as self-defense targets.

Next, the students paired off, and Sifu Mark began demonstrating simplified self-defense techniques that he wanted everyone to learn that night. Bruce was opposite a senior student who had been training with Sifu Mark for a number of years. For the next two hours, they were alternately the defender and the attacker while practicing various grabs, pushes, punches, and grappling assaults. Each participant was to use his most aggressive and brashest attempts to try to subdue their partner. Naturally, the recipient of the aggression improved in their defensive abilities with each renewed attack until it was virtually impossible for the other to penetrate the defense successfully. That evening, even though Bruce had thought it would be a rather dull experience after Sifu Mark had not permitted him to spar, but it had been a very enriching and highly educational experience in the art of realistic self-defense after all.

The following evening Sifu Mark began his formal class with a discussion of fighting theory. This topic was of special interest to Bruce, since it related to what he liked best, that is, fighting and learning every possible aspect of defeating an opponent in empty-hand combat. As with other classes he had attended, a short lecture preceded individual practice and the pairing off with a partner. In that night's discussion, Sifu Mark explained, in great detail, the advantages and limitations found in traditional or classical Chinese gung fu forms. Although he had touched on that subject briefly with Bruce when they were first introduced, Sifu Mark thought it best to expound upon the topic in greater detail for the benefit of all of his students. Bruce relished this conversation, since he had some ideas of his own that related very closely to how Sifu Mark felt about fixed martial art sets and freestyle fighting against another skilled combatant. Sifu Mark said that the best one can hope for was to select a style that most closely resembled the fighting they would expect to use in combat. If a style appeared rigid, still, or too reliant on theoretical, outdated self-defense methods, it would be doubtful that the student would get very far in their training. The student would ultimately become very disappointed at the results after attempting to use their fighting art against someone like a street fighter or boxer, who would have different tactics and experience in fighting. If street fighters are skilled at using tricks such as sucker punches, haymakers, beer bottles, choke holds, spitting, wrestling tactics, or other similar ploys, martial artists that have not learned a style that adequately addresses these types of encounters are destined to be surprised and ultimately be defeated by their own inexperience.

Likewise, the same results would occur if one has not mastered the ways and methods of boxers when they use jabs, feints, bobbing and weaving, uppercuts, left or right crosses, hook punches, and the like. Sifu Mark was animate in emphasizing that the Praying Mantis style that he taught dealt with these types of fighting, and the student should fully appreciate the knowledge and techniques found in the two-man sets. He then stated that the fighter must have a mind and a body that are fluid in expression and in actions, to be like water and fit their tactics to suit their needs at the time. Bruce savored and deeply pondered every word that Sifu Mark said on this most interesting subject. One could learn to react instinctively to an unarranged attack from learning prearranged sets, provided that the practitioner of the style got beyond the point of merely matching the techniques with proper timing and positioning of the expected assault. In essence, this meant reaching a point in training at which the mind and the body were free to respond instinctively. Bruce had heard Yip Man speak of some of these ideas in Kowloon, but back then, Bruce had not fully grasped the real meaning of this type of training. The understanding and clarity with which Sifu Mark expressed his points seemed so much more lucid.

Sifu Mark then shifted the lesson to attacking while using combination ploys, using two different techniques simultaneously against an opponent. The intention of this strategy is to confuse the opponent and penetrate even the most skillful opponent's defense. In some instances, the timing and execution of combinations could be so close that the adversary found it impossible to defend effectively against both attacks. The opponent may block or deflect one attack, but the other would undoubtedly strike its intended target. After Sifu Mark demonstrated a variety of combination attacks, with kicking as one of the two techniques, Bruce began gaining an understanding of just how important low and midlevel circular kicks were to combination technique fighting.

As the class concluded that night, Bruce walked away with a lot of material to digest and many new elements to ponder about the real world of fighting. Sifu Mark had opened Bruce's eyes to a completely new realm of possibilities that would take much contemplation before he could readily use it in his fighting style. Of course, he knew there would be plenty of time to experiment and discover the things that worked best for him.

The remainder of the week, and up until Thursday night, Sifu Mark spent a substantial amount of time working personally with Bruce, for he knew that Bruce would be returning to San Francisco the following Wednesday. While his assistant was teaching the main classes, Sifu Mark was busy introducing Bruce to the concepts behind drawing, hand immobilization, foot immobilization, progressive indirect attacks, and simple direct and singular attacks. All these concepts had a direct application in fighting, in which Bruce could apply the techniques of both his Wing Chun and his newly acquired skills in southern Praying Mantis gung fu. With drawing, he learned unique and clever ways to lure an opponent into traps. One ploy was to create intentional openings in the defense that were too tempting to resist. When the aggressor decided to attack those openings, he was set up for the counterattack. Bruce liked these deceptive little ruses and saw how he could apply them to his own style of fighting. With Bruce's fairly skillful knowledge of Wing Chun Sil Lim Tao set, Sifu Mark had little difficulty teaching him the use of some additional immobilization fighting techniques in which he could artfully use the sliding step combined with techniques of blocking and ultimately entangling the opponent's punching arm, thusly neutralizing of the attacker's forward momentum. Some of these techniques required having the courage and conviction to step into the attack as it was coming toward you. Bruce had no problem moving into an oncoming attack because of the simultaneous blocking and counterattacking he had learned back in Kowloon.

By Thursday night, he was beginning to appreciate the value of the new levels of fighting knowledge that Sifu Mark had taught him. Just when he thought he had a clear picture of Sifu Mark's ability, his teacher would introduce him to something entirely new, like when Sifu Mark started explaining and showing the techniques that involved progressive indirect attack, simple direct and singular attacks. In these techniques, one would use the arrow footwork formula to outwit and outsmart an opponent when one was in the attack mode. Feinting left, moving right, attacking frontally while stepping laterally, feinting frontally while attacking to the right or left was typical of these lightning quick and powerful close-range Praying Mantis maneuvers. When Bruce left class Thursday night, his head was filled with so much additional fighting knowledge that he was not sure how he would ever be able to integrate it into his own fighting arsenal. He did know that it would certainly take time and a lot of practice to assimilate it all.

Again, Bruce spent the weekend socializing with his father's friends and associates from the Chinese opera. Some had bought him small going away presents and tokens of their friendship because he was the son of Lee Hoi Cheun. Bruce spent Sunday morning at the apartment with his father, and they discussed his plans for relocating from San Francisco to Seattle. His father telephoned Quan Ging Ho and confirmed that he would be there to pick up Bruce at the San Francisco International Airport late Wednesday evening. Bruce's father also told Bruce that the lodging he would have in Seattle was a gracious gesture by Ruby Chow. She and her husband, Ping Chow, owned a restaurant there on the outskirts of Seattle's Chinatown. They would be sponsoring him in exchange for his working at their restaurant. After hearing the details, Bruce was agreeable to his family's plans. All the plans were in place, and basically all Bruce had to do was show up and his future was set for the next four or five years.

Bruce spent the remaining two days in New York at the Praying Mantis kwoon on East Broadway in Manhattan. In recapping some of the earlier lessons, Sifu Mark decided to emphasize the complex styles of integration that could be applied to attacks and counterattacks. He did this in a rather simple way, so Bruce could grasp the concepts of intricate combination close-range fighting. Sifu Mark would designate a letter of the alphabet for each specific type of punch, block, and strike. He even gave a designation for some low-level kicking techniques. Bruce was a little puzzled by what his sifu was doing, and he could not see the purpose for such nonsense. Next, Sifu Mark had Bruce assume a fighting pose and remain prepared to initiate an attack. Then, Sifu Mark gave different commands, calling out combinations of letters like ABC, ABD, HIA, FIA, PIA, SDA, or SAA. Bruce stood there motionless, pondering what his sifu was saying. After another brief explanation and a short demonstration in which Sifu Mark told Bruce that an *A* denoted a lead-hand lunge phoenix-eye punch, *B* represented a low-level knee attack, and *C* stood for a circular foreknuckle strike, Bruce understood that this was a system of designing and customizing combinations of fighting techniques. When putting the combinations of letters together, the code would comprise a different fight attack strategy. Literally, he could make thousands of such combinations.

After Sifu Mark demonstrated a few moves while saying their designated letters, Bruce tried this new form of fight training. After about ten minutes, Bruce began to instinctively combine and execute the movements almost as fast as his sifu could finish stating the combination. Sifu Mark was very pleased at the speed at which Bruce could learn this advanced level of training. One of the things Bruce learned during his last night at the kwoon was the importance of awareness. Sifu Mark stressed that a fighter must constantly change with the conditions during any fight. "Real combat is alive," he said, "and requires a constantly changing art and not a dead one. Always apply strategies that reflect this, and you'll always be victorious."

The following morning Uncle Tong arrived at Bruce's apartment and drove him to the airport, where he boarded his return flight to San Francisco. On the flight, Bruce had time to reflect on all of the experiences and things he had learned in New York. He could not help reflecting on the last words that he had remembered Sifu Gin Foon Mark had said.

It was dark when the aircraft touched down in San Francisco. As promised, Mr. Quan Ging Ho was there to greet Bruce and take him back home to his apartment in San Francisco. During the drive home, Quan Ging Ho asked Bruce many questions about his experiences in New York. Bruce had very little to say about the opera or the people he had met that were associated with the production. Most of his conversation centered on martial arts and the enormous amount of knowledge that he had learned from Sifu Mark.

Chapter Two

James Yimm Lee

Life in Oakland

On the first Saturday in September of 1959, the small two-story dwelling located at 584 Valle Vista Street in Oakland, California, appeared to be just another house in the Oakland suburban community that surrounds Lake Merritt. Around the neighborhood, children played, cars were washed in driveways, and domestic chores were busily performed that day. Perhaps the only oddity in the everyday life associated with this suburban community was the sound emanating from the basement of James Lee's home.

Every Saturday and Sunday, James could be found in his cramped basement, secluded from the rest of the world, practicing his "iron-hand" breaking techniques and perfecting his Sil Lum gung fu martial arts forms. Rarely was anyone permitted to witness his training in the art of iron-hand board and brick breaking or his practices in the secretive ways of unarmed self-defense. As the sound of broken boards and bricks resonated throughout the neighborhood, the residents became acutely aware that another individual had somehow gained access to James's private domain. What they did not know was that, for the past year, James had consented to train a fellow martial arts practitioner in the arts of gung fu and iron-hand conditioning.

Since 1958, James had been privately teaching those ancient arts to a large caucasian man named Al Novak. Al was the first student that James had ever agreed to train in these rare skills. The five years that James had spent developing his iron-hand techniques had proven to be time well spent; seriously interested people now sought out his services. Although he was skeptical about teaching these arts to just anyone, especially caucasians, Al Novak truly possessed a desire to learn. James was keenly alert to an individual's sincerity, and he knew that his intuitions about teaching Al were correct.

As the two men perfected their breaking techniques, piles of the pulverized remains of lumber and masonry increased at their feet, and the entire room was permeated with the pungent aroma of dit da jow. This Chinese herbal liniment was the key to successful breaking without causing injury to the hands or arms. James made his dit da jow from a very old and secret Chinese recipe that had been passed down through the centuries by martial arts masters. Since the vaporous liquid took several years to age properly, he usually made five gallons at a time and stored it in the coolness of the dimly lit basement. Between setting up fresh bricks and boards, James and Al would meticulously anoint their hands and arms with the liniment, until it was completely absorbed into the skin. The liniment helped promote circulation and healing of muscle and tissue shocked by the continuous pounding of the breaking exercises. Al was astounded that James could break large amounts of wood or concrete without showing any signs of calluses or abrasions on his hands; they were extremely strong and well conditioned, yet remained smooth and supple. James attributed this to the many years of applying the herbal liniment and practicing the breaking techniques regularly. Al had noticed that, since he had been following James's routine and using the dit da jow, his own hands had increased in hardness while still remaining soft and smooth.

It was amazing to him that the hands could be conditioned to such an extent that they could break incredible amounts of solid substances without causing injury. Any normal person, without knowledge of this ancient Chinese secret, would undoubtedly destroy or severely damage every bone and sinew in their hands by attempting to break even half the amount. Ever since he had first witnessed James demonstrate his iron-hand breaking skills at one of Wally Jay's traditional Hawaiian luaus, Al had been curious how a man of James's small stature could perform such seemingly impossible feats and had wanted to learn how to do it himself. What perplexed Al was the fact that he weighed almost 280 pounds and James weighed less than half that. It all seemed to defy the laws of physics. This added to the mystery of the breaking techniques that James demonstrated. After a short meditative interlude, James hammered the back of his hand into the stack of concrete bricks and actually broke only that particular brick he had chosen in the middle of the stack. This was enough to convince Al that this small Chinese man possessed incredible skills, which he hoped to learn to perform. In retrospect, the many hundreds of hours he had spent training with James had given him much of what he was seeking. James's constant tutelage had produced a deeper understanding of the ancient ways of the gung fu masters. In addition, not only did Al have a great respect for James as his instructor, they had a strong bond of friendship, which had existed since they had first started training together.

Had it not been for James, Al would never have gained the trust and acceptance among the notable gung fu masters in the mysterious inner circles of San Francisco's Chinatown. James was responsible for getting him admission into the T. Y. Wong kwoon of original Sil Lum gung fu. In fact, Al was one of the very first caucasians to be accepted among Chinese gung fu circles. Although James and Al were both students under Professor Wong, the weekend training sessions proved to be more beneficial than the formal classes at the kwoon. Because of the long drive to San Francisco, Al often found it difficult to attend the classes, so he was fortunate to have James as his sifu. Since James usually preferred to work out in private, Al was deeply grateful that James was willing to share his Sil Lum knowledge. The single-minded intent and the individual attention he received from James could not be duplicated.

Al had also gained further insight into the training equipment that James had designed to enhance the effectiveness of a workout. The punching pads, bags full of BB pellets, training tables, striking posts, mechanized kicking and punching equipment, and weight-training apparatuses were all James's ingenious creations. The admiration that Al held for James was obvious to even the most casual observer; he was completely stymied as to where James found the energy to complete all of his martial arts projects.

James's most recent book, titled *Fighting Arts of the Orient: Elemental Karate and Kung Fu,* had received serious acclaim from martial arts practitioners around the world, yet James remained unchanged by their praise. He chose to remain anonymous, while enjoying his pursuits without disruption from outside sources. Al was impressed with James's ability to remain secluded and pursue his own developments in gung fu while seeking ways to reach a higher pinnacle of perfection within himself, and Al sought to emulate these same qualities. By one o'clock in the afternoon, the weekly workout had concluded. Both men were totally exhausted from the intense physical training; all of the Sil Lum sets had been practiced many times, and every breaking routine had been completed. As they left the dusty basement and proceeded upstairs, Al and James reentered the everyday world with a higher understanding of the ancient arts of iron hand and Sil Lum gung fu.

Once in the living room, they would spend the better portion of an hour sitting and sipping Chinese tea. Katherine, James's wife, was always considerate of his guests and liked to make them feel at home. For Al and James, these visits had been a regular occurrence for over a year, and Katherine had come to know Al very well. She was always glad to hear of the progress Al had made in his training, and James would keep her informed of what they had been working on. Even though Katherine was not interested in the martial arts, she understood the discipline that was required to become proficient at anything. After Al had departed the Lee residence, Katherine began preparing to leave for her singing lessons. James had the afternoon to relax and spend time with the children. Karena was now seven years old, and Greglon was five and a half. On these Saturday afternoons, James and the kids could play and enjoy themselves without having any other outside activities. On occasion, they would spend time fishing at Lake Merritt or feeding the ducks and animals at the children's zoo. Sometimes fifteen-year-old Richard, a son from Katherine's first marriage, would join them in the family fun. James thought of Richard as his own son and liked to include him in all the family activities.

On occasions when Katherine was not attending her singing lessons, she could usually be found visiting relatives in San Francisco. She usually took the children along with her when James got involved with his martial arts projects. By early evening, they were back at home in Oakland. As Katherine prepared dinner, she listened attentively as James shared the martial arts ideas that he had been contemplating. He was becoming very interested in selling books and other martial arts related equipment. Although Katherine was not actually involved with martial arts, James valued her opinions on business matters highly. She realized that, regardless of the nature of the business, all business practices must follow a standard format to be successful.

Ever since he had written *Fighting Arts of the Orient*, James had wanted to be independent and expand his part-time company. Over dinner, he unveiled plans for the expansion of Oriental Book Sales. The prospect of James becoming his own boss and possibly quitting his welding job did not please Katherine. He reassured her that, at this point, it was only going to be a hobby; if the venture looked like it was going to be successful, then he could make different decisions about the business. Katherine was relieved to know that James was not going to plunge into a new venture without making careful plans for the future.

Katherine was an excellent cook, but as much as James truly enjoyed her cuisine, he never seemed to savor the true essence of dining. Instead of conversing during the meal, he liked to finish eating quickly. Other than the fact that it sustained life, he viewed dining as a waste of time and felt that idle chatter only prolonged the mundane ritual. This was typical of him. James abhorred senseless talk. And he detested waiting in long lines, regardless of whether it was for food, clothing, or other items needed for daily living. Unless James was deeply involved with a project, he and Katherine would usually spend the rest of the evening watching television talk shows. On a typical Sunday morning, the entire family was at the table eating breakfast by seven o'clock. James was quick to finish his meal and begin his early morning workout. After he had finished training and while the family was at Sunday church services, James would attend to matters that needed attention around the house. He was a fairly proficient handyman and enjoyed making things with his hands; subscribing to *Popular Mechanics* and *Popular Science* magazines helped him achieve some of his expertise with these projects, as well as helping him construct many of his martial arts training devices. There was rarely a Sunday when James did not undertake a project that improved either the house or his training equipment. The solitude that he enjoyed for most of the day also gave him time to draw elaborate blueprints and detailed sketches of future projects. The cabinet in the basement was filled with hundreds of ideas and designs for equipment to help increase the abilities of the serious gung fu practitioner.

After the morning church services, Katherine would usually take the children to San Francisco to visit relatives, often not returning until midafternoon. By that time, James would have completed his work and would be deeply engrossed in a good book. He did not have an extensive library, but he saved books that held his interest even after he had read them. His favorite book was *The Rubáiyát of Omar Khayyám*, and on occasion, he would reread the passages that inspired him. James also enjoyed studying the *I Ching*, an ancient Chinese book that explained the causes and effects of everything in the universe. He held an interest in the writings of Jeane Dixon and Edgar Cayce, the modern-day prophets known for predicting future events. These curious interests proved that James considered himself one who thought on a higher plane, rather than one who never questioned his physical existence. James also constantly read magazines that dealt with science and world events. Among his favorites were *Esquire, Life, Look, Time, Newsweek, Popular Science, Popular Mechanics, Black Belt Magazine,* and *Iron Man,* a magazine that dealt with the principles of weightlifting and bodybuilding. *Iron Man* had been a favorite magazine for several years, and James kept abreast of every new and innovative concept it published. On Sundays, he also had the time to read several newspapers, updating himself on the world affairs he had missed throughout the week.

When Katherine and the children returned from San Francisco, James was always there to greet them. This was the time when they could enjoy each other's company and recount the day's events. By

7:30, on Sunday evenings, the family was enjoying one of Katherine's delectable Chinese dinners. After dinner, the children were readied for bed, and James and Katherine concluded their weekend with the TV evening news before retiring for the evening.

Monday morning came rather early in the Lee household. With James and Katherine working and the children needing assistance in preparing for school, they needed to hire a housekeeper. Sarah arrived every weekday at seven o'clock, and while James and Katherine were readying for work, she was busy making breakfast for the family. By 7:30, breakfast was over and James and Katherine were on their way to work. Katherine was a secretary/receptionist at the Alameda Naval Air Station. Her primary duty was to expedite military supply orders to the various ships and aircraft squadrons that were stationed at the base. The job appealed to her and was financially rewarding.

James had been working as a senior welder at the Universal Window Company in Berkeley, California, for eight years. His job was to insure that each of the window frames and support brackets were properly welded and that they could stand up under the heavy-duty commercial usage. The company considered James to be one of the best welders in the Bay Area, and he was quite proud of his outstanding reputation. He was reliable and known for producing welded joints that could not even be intentionally unfused or forced to break under tension. Over the years, James had acquired many close friends at the plant, and he was well-liked by both management and his coworkers. Of all the employees at the company, Walter Bean was perhaps the closest friend that James had. They had first met when Walter began working there in 1951 and had shown a mutual interest in weightlifting and bodybuilding. Walter was one of several tool and die makers at the plant who also served as a machinist; Walter made many of the intricate and specialized components for James's training devices. Whenever James needed a specific part to make a piece of equipment work, Walter would create the part on the lathe or milling machine during his lunch hour. James and Walter had an understanding with the plant managers; any time scrap metal was available, they could exercise their designing interests during their lunch breaks. The managers knew that James was deeply involved with the study of martial arts, and his dedication to the company proved that he was capable of performing his job without neglecting it in favor of his own projects. James was glad that his bosses did not resent his creative endeavors but rather praised him for the ingenuity he showed in the finished works.

Walter had helped James print his *Fighting Arts of the Orient* book, which was now selling very well through Oriental Book Sales. Together, they had purchased a mimeograph printing machine, and Walter provided the technical expertise in operating it. Walter's wife Barbara had provided the typing for the text, and James had supplied the detailed drawings and photographs. James and Walter's collaborative efforts also produced some unique prototypes of martial arts training devices that were true works of art.

Their daily contact on the job forged a strong bond of friendship that not many people experience. Often Walter would get James to perform some of his incredible breaking feats or martial arts techniques for the other employees. These demonstrations often prompted their coworkers to begin training in gung fu. Although he did not encourage them in any way, James did begin teaching several of the men he worked with during lunch breaks. However, both he and Walter eventually realized that the men were not as serious as they had originally thought and eventually ceased to teach them. James was more content to work on the projects that he had developed, and with the help of Walter, many of his unique creations came to life.

◎◎

By 2:15 in the afternoon, the children had returned home from school. Soon, Katherine arrived home from work and began preparing the evening meal. While she was cooking, the children completed their homework. Both Karena and Greglon were aware that when their mother said it was time to study, there was no playing around. Katherine and James wanted their children to be as educated as possible, because they knew that one day their success would undoubtedly be based upon the knowledge they had received when they were young. Unless he had stopped at a local bar after work to have a beer with Walter, James was usually pulling into the driveway at approximately 4:45 each weekday afternoon. He was quite good about making it home on time, because he knew Katherine would have dinner on the table by five o'clock. After he had taken a shower and changed into fresh clothing, it was time for dinner.

James was always the first to complete the evening meal. While Katherine and the children were still eating, James would excuse himself from the table to go read the newspaper and watch some television. This brief period of relaxation calmed his mind and gave him a chance to redirect his thoughts to his gung fu lessons at the kwoon in Chinatown.

James really looked forward to Monday and Wednesday evenings from seven to nine, when he immensely enjoyed training at the kwoon. Resting before these classes was essential for him to center his thoughts and gather his energies. While Katherine cleared the dinner table, Karena and Greglon would go outside and play with the other children in the neighborhood. By 6:30, James had gotten sufficient rest and had a chance to share a few brief moments with Katherine, talking about things that had happened in the course of the day.

The drive from Oakland to San Francisco's Chinatown had become a routine in James's life. The training was at the Sil Lum kwoon of Professor T. Y. Wong, who was the founder and head instructor of the Kin Mon Chinese Karate–Gung Fu Club. He had been teaching at the Waverly Place address for over twenty years and his reputation as a stern taskmaster was well founded in his community and the Chinese business society. All, including the professor, were quite pleased with the cultural decorum and maturity of his senior students. Most of the respected aikido, kendo, karate, kenpo, and gung fu teachers were well aware of his abilities as an excellent traditional teacher, and visits to the San Francisco Bay Area were not complete until they had paid their respects to the professor.

Professor Wong was very selective in accepting students. Since *Kin Mon* literally translated to mean "sturdy citizen," he felt that every student must have a strong character and live a clean, useful, and moral life. Many of the younger people who sought his knowledge were not interested in attaining better character but were more interested in the fighting aspects of the art. This eliminated many potential students that might otherwise have had a chance to learn his original Sil Lum art. James realized that Professor Wong was very strict in his teachings of the philosophy that accompanied the gung fu training, and James never questioned the professor as to why he did not teach him the fighting aspects of the art. He knew that, when the time was right, he would have an opportunity to experience these advanced levels of training. The kwoon itself was relatively small for the number of students who trained there. Originally, it was a basement area but was converted to an open space training area. The paneled wall on the right side of the entrance held a wide assortment of bladed staff weapons used in Sil Lum advanced weapon training. Specifically designed for use against an adversary who was wielding a weapon of seemingly greater effectiveness, the quan do, tiger fork, spear, or broadblade staff in the hands of a skilled practitioner could be a lethal and devastating tool.

Professor Wong maintained a rigid and disciplined class structure in the kwoon, but he also stressed hospitality and etiquette to each student that entered his temple. A very old and traditional ritual was performed before and after each training session. A long, low table was located along one wall of the training area. This shrine was representative of the past masters of the style; in a time-honored ritual, the professor would place offerings of tea and oranges on the table to exalt these past masters. Each student was expected to give respect to the past masters before they received any strategic martial information or knowledge of their fighting techniques. The ceremony was an important part of the opening and closing rituals at the kwoon, and Professor Wong practiced it as a part of his own daily regimen, in addition to teaching his students. Each student was invited to partake of the tea and oranges, which were always available.

James always arrived early enough to change into his gung fu uniform and participate in the opening ceremonies, knowing that if he did not take part in the formalities, he would not be able to train actively in the Sil Lum classes. Formal salutations were expected of each student, and it was essential that the protocol of the Sil Lum kwoon be practiced in an exacting manner. Not to do so would indicate disrespect for the style, the professor, or both. Students who took their training seriously never omitted this part of the education.

After the formalities were finished, Professor Wong began the training regimen. During the past several years, James had gained proficiency in most of the basic techniques emphasized within the style. A student of Professor Wong's traditional instruction required, in addition to participation in the formal classes, daily practice for at least fifteen minutes to become expertly skilled in the style. The professor had told James on several occasions that he should expect to devote twelve to fifteen years of dedicated practice to achieve a true understanding of the Sil Lum style of gung fu. The first several years had produced favorable results, but James felt that he could learn at a faster rate if he could gain access to the physical knowledge that the professor taught. This was difficult, since Professor Wong would not teach the higher forms until the basic ones had been mastered to suit his high standards. In addition to the fundamentals, which consisted of punching, kicking, and a wide variety of stances that were unique to each maneuver, James had also learned the first form (set of movements), which was comprised of a lengthy pattern of self-defense techniques used against imaginary opponents. This form was known as *lin wand keung*, or "continuous and returning fist," and it was considered to be the cornerstone on which all other successive forms of internal and external systems were based. Professor Wong had told James that it would take over a year to master that one form, and he had been practicing it for almost two years. James was looking forward to the moment when he would be introduced to the second form, *mang fur har shan*, which translates to "tiger descending the mountain."

By the end of the two-hour workout, James and the other students were drenched in sweat. Their muscles ached and their joints burned from the punching and blocking techniques. Although many of the maneuvers were practiced repetitively, James loved the intensity and the way that it made him dig deep within himself to produce more energy. The natural high was something he could not get anywhere else. After the closing formalities, everyone retired to the dressing room to change back into their normal attire. James always made comparisons between Sil Lum and the other styles of martial arts that he had studied. He was constantly posing questions to the professor and required very specific answers to satisfy his curiosity. Though he did not agree with some answers dealing with street fighting, he always chose to be respectful of the professor's knowledge. James also realized that each style had certain techniques that would work effectively against most other methods of fighting, and he hoped that he would have the chance to learn the complete system of Sil Lum gung fu. These possibilities seemed to be the only thing that kept him interested in training, other than the fact that he enjoyed a good physical workout.

෨෧

Tuesdays were quiet for the Lee family, with the exception that James and Katherine would spend the evening hours filling and shipping orders of the *Fighting Arts of the Orient* book. James would advertise his book in magazines such as *Popular Science, Popular Mechanics, The Ring* magazine, and *Iron Man* magazine. Depending upon the market he was trying to reach, he would change the ad to suit the specific interests of the readers of the various magazines.

The response to his ads was astounding, and on any given evening, the mail carrier would deliver a wide assortment of packages and letters from all over the world, containing payments for the books. When James and Katherine opened the larger parcels, they discovered that some of the foreign payments were in the form of jewelry or valued pieces of art. After reading some of the letters that accompanied the packages, they learned that in many foreign countries people could not mail money overseas. They were very surprised that the small ads had reached such a large overseas readership. It was not long before they sold the first thousand books, and James had to print more of them in order to keep his business running smoothly.

James Begins a Writing Career in Earnest

The success of his book prompted James to begin plans for writing another book on the subject of martial arts and he had approached Professor Wong about the prospect of producing a book about the art of Sil Lum gung fu. Since he had printed his first book, he had learned a great deal that could be applied to this next venture. James entertained the possibility that they could collaborate, with Professor Wong demonstrating the techniques and explaining the text while James acted as the interpreter and handled the layout and printing. James had even mentioned to the professor that his first book was doing extremely well and that a book as complete as the Sil Lum book could do better still if the professor would consent to the project. Professor Wong's main concern about the book was how people might respond to it. A book could not adequately express the knowledge and the many years of training required to master the art. James tried to explain that the book's intention was not to convey every aspect of Sil Lum in detail but just to acquaint the public with the style and to help stimulate interest in Chinese gung fu. And Professor Wong would receive greater recognition for his unequaled skill as a master of the original style of Sil Lum gung fu.

The annual lion dance celebration was approaching, and photographs of the performance could possibly be used in the book. James had been learning the lion dance for some time, and interestingly, all of the performers were advanced students at the Chinatown kwoon. The sleeping lion was brought to life by the unique maneuvers, agility, and perfect timing of the dancers. Professor Wong was proud of his team and was always willing to perform the ceremony when a new business opened up in Chinatown. To be blessed by the lion dance meant that the establishment would enjoy good luck and prosperity in the coming years. Returning home from work on Wednesday, James looked forward to his evening workout and the opportunity to discuss some of the details he had been thinking about during the day. Most of his recent conversations with Walter centered on the book project, and James had even mentioned that he was thinking about having this book published by a regular publisher who could finish it in a more professional manner. He had also mentioned that, if Professor Wong was not ready to pursue the book project, he was going to update his book and revise it to include additional photographs and more information pertaining to iron hand and self-defense. After all, he had established a reputation through his first book, and the same people who had read the first one would undoubtedly purchase the latest edition.

By the end of his lunch break on Thursday, James had already compiled much of the information for his project. He knew that all of the preplanning was essential if the book was going to be presented in a professional and authoritative manner; one could never overplan for a work of this magnitude, especially when dealing with a subject as controversial as the martial arts. Once he reached home, after showering and changing clothes, he had some time to play with the children and find out how they were doing in school. While

Katherine was making dinner, James took the time to explain his plans for publishing another book. She thought that it was an excellent idea, providing the profits from the first one could be used to produce the second one. Katherine was the family expert on money management; despite all of James's efforts, he was not one to save money. Katherine was never content with the family's financial planning and always took the initiative to make sure the bills were paid and the groceries were bought. James was content to sign the checks over and leave the money matters to her. The orders pouring in from Oriental Book Sales were enough to convince her that he was indeed serious about his book publishing ventures. If additional money could be made through the sales of another book, the family might be able to move into a larger house. This was why she worked so hard helping James with his small mail-order business.

After dinner, James decided to drive down to Vic Tanney's gym to pick up some tips and training techniques used in weightlifting. Katherine was surprised when James returned home so quickly, but he explained that none his friends were at the gym that night. He preferred to spend the evening at home and lay out an introduction for the book that he wanted to write with Professor Wong. He hoped that, by producing some tangible results, he could show Professor Wong that the work was already in progress and he would consent to move forward with the book. James was sincere about getting the project moving, and his thoughts began to flow quite nicely as he started writing:

> Professor Wong, founder and head instructor of the Kin Mon Chinese Karate Gung Fu Club, has been teaching in America for over twenty years. Little known and less heralded, Sil Lum gung fu was not widely publicized until 1955, when Professor Wong and his Kin Mon Club appeared nationally on Arlene Francis's TV Show.

As head instructor of "Kin Mon," which incidentally means "sturdy citizen," it is the Professor's hope that the knowledge gained from gung fu will help his students live a useful, clean, and moral life. That is why initiation into the deadliest advanced arts are taught only when a student's moral character can be thoroughly trusted, never on a student skilled in the physical aspects alone, no matter how great his knowledge. The club was established as a non-profit institution. All members share jointly in the financial costs of training, equipment, and maintenance of the center. Admittance to the club is dependent upon the prospective member's character.

Professor Wong's emphasis is always on the helpful benefits of gung fu and never used for unlawful purposes that could have potential destructive effects when such a lethal art is misused. Secondly: the constant and diligent training comprised of balance, timing, and harmoniously integrated power- and speed-oriented maneuvers are to only be used for realistic self-defense. A perfect marriage of brain, breathing and fine-tuned body acting as one to exert one's maximum technique, along with a well-devised strategy, to an assailant's vital targets or least-protected vulnerable area. Professor Wong also believes that for one to attain this level of skill for effective fighting requires at least seven years of devoted training. He further feels that for a seriously dedicated student to earn the right to become a fully certified Kin Mon Sil Lum instructor (sifu) calls for twelve to fifteen years. Gung fu makes no fantastic claim that by training at home for 15 minutes a day one will be able to render an assailant helpless in seconds or master the art quickly and easily. Professor Wong was initiated into the aged, proven, and veritably endless art of gung fu at the age of ten. He will be the first to admit that no one person knows all of self-defense. This manual will deal primarily with the basic forms and principles of this internal and external system, as handed down by the Buddhist monks of the Sil Lum Monastery in China. Use it to improve your health, hoping it will be passed on in the same respect. Professor Wong mastered this little-known and jealously guarded Chinese karate system from Professor Leong Tin Chee as a youth in China, and this book will show Sil Lum as it is practiced in China.

Less than sixty years have passed since this system of gung fu was made known outside of the Sil Lum Monastery. Today, through Professor Wong's students, the art has taken root in the United States. This means that the style has not suffered any dilution or variation, as evident unfortunately in some of the other martial arts. All claims to the contrary notwithstanding, not one of the oriental self-defense systems can be quickly mastered in the piecemeal fashion. Only the unscrupulous make such statements. Actually, if one has less than seven years of training, the Chinese consider his art as not fully matured. The stronger and more firm the foundation, the higher one can build. The more one masters the fundamentals thoroughly, the better he can absorb and use effectively the knowledge of this system.

It is the professor's ardent and sincere hope that this modest work will in some small way focus the American attention on the constructive, healthful aspects of the deadly oriental defensive arts. The enduring aim of Kin Mon is to develop healthy, law-abiding citizens whose knowledge of Chinese karate (gung fu) will be a credit to themselves, their communities, and most of all to America; fighting qualities of the arts are of secondary importance.

K. H. Lee
Member, Kin Mon Chinese Karate–Gung Fu Club

◎◎

It was past midnight when James completed the draft of the introduction. He decided to use his original Chinese name of Kein Heir Lee, since he had used that name on his first book. Having the professor as coauthor would add additional credibility to the book and prestige to James's credentials as a writer. Name recognition was an essential part of a writer's trade and would certainly help in the sale of the book. He hoped that the draft of the introduction would convince the professor that a book of this nature would be worth the undertaking. As James retired that night, he had several dreams about seeing the book completed. The next day at work, James was preoccupied with plans for the book and his future projects. He knew that one day Katherine would be proud of him, when he could be his own boss and support the family better than he was doing now. Katherine was always supportive of his efforts, but she knew the reality and stability of a secure income, and she also wanted a larger house.

As always, Al arrived at the house punctually on Saturday morning. He brought a large box of boards and bricks, because James wanted to experiment with different types of materials to determine which were more difficult to break using the iron-hand techniques. Al and James then took some time preparing their hands with the dit da jow liniment, to insure that they were fully prepared for the breaking exercises.

When the iron-hand drills were concluded, the men were surprised by the results. James and Al ultimately discovered that the Roman-style bricks were the hardest to break, even though they were thinner than regular house bricks. This was because they were tempered through a second heating process that made them able to withstand twice the impact before they broke. Normal bricks were not tempered. Thus, they were twice as easy to break, even though they appeared more difficult because of their thickness. James surmised that the logical choice for a demonstration would be the larger, untempered bricks, since most spectators were not aware of differences in texture and usually imagined that the larger bricks were harder to demolish.

Another factor in breaking was that, when bricks were stacked on top of each other without using spacers, they were almost four times more difficult to break due to the compounded density of the material. James preferred to break bricks in this manner, because the knowledgeable martial artist could appreciate the power and speed behind the feat. The next accomplishment was breaking bricks and boards that were suspended from the ceiling by thin cotton fiber strings. This required an enormous amount of velocity, and only the most skilled breaking artists could perform these feats. By keeping the arm completely relaxed, it was possible to generate the maximum amount of speed before making contact with the surface. Just before contact was made, the muscles were tightened so that the mass of the body was transferred to the surface, thus forcing the bricks to shatter. Perfect timing of these two elements was crucial for the success of this type of technique.

After the breaking exercises had been completed, Al and James conditioned their arms, legs, and chests with another application of dit da jow. They then proceeded to pound sections of iron rods up and down their arms and legs until the skin had turned beet red due to the increased blood flow. The dit da jow took effect to promote blood purification in the area while helping to harden the bones underneath. Since the nerves of the skin produced pain in these areas, the herbal liniment helped to desensitize the tissue while healing the damage caused by the incessant pounding of the rods.

The mental confidence acquired through this training made the practitioner realize how tough the human body actually was. Most martial artists never become aware of the incredible amount of abuse the anatomy can take without resulting in serious injury. Both Al and James wanted to know the full extent of conditioning that was humanly possible, and by doing so, they could learn their maximum capabilities, whether used in self-defense or in breaking greater amounts of masonry and boards. James was always testing himself in order to achieve higher levels of proficiency, and most martial artists who knew him acknowledge that there was no one who could exceed him in that respect.

Later in the workout session, James began to teach Al the second Sil Lum form, mang fur har shan. The strong, circular open-hand and closed-fist techniques suited Al's physique perfectly, and James knew that the techniques represented in the form would serve many of Al's self-defense needs. James drilled Al repeatedly, allowing no breaks, until he was ready to drop from sheer exhaustion. James felt that continued training beyond the point of thinking was necessary so that a person could react without having to think about what he was doing. By one on Saturday afternoon, Al and James had completed their workout and relaxed with their cups of Chinese tea as James revealed plans for expanding upon the books that he had written. He wanted to include Al and some of their friends in the book, and he wanted to form a small club to practice the iron-hand training and some of the basic self-defense techniques not specifically emphasized in any one style of martial arts. Essentially, he wanted a club where they and others like them could work out without practicing the rituals of traditional training. James wanted Al to think of a name for the club that reflected some of the Asian flavor he wanted to include in the training. As their meeting concluded, James hoped that Al would consent to be a part of his undertaking.

After Al had left and as Katherine readied the children for a trip to San Francisco to visit relatives, James prepared to write a foreword for *Modern Kung Fu Karate*. There were so many things he wanted to say, but he had a limited amount of book space, so he had to choose his words carefully. After meticulously wording his thoughts, he began to write:

> The original version of this book was written as a hobby. It contains things which I thought some day may be of interest to my young son. In this modest effort, the training apparatuses, principles and techniques which are commonly practiced in Karate and Kung Fu, and some elements of Judo have been touched upon.
>
> In its purest sense, this definitely is not a work per se of the above-mentioned systems as it is written more from a hobbyist's point of view than an expert's. It contains, rather, glimpses into the high points and similarities of the different arts and how we can put these principles to work in home training to be able to develop some methods for keeping physically fit, and perhaps to build a little strength for the protection of ourselves and loved ones. Within the arts are contained many picturesque terms. These movements are as deadly as they are pretty sounding. For instance, "Butterfly Hand," is the start of the deadly chop. "Twin Dragons' Pearl" is a blinding art. "Monkey Stealing the Peach" is the effective monkey grab to the scrotum. Any of these flowery sounding arts can disable a man instantly in the hands of an experienced man.
>
> It is virtually impossible to mention the self-defense system of China without including the names of Hung, Low, Li, Choy, and Mok, the five systems noted for their particular contri-

butions to the defensive arts. "Hung" fist is noted through-out China for its powerful development of the fist. "Mok" leg is equally famous for the development of a powerful kick. The nickname for a fast kick was called "No Shadow Feet," meaning the kick was so fast that no shadow was cast.

In its early origin, the ancient arts were designed to defend against more than one assailant. They disable an attacker in the quickest way possible via kicks, pokes, chops, et cetera, never depending on clothing, submission holds, or the likes.

The whole body of an opponent is opened to your counter-attack, and by the same token, your own body is subject to his ability to counterattack also. The Queensbury rules are not followed in the Ancient Arts. The whole body from head to feet is used as a weapon. The knee, ball of feet, heel, hands, fingers, and back of the hand, etc., are used. The power an experienced expert can exert with his naked hands and feet is almost unbelievable. There is an actual record of an Oriental who fought over a dozen men with Kung Fu years ago in Oakland. This was the subject of an article in *True* magazine several years ago.

In Japan, a Korean expert in the Karate system dropped and killed a charging bull with his hands alone! A friend of mine, while stationed in China, saw a man break a brick by a twisting action and reduce it to rubble with his hands alone.

On close examination, one can see a common thread of similarity which runs through the different Oriental self-defense systems. Especially in certain stances, the yell, and uses of the natural weapons of the elbows, feet and hands is this thread seen. Take the chop for instance: It is used in Judo, Karate, and Kung Fu. It is even adopted by wrestlers of America today. Naturally, it is called by a different name in different countries.

Undoubtedly, the designs of posts, bags, training outfits, differ in the various Asiatic countries, and the way the natural weapons are utilized are not perhaps exactly alike—but the weapons used are the same.

All lands have added their valuable contributions of knowledge to certain phases of the Art. In particular, Judo from Japan, Kung Fu from China, Okinawan version of Karate from Okinawa, Korean version of Karate from Korea, etc.

Although the Oriental system was practiced centuries ago, the human body has not undergone any drastic changes. The old and time-proven system has withstood the test of centuries. The limbs are constructed by nature to bend just a certain way, and the organs can resist only so much pressure. The old masters knew and utilized this knowledge thoroughly, so they simply built the defensive arts against certain fundamental principles which no man can escape, regardless of his physical size. That is why attacks to throat, golden target, etc., are used in all the Oriental systems, though the technique may differ in execution, the results are the same, thus showing once again the same parentage from which all the ancient arts are offsprings. The stances, use of natural weapons, methods to train the hands, feet, etc., show traces of common past influence on the arts as practiced today.

For example, take modern Japan, China and Korea: Today each have their own languages, cultures, yet common words can be *read* and understood by the three different nationalities, though the pronunciation in each case is different. So, as a Japanese is not a Chinese, nor a Chinese a Korean, they are all alike by virtue of being Orientals. Similar points in languages and cultures point to the possibility of a common ancestral relationship in past history.

So it is in the Oriental defensive arts of Kung Fu, Karate, Kenpo, etc. Though they are not alike in certain phases, yet there are enough similarities in some areas that show the adherence to the same training principle of the past.

Kung fu, as one version of the Art is called, was said to be improved by the astute observations of the Chinese monks. They noticed how all wild creatures were provided with certain natural weapons, whereas the relatively weak human being had to resort to weapons of knife, spear, and dagger. The eagle has its beak, the tiger has its claws, but the delicate man, by being gifted with a little brain can easily fashion weapons to kill the eagle or tiger. So for their own defense, they copied freely from nature. They imitated the "Eagle's Beak," "Tiger's Claw," and the "Buffalo Horn." Once again their ingenuity enabled them to forge their hands and limbs into a substitute for a dagger, spear or club. Better than the weapons, they are never seen, but ready for instant use if required. Of course in different Kung Fu systems the names are different. For instance, "Buffalo Horn" is called "Dragon Head," the chop "Kwan Yin Palm."

Many of the Arts were developed in the Sil Lum Monastery of centuries ago, taught by the monks to their disciples. From there it spread throughout the Orient. This is perhaps why there are so many parts of Oriental arts that seem to be copied from each other. Just as the son will look somewhat like the father, the father always precedes the son. In itself Kung Fu, Karate, Kenpo, Judo, or Boxing, etc., shouldn't be suppressed from the public any more than the stores which sell bricks, pipes, or ball bats. When misused, a brick or bat can easily kill or injure a man. Any knowledge or implement when used without moral conscience can be a force for destruction. This is equally true whether it is physical or atomic power. If mayhem is the sadistic desire of anyone who takes up the fighting arts of the Orient, I really think it is much easier to get an axe, hammer, or pistol. Why spend weeks, months, or even years to develop the skill and power to hurt someone?

But on the other hand, if we approach the training sessions as a means of keeping physically fit, and mentally alert, to develop some degree of co-ordination between brain, breath, and body, to provide healthful stimulation of the blood it will be more enjoyable and less tiresome. You should develop the mental attitudes of people who box, wrestle, or fence for fun and health, not necessarily hoping for a chance on the outside to "knock a man's block off" or a chance to dislocate a persons shoulders, or even of driving a blade through an opponent's midsection.

Fortunately, or unfortunately, there is no absolute control over knowledge. When you buy a gun, the way it is used is up to the purchaser. When you develop power, the way it is used is of your own volition. It is sincerely hoped that this book, inadequate as it is, will be used in a constructive way by all. Use this knowledge to keep physically fit, always remembering that this sort of knowledge is a two-edged sword; it can cut both ways.

Perhaps by arousing the American interest in this facet of Oriental Art, this may in some small way become the wedge to keep open the door to understanding and good will between the different cultures of the East and the West. There is an old Chinese saying "Tin ha, yat gat," which means, "Under Heaven, there is but one family." I, for one, certainly agree."

@@

James was suddenly interrupted when the telephone rang. It was Professor Wong calling to say that he was interested in starting the book project as soon as possible. Evidently, the draft of the introduction section of the manuscript had a definite impact on the professor. He was now firmly committed to the project. Professor Wong informed James that he would start putting together some early historical documentation and information about the founders of the Sil Lum style. He instructed James to begin the layouts of the first two Sil Lum forms, and to determine the cost of the book. After the conversation concluded, James realized that his own book would have to be put on hold until after the Sil Lum book was finished. That evening, while the family ate dinner, James was busily working on the new project until, at two o'clock in the morning, he was exhausted.

The following morning, after Katherine took the children to Sunday school, James brought several hundred of his books to Chinatown to replenish the stores that had sold out. By early afternoon, James had put all of his available books on display and opened twenty-two new accounts. The money he had collected from the sales meant that Oriental Book Sales had made over five hundred dollars in the past two weeks, and he knew that it would please Katherine very much. The remainder of the day was spent at Professor Wong's home, where they went over the entire layout in detail. James had figured out the details on printing, typesetting, and cost factors, which would be shared on an equal basis. Professor Wong suggested that most of the photography be done in the kwoon, so that the action sequences and techniques could be performed in the traditional environment. Once the meeting was concluded, it was past 7:30 in the evening, and James began the trip back to Oakland.

The following week, James spent every available moment working on the book. He and Professor Wong decided to include several very prominent local martial artists of different styles to help broaden the respectability and credence of their collaboration. Paul Pung, a second degree black belt and head instructor at Paul's Kenpo Karate Studio in San Francisco, added several paragraphs to the text to represent his style. Another inclusion was Herman Cheong, a second degree black belt in the Japanese art of jujitsu who also sponsored the annual Hawaiian Islands Championships in weight-lifting and wrestling. Also included was Wally Jay, whose judo and jujitsu school in Alameda was a landmark in martial arts and had produced world-champion students on a consistent basis. The inclu-sions of these great martial artists gave the book an added author-itative respectability that would create a broader readership among the different styles, as well as recognizing these men for their con-tributions to the arts.

The kwoon photo sessions showing the professor demonstrat-ing the first two forms and a broad assortment of basic techniques had turned out quite well. The professor wanted James to be the model for several of the self-defense techniques and also wanted him to demonstrate the iron-hand breaking techniques as well. His idea was for James to appear on the back cover of the book per-forming one of his incredible breaking feats while demolishing two large bricks. After several weeks of constant shooting, all of the pre-liminary graphic illustrations and photos were ready to assemble.

By the time the holiday season approached, virtually every phase of the layout was complete, and it looked like the book would be available for sale in the next few months. James was proud of the fact that he had teamed up with the top authority of true Chinese gung fu in the United States. He felt that their collaboration would appeal to all martial artists who wanted to expand their knowledge of true Sil Lum and self-defense. The Christmas holidays were a special time of the year when all of the relatives got together to share time together that they did not normally have during the rest of the year. Traditionally, Christmas Day was spent at the home of James's parents for a yearly family reunion. It was a time to gather and reaffirm commitments to themselves and their elders. Over the New Year, James and Katherine hosted several parties at their home, and the friends that they did not often see would drop by to share in the holiday cheer.

Quicker than expected, the first week in January arrived, and James was excited that his book was being typeset at a local printer. Each night that James went to the kwoon, the first thing he would do was update the professor on the progress of the book. James was fast becoming one of the professor's best students and was progressing at an exceptional rate. Professor Wong knew that James was an outstanding example of what a person could accomplish if he set his mind to it. Since the Chinese New Year was quickly approaching, James and the other students were diligently working on the lion dance that they would perform at the parade. When the day finally did arrive, the lion dance team performed precisely and flawlessly, to the professor's expectations and standards.

When the family arrived home that evening, they were saddened by a phone call from James's brother, Jon, telling them that their father, Look On Lee, was seriously ill with a kidney malfunction. The next few weeks were spent preparing for the inevitable passing of James's father, and he tried to dispel his frustrations by working out even harder than usual. All of the anxiety caused James to have a relapse of malaria, which weakened him considerably during this critical stage. Just as he began to regain his health, James received word that his father had passed away during the night. The eighty-year-old Look On Lee was laid to rest in the Mountain View Cemetery in Oakland in January of 1960.

By the summer of 1960, the Lee family had resumed their normal daily routine. James's major concern was the possibility of a strike at the Universal Window Company, where the workers were demanding higher wages. Three weeks later, the strike occurred, so James decided to use the time to complete all his book projects and construct several new pieces of training equipment. His books, which were displayed in Chinatown, were selling well enough to help support the family during the strike, and soon his book with Professor Wong would be ready for distribution.

The first week in September arrived quickly, and the printers had finished the initial one thousand books. As soon as James loaded the books into his car, he was on his way to San Francisco to show them to the professor. When the professor saw the results of their work, he was quite pleased with the product; James had presented the Sil Lum style in a clear and concise manner without exploiting the art for the sake of glamour. The well-balanced blend of explicit pictures and authoritative chapters made the book the first of its kind written in the United States.

At the workout session that evening, James was introduced to his first advanced weapons form using the quan do, a large staff with a broad cutting blade that resembled an axe. The professor only taught this ancient art to those students whom he considered extremely proficient in unarmed combat skills. Trust and dedication were two essential elements that each student must also possess before entering the inner sanctum of weapons training, and those who did not meet the requirements had to leave when the training began. By the time the session had ended, James's muscles ached from the intense workout, but he felt that the challenge made him go deeper inside himself to exude more energy and strength than he had ever thought possible.

The following week brought great joy to Katherine, when James announced that he wanted to buy a larger house. While Katherine checked out locations for schools, hospitals, and other conveniences, James spent the next few weeks fixing up the old house, so they could get a better price when they sold it. By the time they were ready to move, the old house appeared completely refurbished and with expertly placed landscape.

Once they were settled in their new home, James wasted no time in converting a lower-level den into his workout area. He immediately began constructing new and improved training equipment and then decided that he would need additional space to store these pieces. His solution was to expand the gym to include the attached garage so that he could mount all of the equipment and still have room to practice. Al Novak had resumed his weekly training, and he and James were planning to create several special training apparatuses to help sharpen their skills. James's new book was selling extremely well, and Al was impressed with the way he dealt with his newfound notoriety. The orders were constantly flowing in, and it was becoming obvious that James was receiving some long overdue recognition for his martial arts acumen. The influx of mail prompted James to get a post office box to give the business a more professional appearance. If everything proceeded as he had planned, it would not be long before all of their expenses had been recovered and he and the professor would begin to reap the profits.

After James and Al had completed their workout, James received a phone call from two noted instructors of kenpo karate. Ralph Castro and Ed Parker had spotted one of James's books in San Francisco and decided to locate him to discuss his training techniques. James had several friends who were acquainted with the two men, but he had never had the opportunity to meet them. Ralph suggested that they meet to share knowledge about their respected styles and martial arts in general, and twenty minutes later, the two arrived at James's house. Ralph, Ed, and James became very comfortable with each other as they shared a mutual admiration for all styles of martial arts. Ralph and Ed were broadly versed in a wide spectrum of styles and methods and could express ideas without showing favoritism for a particular system. James could see that they were sincere, and this caused him to open up and reveal the deeper levels of knowledge that he possessed.

The two men were impressed with the great strength James possessed for his small stature, and they could see that he was willing to share knowledge of his system. Unlike many Chinese, who were secretive about their styles of gung fu, James liked to discuss, with great depth, the intricacies of such a deep and mysterious art from his ancient culture.

He was equally impressed that Ralph and Ed spoke openly and frankly about their style of kenpo karate, and they appeared to have open minds and clear visions of what the martial arts were all about. In James's mind, true martial artists were always willing to make new friends and broaden their horizons; the arts should never be so secretive that only a select few have the opportunity to experience their benefits. Soon after their initial meeting, James began paying regular visits to Ralph Castro's kenpo school in San Francisco. Ralph viewed James as an honored guest and always had the students give him a formal salutation to show their respect. James reciprocated by introducing Ralph and Ed to many of the gung fu masters in the inner circles of San Francisco's Chinatown. The three men also spent many afternoons discussing innovative ideas at James's home in Oakland.

The following week James was engrossed in his martial arts activities and in the sale of his latest book. The two thousand dollars that James had laid out to get the book published had almost been recovered. He and the professor would soon be turning a profit from the sales. And Wally Jay had asked James to demonstrate his iron-hand breaking feats at his upcoming luau. James dedicated most of his spare time to getting his hands into prime condition for the event, and by the time the luau arrived, he was ready. James was a huge success, as were the other martial artists assembled for the gathering.

Christmas of 1960 brought a remorseful turn of events for James. The professor and James had had a misunderstanding about the profit-sharing arrangements for the book. While they had agreed that all the profits would be divided on a fifty-fifty basis, the professor failed to realize that James had supplied all of the finances for the printing of the book and he had yet to reach a break-even point for his initial outlay. The professor, on the other hand, thought that the profits should have been divided evenly from the first dollar received, rather than waiting until the original working capital had been recovered. The tension created by this misunderstanding meant that James's workouts at the Sil Lum kwoon would never be the same, and the uncertainty of the future plans for the book loomed in James's mind.

The East Wind Modern Kung Fu Karate Club

The new year became the turning point that prompted James to make some resolutions concerning his martial arts training. Since he would probably no longer be associated with the Sil Lum kwoon, he would start a small club for some serious students who wanted to learn iron hand and basic self-defense. The sudden change in his habits was not going to be easy, but it was necessary to prevent losing his dignity and respect from the people he had trained with in past years.

James and Al wasted no time in starting regular workout sessions at the Monticello home. They decided to name the group the Modern Kung Fu Club, since it held both an Asian interpretation as well as a Westernized meaning. Although James had never been authorized by Professor Wong to teach Sil Lum gung fu, he did possess the knowledge of an authentic black belt in any style of martial arts. Al was concerned about how other martial artists would accept him without a valid certification from an authentic style, but James readily explained that his intentions were not to teach a traditional style, but more a basic, condensed course in self-defense that was both practical and effective. He also wanted to eliminate the many years of training spent on practicing the forms that represent a specific style. After a lengthy discussion, James and Al decided to recruit a select group of serious individuals who were interested in learning practical self-defense without the traditional formalities. James also wanted to write a manual that represented the course of training for the club members. Al mentioned that he had several close friends who would be interested in studying self-defense but did not have the time to pursue the classical arts. As the meeting concluded, Al saw that James was somewhat ahead of his time, venturing into new areas and presenting new concepts that had not been stressed before. The challenge would prove interesting, and the gamble was decisively worth the effort. Later that night, James began to write the guidelines for the study course of the future students of the Modern Kung Fu Club. As his ideas came together, he wrote:

Fundamentals of Modern Kung Fu Karate

Progress must be gradual. "Make haste slowly"—especially for those who are interested in breaking bricks the "exhibition way." Remember, 3,5,7 years will pass by anyway—so training should be of a slow gradual progress. Of course, breaking a brick the "training stunt" way can be accomplished within 100 days or less. But this is no true power. Just for sideshow.

Perseverance is of vital importance. There is an old Chinese saying, "Fist cannot leave the hand, Song cannot leave the mouth"—or in other words you can't train half-heartedly only to lay off and resume again. To be a good vocalist you must keep in constant practice through singing. In Kung Fu in 3 years you should show some progress; 5 years half the art is mastered; 10 years you should master one particular system. You cannot master 2 different systems at the same time.

After you learn a little about Oriental fighting, refrain from an attitude of conceit and arrogance. As Ed Parker says in his wonderful book *Kenpo*—develop an attitude of humility and self-restraint.

Use your Modern Kung Fu Karate training for physical fitness—only in extreme cases, perhaps to help the aged and weak, or in defense of your own safety—then use it as a deadly weapon. Kung Fu won't say you will always be victorious, but it will give you the courage to fight back whole-heartedly.

Avoid all physical excesses. If you must smoke or drink, confine it to after meals. Avoid nightlife, insufficient sleep, burning the candle at both ends.

Avoid emotional entanglement. This is why Monks make the best Kung Fu fighters. Their life of celibacy frees them from domestic strife, petty bickering, etc., so common among the American marriages of modern life.

They always maintain an air of tranquility.

Never start any blow from the head downward. This exposes your armpits—a fatal mistake against a trained opponent.

Whether you are chopping, poking or punching, never extend arms completely straight. This is a weak position—can be broken easily when straight.

Never fight from a stand up position. Always assume one of the basic "horse stances." An erect person has no solidity.

◎◎

Upon retiring that night, James was pleased with the master plan he had formulated for his new organization. While he slept, he had several dreams about the name of the club and wrote them down as he woke during the night. The next morning, he studied the suggestions and chose the name East Wind Modern Kung Fu Karate Club, because he felt that it incorporated more of the Eastern culture involved with the martial arts.

For the next three months, James devoted himself to writing guidelines for the club. When Katherine happened to read some of the notes he had made, she was surprised at how quickly his organizational plans were taking shape; he was writing and revealing wisdom about the martial arts that few were aware of. As Katherine continued to read, she was fascinated with the factual accounts of his art and future plans, which read:

> The early forms of karate, which consisted of basic fundamentals, were introduced into China from India by a religious man named Dot Mor. As the years went by, these forms were improved and added to by the monks of the Sil Lum Monastery in China. From there, certain aspects of the art spread to Okinawa and Japan, where it became known as "karate." "Kara" is the Japanese word for "empty," and "te" signifies "hand," thus the word "karate" is the common reference for many systems of "empty hand" fighting arts.
>
> The basic goal of Modern Kung Fu Karate is to base our teachings on the old and proven Chinese saying, "Yut dom, yee lik,

som kung fu," or "First is courage, second is power, third is the art of kung fu." Having two of these qualities without the third is equivalent to sitting on a three-legged stool with a missing leg.

The "East Wind Club" training will emphasize the fist art, since the mastery of knives, staffs, etc., is actually a waste of time in this modern world. Since we are not interested in monthly fees, we will try to give members a basic groundwork in health building and the fundamentals of self-defense in the least possible time. Within our non-profit club will be members who hold black belts in Judo, as well as some with weightlifting experience. At "East Wind" there is no student/teacher relationship, as we are all training partners. We learn as much from other members as they do from us, and we do not close our minds toward any other self-defense systems, since no system is better than the man using it is, nor is any system necessarily the best.

Modern Kung Fu Karate is constantly being revised to eliminate the bad features and improve the good ones. We try to present the American public at large with a true perspective of the Oriental art of defense, rather than the exploitation and exaggeration they have become accustomed to. Any Oriental system of karate is good, and certain systems are more suitable to people with a specific build or stature, so pick the one you like and specialize in it. Through your everyday conduct, be living proof that karate enthusiasts are not necessarily violent people who like to show off their prowess in fighting.

Remember, in this day and age, to injure someone unjustly may cause the same person to resort to vengeance with a revolver. It is our sincere hope that we can contribute what little knowledge we have toward increasing the American public's incentive toward physical conditioning. Our aim is to decrease the all too many "flabby" Americans; not to make them bare-handed men of violence.

J. Y. Lee
East Wind Modern Kung Fu Karate Club

◎◎

As Katherine and James perused the notes, the telephone rang. Al was calling to inform James that he had several friends who were interested in joining the club. These men represented a broad spectrum of martial arts and law enforcement, and most of them had trained in judo, weightlifting, boxing, and wrestling as well. After Al had given James some background information about the men, James felt sure that they would be assets to the club. James revealed that he wanted to form a club that included lifetime memberships and a board of advisors to give the group an established reputation among the community. As the conversation continued, Al was quite impressed with the thorough way in which James had planned the entire organization. It was possible this concept could become a history-making event. In any case, the knowledge that all of these men could contribute would certainly increase their awareness of self-defense and the martial arts.

On the following Saturday, all of the initial prospects gathered at James's house for a meeting, and they were very impressed with the arrangements for the club. They were excited to be a part of a growing idea that offered so much potential for them to learn and share knowledge from their broad backgrounds. They had a chance to review the notes for James's book project, which would be used as a training manual as well as a means for generating income to sustain the organization. James planned to take photographs of the development of the original members to illustrate the effectiveness of the course to the readers and future members. The men agreed to hold regular workout sessions on weekends, and they would be training in the garage of James's house. After the training was finished, they would discuss and evaluate the progress they had made. The overall format for the book would be based on the results of their training, and the guidelines set forth by James would be amended to match their progress. To insure that the group kept its high moral character, potential members would be evaluated and approved by the original members, which would serve as an excellent safeguard of the standards upheld in their unofficial charter. This would be a golden opportunity to experiment and improve their talents while sharing their wisdom.

After the meeting was adjourned, James sat in the den and tried to put all of his ideas in perspective. He hoped that the new club would serve a useful purpose that would lead to more significant martial art achievements. His primary thought was to one day form an institution that could possibly bring all of the martial arts disciplines together under one banner. This would be the ultimate martial arts institute, where everyone could learn from each other in a friendly and cooperative environment without any single style claiming superiority.

The following week, the serious group of recruits began training in earnest. James introduced them to several of the traditional forms, so their bodies could become accustomed to the flowing movements that were needed to deal with a wide assortment of adversaries who might maneuver against them in different ways. At the same time, they were becoming acquainted with the rudimentary forms of iron-hand training, along with the application of dit da jow to condition their hands for the more intense training that would later follow. The newer members contributed their knowledge of judo, which was effective in close-range fighting, but James felt it wise to emphasize the importance of changing the fighting ranges as it became necessary.

James gave the members a rigid training schedule, which would have to be maintained if they were to progress at the desired rate. Since most of the men were not familiar with the deeper realms of knowledge within the gung fu arts, they were quite impressed with the focus power that James possessed. James began teaching them the little-known art of putting the entire body weight into one blow, then concentrating it all in a given point at a specific time. When this was performed properly, it gave the practitioner the power of three men. James also emphasized that technique and intense mental attitude were required if one was to master this unique power-achieving method. Perhaps the foremost quality possessed by James was that he could designate specific fighting techniques that would suit each particular member's needs without standardizing methodologies that might not work effectively for that individual. James's wisdom proved to be the basis for most of the members' learning, even though each member contributed to the general learning process. After several weeks of introduction to the training regimen, James suggested that the group begin meeting three times a week, on Tuesdays, Thursdays, and Saturdays; this schedule worked perfectly for everyone.

Soon after the new training schedule had begun, James met several new individuals who were interested in joining his classes. It soon became apparent that the garage would outgrow its usefulness as a gym, since it lacked the professionalism to maintain the club's character. Until James could locate a vacant storefront, some of the prospective members would have to wait.

Since the main characteristic the men had in common was their ability to perform the iron-hand techniques, it was not long before the word of their breaking skills spread far and wide. *The Al Collins Show,* a popular local television program, asked the club to appear on the show to perform their incredible feats. On the day of their appearance, the station's telephone lines were busier than they had ever been for the program. Soon after their demonstration, word spread even further about James's and Al's unbelievable skills, and everyone who had martial arts experience was seeking them out for instruction in the iron-hand training. Through James's efforts, martial artists were developing a renewed interest in breaking techniques.

James was acutely aware that, if he and Al started teaching in a commercial location they should not advertise, because they would soon be flooded with people who did not take their training seriously. James liked the idea of working with a small group of students, since each individual had different needs and required proper guidance to become proficient. He wanted to share as much of his wisdom as possible, but he also wanted to be selective and secluded. In his teachings, James always felt that if a student was not serious, the training was a complete waste of time for both student and teacher alike. Many people wished to become proficient in the martial arts but were not willing to make the sacrifices necessary to develop the skills. It took hard work and dedication to master even the simple techniques, and Al and James were not sure how many prospective students packed the gear to handle the rugged training.

A Martial Arts Kwoon Emerges

By March of 1961, James and Al had finally decided to open a small gung fu school in Hayward, California. The building was much in need of repair, but after several weeks of hard work and maintenance, it took on an entirely different look. They had decided that they would keep a low profile and only recruit serious members who were truly interested in progressing in the arts, rather than advertise the club. Problems began when they could not gain approval for a business license from the city of Hayward. The safety inspectors declared the building a hazard, due to the weights and heavy equipment on the second floor, so after three months of training in obscure secrecy, Al secured another location in downtown Hayward.

The new school was in a prime location, and James and Al decided to increase their enrollment and charge the students enough so they could pay for the rent and utilities. Within a week, they were teaching several dozen new students, and James had organized a schedule for the beginners, so they could learn the basics without slowing down the more advanced students. The rotation of teaching duties with Al gave James more time to pursue his book project, which he intended to publish in the near future.

The most difficult problem with the book was the "poison hand" training that he proposed to include within the text. Even many of the advanced students had difficulty comprehending the deeper levels of poison hand's many techniques. It was hard for them to believe that a certain hand technique applied to a specific part of the human anatomy at a precise time of day could cause severe internal injury or death without showing any visible signs of damage. James had learned these techniques many years ago, and while they were regarded as one of the most advanced phases of gung fu, many of the old masters realized that poison hand could be used for healing as well. James wanted to reveal the existence of poison hand or dim mak kung fu, as it was called in Chinese, to the person who was seriously interested in the martial arts, without divulging so much information that a novice who read the book could start experimenting on people without being fully aware of his actions. Al and James carefully deliberated the wording of the chapter, and decided to print it in this manner:

> Dim Mak Kung Fu cannot be learned from a book. All we are doing is bringing the American people some general knowledge of the Dim Mak system. It is possible, by striking with one finger in the proper spot at the proper time, to render an assailant immobile, and yet to revive the victim all that is required is a slap in the appropriate place, and he will recover and act normally. With this deadly system, it is possible to cause death either immediately or belatedly through the formation of blood clots in major arteries of the anatomy.

> To understand how such a deadly system was devised by the ancient Chinese monks, one must realize that kung fu is not just a hodge-podge system of dirty fighting, but a carefully thought out and perfected system based on their knowledge of nature and the inescapable cycle of life and death. The monks made careful observations of nature, and concluded that nature had provided all birds, beasts, and fish with some measure of self-defense. For some, the weapon was teeth and claws, others possessed protective coverings, and still others had the ability of flight.

> Since the brain is the most vital organ of the human anatomy, nature protected it with a skull; the heart and lungs are protected by the rib cage. As surely as there are vital organs which are hard to injure because they are so well protected, there are others which are located more closely to the surface, and it is this basic principle on which "Dim Mak" is based. By hitting the weak points with our hard surfaces, we can easily disable the largest or strongest assailant. Chinese Kung Fu Karate is based on three basic fundamentals:

1. Attacking the vital organs. This is imitated in all other self-defense systems.

2. Attacking the blood vessels. This causes blood clots to form, which disables the attacker.

3. Attacking the centers that cause paralysis or unconsciousness. This can result in death, depending on the experience of the executioner.

The system of Dim Mak utilizes a timetable to determine which points on the body are vulnerable at a certain time of day. The timetable is divided into twelve two-hour periods, and a strong attack to certain points at these times of day can cause death. This chart will never be proven by the general readers simply because they lack the other knowledge to make the art complete; the missing links are technique, internal strength, and personal instruction from a master of the art. Listed below are the times of day and the corresponding areas of attack:

12 noon–2 P.M.	Wrist area where pulse is felt
2 P.M.–4 P.M.	Sternum
4 P.M.–6 P.M.	Two inches below the navel
6 P.M.–8 P.M.	Inner thigh
8 P.M.–10 P.M.	Between thighs and behind scrotum
10 P.M.–12 A.M.	Bottoms of the soles
12 A.M.–2 A.M.	Beneath nostrils
2 A.M.–4 A.M.	Bridge of the nose
4 A.M.–6 A.M.	Crown of the head
6 A.M.–8 A.M.	Underneath the jawbone
8 A.M.–10 A.M.	Temples
10 A.M.–12 P.M.	Above the nipples

Always use caution in practicing against these centers. You may accidentally master the Dim Mak technique, and the results can be fatal.

 created

James then suggested that they insert an anatomy chart to show the exact target areas, so that the practitioner did not accidentally strike the points that were vulnerable at that time of day. Al and James also collaborated on the amount of knowledge they should convey to the reader without falling short of their intended focus on the subject of poison-hand training. The charts revealed the approximate locations of the actual dim mak target areas. James then decided to include specific details dealing more on how to train in the poison-hand arts, and he managed to divulge this information in the following paragraphs:

> To memorize the lairs, get a piece of hide approximately two feet by five feet and install an eyelet on each corner so that the hide can be stretched taut. Draw a diagram of the human anatomy that shows the vital centers prior to hanging the hide. Through daily practice of kicks, pokes, and chops, you will memorize the lairs and find the most convenient ways to attack them. After consistent drilling, you will be able to look at an assailant and immediately recognize his unguarded and weak areas.

> The heart of Oriental fighting is based on muscle memory, and through constant training your reflexes will become automatic to your assailant's vital areas. If you train properly, your counterattack should come without thinking. In leather training you are not trying to develop great strength, but rather concentration of strength to a small area along with speed and accuracy. As you progress, you should hang additional pieces of hide so that eventually you can attack to the north, south,

east, and west simultaneously. In a year's time, you will be amazed at how quickly you can change positions, weapons, and variety of your counterattacks.

Poison Hand is a method of developing fighting strength to disable an assailant without resorting to exercises that increase bodily strength. It is not effective for breaking bricks or planks, nor will it enable you to lift enormous weight. It is primarily a technique used only to defend against someone stronger than you, so that you can disable him through hidden strength rather than muscular power. The most common methods of Poison Hand training are the use of paper, water, leather, candles, and body resistance.

Before signing a contract in any course of martial arts study, you should be sure that the instructor is well qualified. A simple guide to finding a bona fide instructor is to ask him the following questions:

1. Where did the instructor learn his art, and who was his teacher's teacher?

2. If a certain system you are interested in uses black belt ranking, did the instructor get his belt through competition, self-promotion, or by finishing a course of study in a well-established school?

3. To be avoided at all costs are instructors who tell you that by learning their particular system you will become a better fighter than anyone regardless of their strength or size.

4. Avoid any teacher who badmouths other styles and says that his system is far superior to all others.

5. Beware of an instructor who claims to be an expert of kung fu, aikido, jujitsu, judo, karate, and other styles as well. It is a physical impossibility to master so many techniques

in a lifetime, especially if he has lived in a country where there is a lack of bona fide instructors in these particular systems.

Of course there are many qualified instructors in the United States, but I am advising caution due to some of my past experiences. I believe it was Lincoln who said, "You can fool part of the people all of the time, all of the people part of the time, but you can't fool all of the people all of the time."

☺☺

Al was deeply impressed when he finished reading the treatise, and he wondered why James never gave himself any recognition for his many years of training within the martial arts. James was one of the most modest martial artists he had ever met; while he had greater skills than many other practitioners did, he did not consider himself an expert, but simply a person who was deeply committed to the study of the arts he loved. The students were also impressed by James's lack of arrogance, and they liked the way he maintained a personal closeness without acting superior to others. It was not long before word of James and Al's kwoon spread far and wide, and interested students were coming in from as far as Modesto, Sacramento, and Vallejo. Most of these people were already skilled in various forms of the martial arts, but they knew that James could offer them more than just a belt or degree for their efforts. James chose not to issue ranks or degrees because he felt that the experiences of life and serious training were more important than the wearing of a belt to symbolize one's knowledge. Traditionalism was not stressed, since James believed that if he could offer someone a piece of knowledge that they had not learned in their previous training, then he had contributed in his own small way to their success in the martial arts.

James was quickly realizing that although most of his students were capable at other forms of martial arts, they were somewhat naive to the practical applications of self-defense. Most traditional schools had limited their training to kata and prearranged fighting sequences, so when the students had to deal with an outside fighting situation that did not comply with what they had been taught, they had difficulty in adapting to a spontaneous confrontation. He and Al devised a basic course to teach spontaneous techniques for self-defense that were direct, powerful, and never gave the opponent a chance to recover. In order for the techniques to work, they had to be free of traditional regimentation and the students' reactions had to be sharp. Al and James began to evaluate every movement to determine its effectiveness, and they stressed that each student should use what was best suited for himself rather than teaching everyone a rigid set of techniques that would not work in a real fighting encounter.

In June, James was forced to take several weeks off due to ulcers; the restrictions on his physical activities gave him time to finish his book project. He used his rest period to finish shooting the pictures for the action sequences, using Al and the students as models, and by the time he went back to work, the book was at the printer.

In the next several months, many exciting events took place in James's martial arts career. First was the printing of his new books, which were distributed throughout San Francisco and Oakland's Chinatown. They were extremely well received by the public, and James felt that the printing costs would be recovered much sooner than he had originally expected.

Soon after the publication of his latest work, James received a phone call from Dr. Arnold Wong, an ear, nose, and throat specialist who was also a noted entrepreneur in the grain industry. Dr.

Wong had heard of James's skills through a mutual friend and deeply wanted to begin training with him on a private basis. James agreed to start a small class in the doctor's home for him and several of his business associates, and he planned a schedule that coincided neatly with his classes at the nearby kwoon.

Between working his regular welding job, teaching at the kwoon and Dr. Wong's home, and training still more students at his own home, James began to wear himself out. He was able to assign most of the teaching duties at the kwoon to Al, but by the summer of 1962, he had tired of the long trips to Fremont to teach at Dr. Wong's house. James suggested that any of the students who were seriously interested were welcome to participate in the classes either at the kwoon or at his home in Oakland.

Chapter Three

Bruce Lee's Formative Years

Life in Seattle

T he flight from San Francisco International Airport to Seattle had been uneventful, except for the slight turbulence and the mild and icy rains that pelted the Boeing 707 as it crossed over the airspace of Oregon's northern border. Bruce, sitting next to his older brother Peter, pondered the reality that shortly the plane would reach its destination and he would be required to begin a new chapter in his life. Peter would catch a connecting flight and would continue to Wisconsin, where he would attend the University of Wisconsin. Prior to leaving San Francisco, Peter had made a long-distance telephone call to notify Ruby Chow of their 3:10 P.M. arrival at the Seattle-Tacoma International Airport. If everything went as planned, a Chow family member would greet and chauffeur Bruce to the Chow family business establishment, located just outside Seattle's Chinatown district.

For now, Bruce Lee was content to just sit back and contemplate what awaited him once the plane landed in Seattle. Although the prospects of working as a waiter—or worse yet, a busboy—in Ruby Chow's Chinese restaurant would never satisfy his ideal of becoming independent, he knew only too well that his livelihood and lodging arrangements were hinged on honoring the wishes of his parents. He would need to temporarily lower his standards and accept that he was about to begin a journey in which menial labor would be his station in life. It would be the first time in his life that he would actually be on a payroll as an employee. He thought he would give it a try, at least until he had adjusted to American mores and fully understood where his true niche would be in this new culture.

Bruce had vague memories of the particulars surrounding Ruby Chow's association with his parents, but Peter, being older, remem-

👁👁 **1** (top) The type of ship Bruce Lee sailed on when he crossed the Pacific Ocean on returning to San Francisco (the place of his birth). Photo courtesy of Sid Campbell's archives.

👁👁 **2** (bottom) Bruce Lee, as he looked upon his arrival in San Francisco in 1959. To help Bruce earn money before he left for Seattle to enter Edison Technical Vocational School, Quan Ging Ho made arrangements for him to teach cha-cha to associates and friends in San Francisco and Oakland. Photo courtesy of Quan Ging Ho.

◎◎ **3** Bruce was no stranger to being in front of a camera. The television production staff for Seattle's local TV station was duly impressed with his professional demeanor and screen presence. Though his English was somewhat limited, his proper choice of words and gung fu talent more than made up for it. Bruce Lee's First Students in Seattle Back row (left to right): Jesse Glover, Bruce Lee, Skip Ellsworth, Tak Miyabe. Front row (left to right): James DeMile, LeRoy Garcia, Taky Kimura.

◎◎ **4** In an effort to generate interest in his martial art, Bruce Lee and his small cadre of students performed many exhibitions in and around the Seattle, Washington, area. Here "Skip" Ellsworth takes the center stage to demonstrate some gung fu form and self-defense techniques. Since some of the students had skills in judo and fighting in general, Bruce would integrate that into his performances. Photo Courtesy De Welle F. (Skip) Ellsworth.

◎◎ **5** Bruce Lee demonstrating a self-defense technique at one of the martial arts exhibitions he and his students performed in and around Seattle. These impressive performances spread the word quickly, and Bruce's reputation as a sifu rapidly spread among the students on campus at the University of Washington. Photo Courtesy De Welle F. (Skip) Ellsworth.

@@ **6** This was the quite unimpressive storefront of Bruce Lee's very fist commercial Jun Fan Gung Fu Institute in Seattle's Chinatown district. He conduced his classes downstairs and had, at first, a rather exclusive group of devoted followers. Later he would relocate to another, much nicer, school closer to the University of Washington and then eventually return to this location. Photo courtesy of Sid Campbell's archives.

@@ **7** After Bruce Lee started teaching in Seattle, he designed his own martial arts uniforms (jing mo) for his students and himself.

@@ **8** Bruce Lee spent $100 to buy a white Chevrolet Corvair to get around while he was in Seattle. It wasn't in the best of shape, but it gave him satisfaction to know that he did not have to rely on his students or public transportation to get around town.

@@ **9** Bruce Lee (above and right) working out with his student Taky Kimura in Seattle. Before Bruce Lee formally opened his kwoon, they would work out in parks, student's backyards, and even parking lots. Photo courtesy of Joseph Cowles.

@@ **10** This is the basic yin-yang logo design that Bruce Lee developed during the time he was teaching his Wing Chun–based gung fu in Seattle. Over time this design was embellished to include the Chinese characters that stressed his philosophy and his Jun Fan Institute. Photo courtesy of Sid Campbell's Archives.

⊚⊚ **11** (Left to right) Allen Joe, Bruce Lee, and James Lee sharing a celebratory moment during Bruce Lee's Christmas break from the University of Washington. He would drive down and spend time with James Lee during these breaks from classes. Photo courtesy of Allen Joe and the James Yimm Lee estate.

◎◎ **12** A mook jong typical of the one Bruce Lee received from Hong Kong when he was living above Ruby Chow's Chinese restaurant in Seattle, Washington. Photo courtesy of Sid Campbell.

◎◎ **13** Wally Jay as he looked at about the time he first met Bruce and James. Photo courtesy of Wally Jay.

◎◎ **14** Wally Jay (kneeling, left) with his Island Judo team at about the time he visited Seattle and met Bruce Lee for the first time. Photo courtesy of Wally Jay.

JXDO + GXNG FX
DEMONSTRATION

PLACE   YESLER TERRACE GYMNASIUM
         (AT THE FOOT OF BROADWAY ON YESLER)

DATE   14, FEB., 1961 (TUESDAY) AT 8:30 P.M.

BY
BRUCE LEE
AND
CHARLES WOO (BLACK BELT),
TAK MIYABE (BLACK BELT),
PAT HOOKS (BLACK BELT),
JESSE GLOVER (PACIFIC N. W. CHAMPION),
ROY GARCIA,   SKIP ELLSWORTH,
JIM DEMILE,   TAKY KIMURA,
JOHN JACKSON,   GEORGE MACNAMARA.

FREE

國術柔道表演。

◎◎ **15** On February 14, 1961, at 8:30 P.M., at the Yesler Terrace Community Recreation Center gymnasium, Bruce conducted a judo and gung fu demonstration that featured his senior and top students. Bruce Lee, Charlie Woo, Tak Miyabe, Pat Hooks, Jesse Glover, Roy Garcia, Skip Ellsworth, Jim DeMile, Taky Kimura, John (Jon) Jackson, and George MacNamara are featured on this flyer.

◎◎ **16** Professor Wally Jay was one of the first intermediaries to know both Bruce Lee and James Yimm Lee personally. In fact, the two men met through his introduction. Through all the years that James and Bruce were developing JKD, Professor Jay remained close to them, even until their last days. Photo courtesy of Professor Wally Jay.

◎◎ **17**　Not long after Bruce Lee met James Lee, Bruce discovered James's incredible breaking skills. Here James teaches Bruce how to break lightly supported and suspended boards. Photo courtesy of Greglon Lee and the James Yimm Lee estate.

◎◎ **18**　A young Bruce Lee hamming it up in the meat department of Allen Joe's grocery store in Oakland, California. Even as a butcher, Bruce dressed extremely well and was very dapper. Photo courtesy of Allen Joe and the James Yimm Lee estate.

◎◎ **19**　James Yimm Lee had developed the iron hand breaking techniques to the point that he could smash through dense slabs of concrete without the use of spacers or other gimmicks. In fact, he could break only a single selected brick in a stack of six or more. Photo courtesy of Greglon Lee and the James Yimm Lee estate.

@@ **20** Allen Joe (left) and Bruce Lee (right) posing together at Allen Joe's grocery store in Oakland, California, during one of Bruce Lee's visits to the Bay Area from Seattle. Bruce would always stop by and pay his regards to Allen Joe and other friends in the Bay Area on these special visits. Photo courtesy of Allen Joe and the James Yimm Lee estate.

@@ **21** A dapper Bruce Lee (left) and James Yimm Lee (right) sitting together at Allen Joe's home at a Christmas party. Sharing Christmas with his martial arts friends in Oakland was very special to Bruce Lee. Photo courtesy of Allen Joe and the James Yimm Lee estate.

@@ **22** Al Novak was one on the very first Caucasians to be admitted into the secretive martial arts world of gung fu back in the late 1950s and early 1960s. James Yimm Lee taught Al the art of "iron hand" breaking, in addition to many other aspects of ancient Chinese gung fu training. Photo courtesy of Greglon Lee and the James Yimm Lee estate.

@@ **23** James Yimm Lee was a staunch advocate of physical conditioning and body toughening. Here he trains with his student Al Novak, working on arm conditioning. Many times this intensely and physically demanding training was conducted in James Lee's garage. Photo courtesy of Greglon Lee and the James Yimm Lee estate.

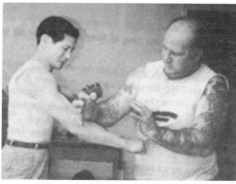

@@ **24** An assortment of specialized martial arts training equipment pieces that James Yimm Lee designed and built to enhance his fighting skills. Bruce Lee was duly impressed with James's ability to weld and construct such ingenious pieces of equipment. Photo courtesy of Greglon Lee and the James Yimm Lee estate.

@@ **25** After Bruce Lee first met James Yimm Lee and discovered his phenomenal welding and construction skills, they collaborated and built a human-shaped training dummy that integrated mook jong characteristics and spring-loaded qualities. James designed the dummy so that the head and arm attachments could be changed, thus adding more diversity than was previously ever considered for such devices. Photo courtesy of Greglon Lee and the James Yimm Lee estate.

@@ **26** An assortment of heads and features that could be attached to James's training equipment pieces. Some had eye targets, temple targets, and the likes. These attachments could be changed in minutes. Photo courtesy of Greglon Lee and the James Yimm Lee estate.

@@ **27** James Yimm Lee was among the very first martial artists to integrate weightlifting into his training regimens. Here we see an inclined bench that was ahead of its time with respects to weight training. Photo courtesy of Greglon Lee and the James Yimm Lee estate.

@@ **28** James Lee was incredibly creative with regards to specialized martial arts training equipment. This ingenious device is a first-of-its-kind neck-choking trainer. To develop the muscles used in choking a person, James created this device with springs and variable tension. Even today, devices of this nature are nonexistent in the commercial market place. Photo courtesy of Greglon Lee and the James Yimm Lee estate.

@@ **29** Another artful James Lee creation that struck Bruce Lee as an ingenious work of art was these dumbbells made from semi truck ball bearings. They were very heavy yet compact, and Bruce Lee liked this in training equipment. Photo courtesy of Greglon Lee and the James Yimm Lee estate.

@@ **30** James Yimm Lee was quite an inventor of martial arts training devices. Though somewhat crude by today's training equipment standards, his equipment designs were extremely durable. Bruce Lee was amazed at the advanced knowledge James had regarding training devices. He was ahead of his time. Even today some of his designs have not been commercially manufactured. Photo courtesy of Greglon Lee and the James Yimm Lee estate.

☺☺ **31** James Yimm Lee during his teenage years. He was rather lanky and felt that bodybuilding would help develop his physique. Photo courtesy of Greglon Lee and the James Yimm Lee estate.

☺☺ **32** James Yimm Lee was fifteen years old when this picture was taken, November 30, 1935. It was given to his Godmother Hall (standing with him). Photo courtesy of Greglon Lee and the James Yimm Lee estate.

◎◎ **33** This professional portrait of James Yimm Lee was taken in 1941 on his twenty-first birthday. Photo courtesy of Greglon Lee and the James Yimm Lee estate.
◎◎ **34** James as a teenager. This was taken in the 1930s. Photo courtesy of Greglon Lee and the James Yimm Lee estate.

◎◎ **35** James Yimm Lee playing with his daughter Karena at home. Karena would later be selected by her "Uncle Bruce" to be the president of his unofficial fan club when he garnered the role of Kato in the Green Hornet television series. Photo courtesy of Greglon Lee and the James Yimm Lee estate.

◎◎ **36** James Yimm Lee holding his daughter Karena Lee shortly after she was brought home from the hospital. Photo courtesy of Greglon Lee and the James Yimm Lee estate.

◎◎ **37** Circa 1952, James's wife Katherine M. Chow Lee. Photo courtesy of Greglon Lee and the James Yimm Lee Estate.

⊚⊚ **38** A dinner party that James and Katherine attended in 1951. Photo courtesy of Greglon Lee and the James Yimm Lee estate.

⊚⊚ **39** James's wife Katherine (Left, back row) posing with her three children standing in front: (left) coauthor Greglon Lee, (middle) Karena Lee, (right) Jacob Louie. Photo courtesy of Greglon Lee and the James Yimm Lee estate.

⊚⊚ **40** James Yimm Lee and his bride Katherine on their wedding day in 1951, after returning from Reno, Nevada. Photo courtesy of the James Lee estate.

⊚⊚ **41**　The siblings of James Yimm Lee.
⊚⊚ **42**　(Left to right) Phil Lim, Charlie
Low, James Yimm Lee, and Stud Wong
dining in Oakland's Chinatown. Among
the locals in the area James was known as
the "unofficial mayor" of Chinatown,
because he was so well acquainted with
everyone there. Photo courtesy of Greglon
Lee and the James Yimm Lee estate.
⊚⊚ **43**　James Yimm Lee featured on Al
Collins's television show demonstrating
his brick breaking skills. This show would
garner attention for James in the Oakland-
San Francisco area for his martial arts
prowess. Photo courtesy of Greglon Lee
and the James Yimm Lee estate.

MODERN KUNG-FU KARATE

iron, Poison hand training   book 1

唐手功夫

break brick in 100 days   by J.Y. LEE

◎◎ **44** James Yimm Lee's Modern Kung-Fu Karate Iron, Poison Hand Training: Break Brick in 100 Days BOOK 1 was divided into two parts. These books are very rare and are valued by martial arts book collectors. James had some printed using various colors: pale green, pale yellow, and powder blue. He also featured various single and double cover photos for illustration purposes. On some of the very rare editions, Al Novak is featured on the front cover. These were among the very first English martial arts books published in the United States. Photo courtesy of Greglon Lee.

@@ **45** James Lee published some of the very first martial arts books to be produced in the English language. He occasionally used his original birth name, Kein Heir Lee, and sometimes simply used his initials, K. H., or Kein H. Lee. On the book Chinese Kung-Fu Karate, which he coauthored and self-published with San Francisco gung fu master Professor T. Y. Wong, he used the moniker K. H. Lee, and on his Fighting Arts of the Orient: Elemental Karate and Kung-fu (illustrated for home training) (below), he decided to use Kein H. Lee. Photo courtesy of Greglon Lee and the James Yimm Lee estate.

@@ **46** By late 1957, James had begun training at the Kin Mon Chinese Institute on Waverly Place in San Francisco's Chinatown, under the tutelage of Professor T. Y. Wong, a noted authority in the Sil Lum art of Chinese gung fu. This proved to be a very valuable martial arts experience for James, and he spent more than three years pursuing the ancient methods of self-defense taught by Professor Wong. Photo courtesy of Sid Campbell.

◎◎ **47** James Yimm Lee in top fighting form. Bruce Lee was deeply inspired by James, because James's physique was incredible for someone over twenty years older than Bruce. James Lee's regimen combining martial arts, weightlifting, and equipment training had a profound impact on Bruce Lee, lasting his entire lifetime. Photo courtesy of Greglon Lee and the James Yimm Lee estate.

◎◎ **48** Fighting Arts of the Orient was James Yimm Lee's very first self-published work. It was among the very first martial arts books to be published in the United States and in the English language. This is a very rare collector's item. Photo courtesy of Greglon Lee and the James Yimm Lee estate.

◎◎ **49** When James Yimm Lee dressed up, he could very easily be perceived as a businessman or a member of the clergy. He usually dressed up when he went out to dinner or social engagements with his friends. Photo courtesy of Greglon Lee and the James Yimm Lee estate.

@@ **50** The birthplace of Jeet Kune
Do. James Yimm Lee's home on 3039
Monticello Avenue in Oakland, California. Bruce and Linda Lee lived here for
more than two years while they
developed the concept of Jeet Kune Do.
@@ **51** A handsome and dapper James
Yimm Lee the night he proposed to the
beautiful and lovely Katherine in
Oakland, California. Photo courtesy of
Greglon Lee and the James Yimm Lee
estate.
@@ **52** Greglon Lee (coauthor) with a
group of neighbor friends at a birthday
party at their Monticello
Avenue home in Oakland,
California. Photo courtesy
of Greglon Lee and the
James Yimm Lee estate.

@@ **53** James Lee (second from left) with weightlifting buddies. This photo was taken in 1946 in Oakland, California. James was sometimes known as "Shoulders" or the "Vee Man" and this photo attests to his hulking physique when he was a training to become a bodybuilding champion. Photo courtesy of Greglon Lee and the James Yimm Lee estate.

@@ **54** James and his new wife Katherine visiting his parents on their wedding day.

@@ **55** James with his wife and daughter.

@@ **56** Katherine and Karena at Lake Merritt in Oakland.

◎◎ **57** Waverly Place in San Francisco's Chinatown is where James trained in Kin Mon Kung fu under the tutelage of Professor T. Y. Wong. Photo courtesy of Sid Campbell.

◎◎ **58** James and students in the early 1960's.

👁👁 **59** Sifu Gin Foon Mark was the gung fu teacher and acupuncturist on New York's Manhattan Island that introduced Bruce lee to and expanded Bruce Lee's awareness of the Praying Mantis style of self-defense. Sifu Mark was skilled in many weapon arts, which fascinated Bruce very much. Photo courtesy of Sifu Gin Foon Mark.

👁👁 **60** This is the way Bruce Lee would have perceived Sifu Gin Foon Mark when he witnessed the Praying Mantis master demonstrating his expertise with the Chinese sword for the fist time. Photo courtesy of Sifu Gin Foon Mark.

61 Bruce Lee was exposed to many different arm-conditioning and strengthening devices that he was previously unaccustomed through Praying Mantis Sifu Gin Foon Mark. He shared his knowledge with Bruce about these simple, yet very effective, homemade training concepts. Photo courtesy of Sifur Gin Foon Mark.

62 The hanging bundles of chain were another simple training device that Sifu Gin Foon Mark introduced Bruce Lee to when he trained for two weeks in New York City while visiting his father (Lee Hoi Chuen). Photo courtesy of Sifu Gin Foon Mark.

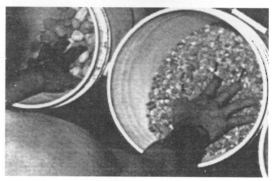

63 Strengthening the fingers and toughening the skin was another method of conditioning that Bruce learned while training with Sifu Gin Foon Mark. Buckets of sand, coarse stone, ball bearings and the likes were used for this purpose. Photo courtesy of Sifu Gin Foon Mark.

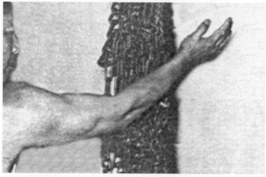

64 Toughening and conditioning the forearms was a prerequisite for students of Sifu Gin Foon Mark's Praying Mantis kwoon in New York City. Bruce found using the assorted iron rings to toughen the arms very interesting. Photo courtesy of Sifu Gin Foon Mark.

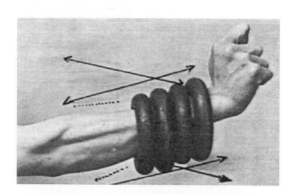

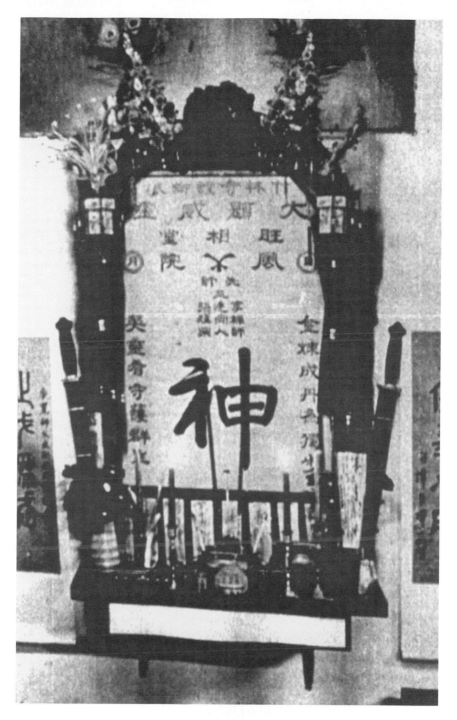

⊚⊚ **65** The altar that Bruce Lee found fascinating at Sifu Gin Foon Mark's Praying Mantis kwoon in New York City when he visited there in 1959. Photo Courtesy of Sifu Gin Fook Mark.

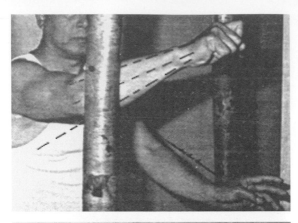

66 Toughening the skin and internally conditioning the sinew was another training method that Bruce Lee learned from Sifu Gin Foon Mark. The use of saplings that had been cut into lengths and affixed so they could rotate in a housing served those means quite nicely. Photo courtesy of Sifu Gin Foon Mark.

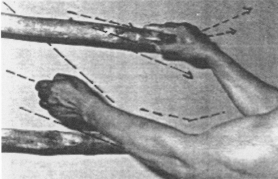

67 The Praying Mantis style had its own version of the yan mook jong (wooden dummy). It was fairly similar to and less elaborate than the one Bruce was familiar with back at Sifu Yip Man's kwoon back in Kowloon. Photo courtesy of Master Gin Foon Mark.

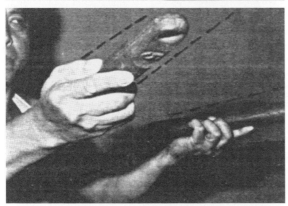

68 Sifu Mark was an advocate of total body conditioning, which Bruce Lee found very interesting. The kwoon in New York used simple equipment to produce phenomenal results for the students. Here simple windowsill counterweights are used to strengthen the muscles of the arms. Sifu Gin Foon Mark felt that results were more important that the sophistication of the training devices. Photo courtesy of Sifu Gin Foon Mark.

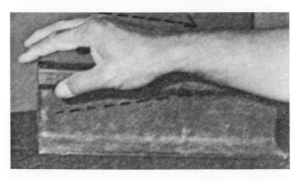

69 Finger strength was another vital consideration when mastering the intricacies of Praying Mantis gung fu. Bruce liked the idea of strengthening the fingers and hand by isolating the muscle groups and lifting a cut off section of iron railroad track. Photo courtesy of Sifu Gin Foon Mark.

70 Rolling and avoiding attacks by artfully tumbling and flipping helped a student develop incredible agility. Bruce Lee felt this had valuable importance with regards to the fighting arts. Photo courtesy of Sifu Gin Foon Mark.

71 Praying Mantis master Gin Foon Mark as he appeared at the time Bruce Lee visited and trained at his kwoon in New York City during 1959. Photo courtesy of Sifu Gin Foon Mark.

72 Sifu Gin Foon Mark was brilliantly elusive with the Chinese sword. Bruce Lee liked the swiftness and unpredictability of such a weapon. Photo courtesy of Sifu Gin Foon Mark.

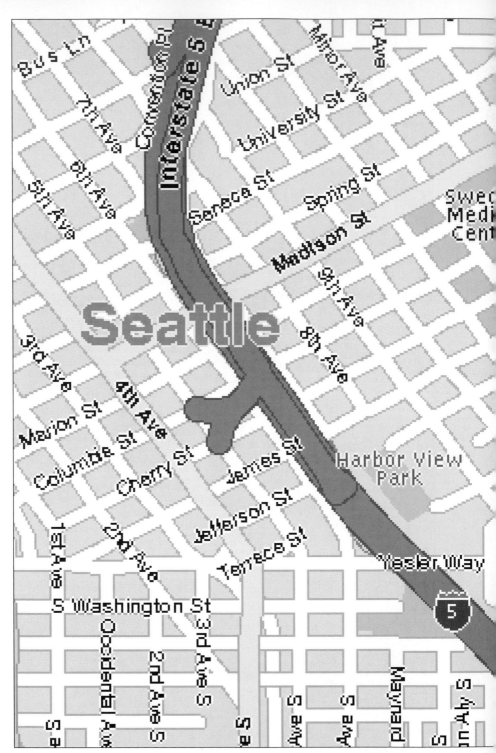

◎◎ The included maps show the geographical locations where Bruce Lee traveled, studied, lived and trained when he was residing in Seattle, Washington.

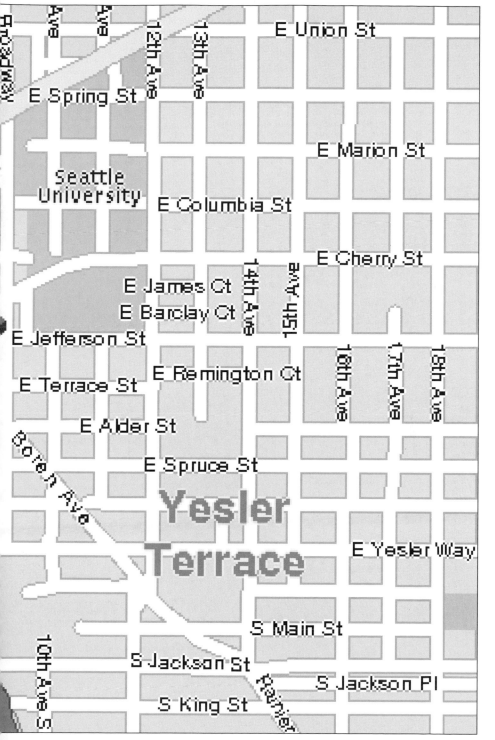

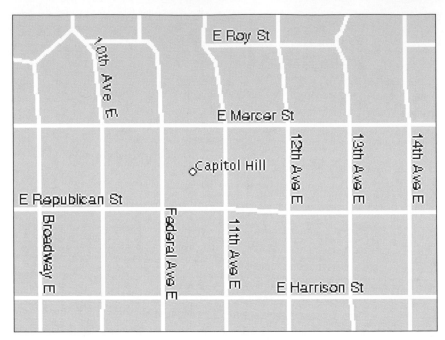

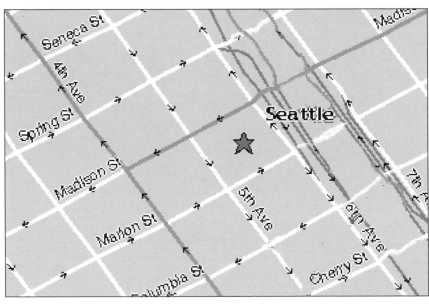

@@ ALL MAPS are courtesy of MAPQUEST®.

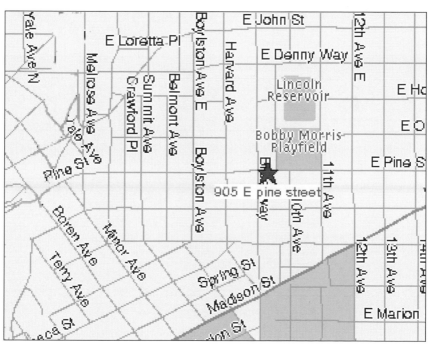

905 E pine street

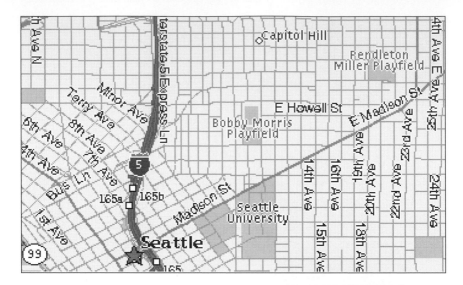

👁👁 **73** A model of a car like the black Ford Fairlane that Bruce Lee had when he was in Seattle. He called it his "police car." This was the second car that Bruce Lee ever owned, and his student LeRoy Garcia taught him how to drive. Photo courtesy of Sid Campbell.

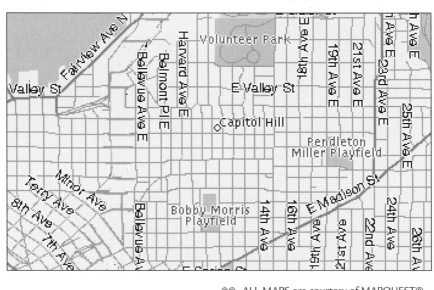

👁👁 ALL MAPS are courtesy of MAPQUEST®.

bered more of the obscurities surrounding Ruby's and their parent's relationship. Ruby Chow had been born with the Chinese name of Mar Seung Gum. Her father, Mar Jim Sing, was an immigrant from the Guangdong village of Hoi Yuen and ran the San Juan Fishing and Canning Dock in the Puget Sound. In Seattle, he was a wealthy and influential Chinese businessman and, because of this, even had his own bodyguards. Ruby's mother had a twin sibling who drowned in a flood at an early age. When her mother died, Ruby assumed the matriarchal role in the family.

Ruby married Ping Chow who was a celebrated opera singer in the same Chinese opera company in which Bruce's father Hoi Cheun performed, the Hong Kong Cantonese Opera Company. During World War II, around the time the United States had declared war against the Japanese government in 1941, Ping Chow became ill while performing on tour with the show in New York City. The tour continued without Ping Chow as he recovered. Ruby Chow helped nurture him back to health. Shortly thereafter, Ping Chow decided not to return to Hong Kong. He chose to remain in the United States and marry Ruby. After relocating back to the Northwest, Ruby began working, in the early 1950s, as a barmaid-hostess at the Hong Kong Cafe in Seattle's Chinatown.

Bruce let his mind drift to memories of his father and mother discussing Ping and Ruby Chow over evening dinners at their home in Hong Kong. He had never paid much attention to any of it, but what he did remember for sure was that Ruby Chow was a pretty tenacious woman, with a lot of ambition. She could be very vindictive and coldhearted to anyone that crossed her or got in her way.

Bruce smiled to himself as he remembered his father saying that Ping Chow was probably the best thing that ever happened to Ruby Chow. In America, Ping Chow attracted opera fans that had known him in Hong Kong; he had style and class; he knew many wealthy people in Chinatowns all over the United States; and he was definitely a gentleman with an eye for business opportunities. It was his idea to name the restaurant Ruby Chow's, after his wife. He and Ruby were the first Asians to open up a truly first-class Chinese dinner establishment outside of Chinatown in Seattle. With Ping as the head chef, occasionally singing Chinese opera, and Ruby hosting and running the dining room operation, their mutual business acumen had proven to be very successful. The restaurant was quite popular with the Caucasian and African American customers that would have probably never traveled into Seattle's Chinatown to dine. And, it did hold a modicum of popularity with the older longtime Asian population, who knew of Ruby from her days as a barmaid and Ping from his performing career with the opera company.

The aircraft was several minutes behind schedule in landing, due to delays in control tower operations caused by flight congestion on the runways. However, barring this annoyance, they had a smooth touchdown and were off the plane and in the terminal before they knew it. It would be a short good-bye, since Peter had to hurry to his connecting flight. They embraced and said good-bye. Bruce continued to watch his brother for as a long as he could, as Peter proceeded down the long corridor and disappeared into the crowd; Bruce knew it would be a while before he would see him again.

Despite intently watching for anyone looking for him and trying to navigate through the crowded corridors, while deciphering the somewhat confusing directional signs, Bruce managed to find the baggage claim area of this huge terminal. As he was busy retrieving his luggage and searching for his claim check, the matronly Ruby Chow suddenly appeared next to him and tapped his shoulder. He turned to be greeted by a broad smile and outstretched arms. They immediately hugged and exchanged greetings. It was as if a long-lost friendship had finally been reunited, although Bruce had never met Ruby before.

After departing the airport terminal parking lot and settling in on the north interstate highway, Bruce and Ruby had time to acquaint themselves and talked about the times her husband, Ping, and Bruce's father, Hoi Cheun, had years ago with the Hong Kong Cantonese Opera Company. Between breaks in Ruby's incessant talk about the opera, her restaurant, life in Seattle, and how the Chinese were finally getting respect in the area, Bruce interrupted from time to time with cordialities that expressed how his family sent their best wishes and was most appreciative of her generosity in providing living quarters for him. Likewise, he conveyed his gratefulness and expressed his deep indebtedness for her kindhearted hospitality. It was most reassuring for his mother and father to know that he would have lodging and gainful employment while in Seattle pursuing his academic studies.

Ruby's natural straightforwardness and inquisitive nature became evident in the way she broached questions pertaining to his adolescent years in Kowloon and Hong Kong, and his more recent months in the United States. Her probing questions about recent girlfriends, his sexual promiscuity, his friends and their reputations, and the nature of his ambitions evoked uneasiness. Bruce did not know where her inquiries might lead. Bruce became mildly flustered, uncomfortable with the idea that his not-so-favorable past might be revealed. Ruby's inane questions began to feel like the police interrogations he had experienced in Hong Kong on numerous occasions. He hated to be embarrassed by answering probing questions of this nature, whether it was by the police authorities or by anyone else that he did not know personally.

⊚⊚

By the time Ruby's new Cadillac turned onto Minor Avenue and had pulled into the private delivery entrance adjacent to the restaurant and come to a stop, the household arrangements had been settled. Bruce would have his own room on the third floor above the restaurant and would work some of the weekend lunch shifts and the evening hours. Ruby had promised him a position as junior waiter, but sometimes on the busy weekend nights and at dinner parties or banquets, he would have to double as a busboy. Ruby was reluctant to discuss a salary in detail until she knew exactly how well he could perform his duties. This was fine with Bruce since he knew that, with free lodging and dining privileges, a nominal salary combined with customers' tips would undoubtedly be more than what he needed to cover his day-to-day living expenses during the interim that he was attending school. He didn't know how well he would handle being a waiter and busboy, though. As he stepped out of the vehicle and stood studying the restaurant premises, it occurred to him that this restaurant was quite different from any he had ever seen before. It was located on a triangular intersection, with three streets surrounding the three-story building. On one side was an acute intersection where Jefferson Street and Minor Avenue met, along the north side of the restaurant was James Street, and along the east facade was Broadway.

Upon further inspection of the restaurant, Bruce figured that the establishment had at one time been a very large and palatial estate, probably owned by some wealthy family. It looked like it had been renovated to include several structural additions.

As they entered the front of the building and as Ruby showed Bruce around the premises, his deductions proved correct. The additions had made it possible to extend the size of the dining room and give the interior structure an L-shaped appearance. He estimated that the dining area had about thirty tables and could probably seat over a hundred people at any given time. From what he could see, the lengthier portion of the restaurant had been built on what would have been the back yard of the house. Bruce's attention became captivated by a large multiarmed statue that was prominently situated at the other end of the dining room. Ruby, sensing his fascination with the statue, told him it was the deity Vishnu, or the image of the Buddha reborn. As he approached it and touched the array of extended arms, she told him that Vishnu represented the god of home and family values and was intended to represent stability and order. As Bruce continued to gaze upon the statue, Ruby pointed out that each arm carried a symbol: the discus, conch, club, and lotus. The discus and club are both weapons, signifying Vishnu's absolute might in destroying evil. The lotus represents fertility and regeneration, the nourishment of the soul that occurs through devotion to this deity. The conch shell is blown in India like a trumpet during many sacred rituals. It is considered to make the purest sound, from which creation springs.

A collection of large framed pictures adorned the restaurant walls, all featuring a costumed performer that appeared to be an actor with the Hong Kong Cantonese Opera Company. The costumes were all similar to the many Bruce had seen his father wear during his performances with the opera company. As Bruce approached these colorful portraits to inspect them more closely, Ruby told him the portraits were of her husband, Ping, when he had acted with the theater in Hong Kong. Bruce nodded and casually added that they reminded him of his father when he was performing there as well. As he walked along the walls gazing at the pictures, Ruby walked alongside and gave a brief narration of the time and shows that Ping had performed in during his tenure with the troupe.

Then, almost as quickly as it began, Bruce's impromptu history lesson was cut short, when Ruby stated rather matter-of-factly that it was time to get him settled in his quarters. She said that he would be staying on the third floor. She added that the family quarters were upstairs on the second floor and that he would have a room above them, just off of the lady's lounge.

Ruby then assigned an employee to show Bruce his quarters. They exited the restaurant and walked back toward the side of the building to retrieve his luggage from the car. As Bruce followed, the employee led him up an outside stairway to the third floor. Entering the third level from the outside and walking down the hallway was almost a surreal experience. Just the sound of their footsteps echoing off the bare walls made Bruce apprehensive about what awaited him at his quarters. He had envisioned himself as a houseguest at a stately home, where many of the amenities he was used to would be at his disposal. Comfortable rooms, modern kitchen facilities, and a personal bedroom were what he had expected as his abode. However, things were not looking very promising. As the door was opened and Bruce peered inside, a feeling of despair and trepidation suddenly hit him.

With baggage in hand, Bruce entered the gloomy confines of a single room with nothing more than a small dresser, a cot, and single bare lightbulb hanging from the ceiling. This had a dampening and all too sobering effect on Bruce's expectations. The employee, sensing that his assistance was no longer needed, turned to make his departure. On the way out, he pointed toward the corridor and, almost as an afterthought, mentioned that the toilet and bath area was down the hall. After somberly assessing this unexpected turn of events, Bruce began having reservations about having agreed to this work arrangement in the restaurant. But, unfortunately, this was the agreement that his parents had made for him with Ruby, and he had promised to abide by her terms during his tenure under her guardianship.

The first night working the dinner shift turned out to be a great deal more demanding than Bruce had imagined. Ruby had assigned him duties at the very bottom of the labor stratum but implied that, once he was familiar with the routines, he would be elevated to the position of waiter. As a busboy, Bruce did nothing more than remove used tableware and renew the place settings for the next customers. It seemed simple enough, but it wasn't. Usually Ruby positioned herself at the cashier counter, so she could greet the customers and simultaneously monitor the waiters and busboys covering their stations. From this vantage point, she saw Bruce's every move. On several occasions, after observing Bruce go about his chores in an unorganized and inefficient manner, she politely but sternly admonished him for his lack of professionalism.

Bruce soon found out that Ruby had very rigid and exacting procedures for performing every minute detail of running the restaurant, right down to how the dinnerware and tablecloths would be removed from the tables after a dinner party had departed. This particular procedure had an order and proper technique that would minimize any inconvenience to nearby guests. Ruby believed in placing the used linen napkins in the tray-laden pushcart first, so they would muffle any sounds as the busboy stacked the glassware and minimize the risk of accidental breakage. She thought that a well-trained busboy should try to remain out of sight, until the station waiter had collected the tips, before moving in to clean a table.

During peak business hours, the busboy should also have fresh table linen already prepared after the old linen was removed, to minimize the amount of time a table was out of service. To insure against theft, she felt that the busboy should account for each and every fork, spoon, and knife that was assigned to a table. She liked her busboys to arrive an hour early for work to fold the linen napkins in a precise manner so that they looked like blossoming flowers poised on the freshly set table. Until his crash course in "busboyology," Bruce never realized that the staff was doing all of these seemingly idiotic procedures and preparations before the customers had even been seated, but Ruby expected and insisted that these procedures be performed on each and every table in the establishment—every night of the year.

After his first night shift, Bruce felt that regardless of how hard he worked or how well he performed his duties, Ruby was always going to be stern and strict with him. She was a perfectionist in every sense of the word. Nothing escaped her attention when it came to providing the very best in Chinese cuisine and first-class service to her customers. The more he thought about his situation, the more it played on his mind. He noticed that the waiters working at the restaurant were very proud and content with their jobs, and most had been longtime employees. Almost all of the regular customers knew the waiters' names and requested particular waiters when they came to the restaurant.

Bruce was only biding time there to satisfy his parents' wish for him to get a higher education. He considered the job a small price to pay for that. Deep inside he knew that doing this type of subservient work would, in no uncertain terms, mean that there would be conflicts because of his general temperament, his sense of humor, his fairly large ego, and his sense of pride. He realized that any such conflicts would have to be stymied if he was to maintain the respect and good graces of his benefactor.

In the short weeks that followed, working at the restaurant became routine, and Bruce got a lesson in the harsh realities of how many Westerners typically treated Asians who worked in dining establishments. He experienced firsthand the way in which the bus-boys and waiters were treated, which confirmed his suspicions that Western culture had a strong stereotypical image of Chinese. He had seen the Western tourists shopping and sightseeing in Hong Kong act the same way. The mental anguish and resentment that arose from these experiences were very hard for him to hide from his fellow Chinese workers at the restaurant, many of whom had worked there many years and were content with their station in life. Bruce verbalized his malcontent without worry of reprisals. He sometimes even berated his coworkers for being spineless in allowing them-selves to be treated disrespectfully. Perhaps, more than anything else, Bruce took exception to the way he thought people perceived him when he was dressed as a waiter. In addition, his obstinacy was bordering on contempt whenever inebriated customers talked down to him or snapped their fingers to signal his service for another cocktail. The other waiters knew Bruce had reached his limit when his body language took on a decidedly resistant posture. He would stand with his feet about shoulder width-apart, with his arms defi-antly positioned across the front of his chest, all the while, glaring at the person with his eyelids half opened and his head slightly tilted sideways.

His lack of recognition at the restaurant continually gnawed at him. At times, his temperament was such that senior waiters and kitchen cooks would become very uneasy in Bruce's presence. They felt that he was a time bomb ready to explode whenever he was assigned the unpleasant duties around her establishment. It was even worse when he was assigned to wash dishes and remove the garbage. At the busier times of the day, such as noon and the evening dinner hours, when he had double duty as both waiter and busboy, his patience was tried almost to the breaking point. At these times, Bruce had to use self-control and forced humility to subdue his contemptuous side. His trials and tribulations even carried over into his sleep, as he would toss and turn restlessly while he seemed to fight off unknown forces that were holding him back or keeping him from getting ahead in life. He attributed most of this pent up anger to the fact that he detested being the only worker who was assigned what seemed like almost all of the less desirable chores. Even laying in his small cot in his upstairs room, staring at the single bare light bulb hanging from a ceiling lathed with cracked plaster and faded paint made him aware of his status. This lightbulb was the last thing that he saw before he closed his eyes at night and the first thing that he saw when he awoke in the morning. In the darkness of night, when he could not sleep, he could stare into the ceiling and see the faint image of that grayish bulb suspended so precariously in the blackness of space. He sometimes wondered if that was his destiny—to be a lone figure in a void of nothingness. These solemn moments of coming face-to-face with himself in this bleak darkness only strengthened his will and fortified his desire to make something of himself.

Although he shared in the tips and gratuities left by the customers and was as cordial as the situation required, he felt his lack of seniority and his temporary status were the primary reasons that he had been cast into this unfortunate role. It had also occurred to him that Ruby might be using him, just like several of the other students that were temporary employees. He felt that if something better came along, it would be fair play to take it. At least the position was only temporary, and he would definitely change his situation for the better once an opportunity availed itself.

Bruce contemplated his ironic situation, the contradictions in his life. On the one hand, he wanted to present an image of a proud Chinese American with refined taste, possessing social amenities befitting someone of his family's status in Hong Kong, and on the other hand, he felt no better than a Chinese coolie, with a menial job toiling as a lowly, subservient waiter-busboy.

He slowly convinced himself that, in order to remain on favorable terms with Ruby, as his parents would have expected, he would have to curtail his obstinant behavior while on the premises of the restaurant. Besides, a short temper was assuredly not worth losing his job and living quarters over, both of which he needed desperately. Therefore, in most instances, he remained content to contain his anger and keep his thoughts to himself, at least until he had more control over his destiny and independence.

Over time, Bruce slowly became a model restaurant employee— most of the time. While at the establishment, he tried to conduct himself in a very businesslike manner and tried to put aside his differences with Ruby. Most of the petty disputes now stemmed from grievances reported by the kitchen chefs. They complained to both Ruby and Ping that Bruce's waiting and busing duties were inconsistent. They claimed that his intermittent ineptness reflected on them and made their work appear to be substandard, especially when dishes arrived cold or when orders were not delivered correctly. Ruby tolerated this but, on occasion, berated Bruce for his poor service efforts. Sometimes, she did this in front of customers and, at other times, in the kitchen within earshot of the chefs to appease them. She hoped to embarrass Bruce enough to coerce him to get along and work with her cooks.

When Bruce was off duty, he rarely remained on the restaurant premises. He was there only for meals, which Ruby's employees were entitled to, or to see how his weekly schedule was changed to accommodate special parties or banquets. His upstairs room, although small and bordering on dilapidation—even by Hong Kong standards—was a sanctuary that afforded him privacy and solitude when he chose to be alone. Sometimes he would simply study English, write letters home, listen to the radio, and periodically change radio stations so he could become familiar with a variety of American music styles. He also used the radio as a way to practice his English enunciation, by mimicking disc jockeys and emulating colloquial phrases. Bruce could keep himself preoccupied for hours at a time with nothing more than a radio, notepad, and any old periodicals that were mailed to the restaurant. He also spent time practicing his penmanship and meticulously forming each letter of the alphabet. He wanted to create a style of writing that was both articulate and elegant in appearance. By studying signatures and styles of handwritten paragraphs that he saw in magazines and other printed matter, Bruce began to create his own distinct style. He liked the flare and flowing symmetry of his own name and practiced writing it for hours just to get it natural looking.

Not long after settling in, Bruce began collecting and perusing American magazines, and he was particularly interested in the men's fashion advertisements. He still retained some of his customary dressing habits, though he constantly kept up with the latest fashion trends of the United States. Sometimes he chose to dress in the westernized Chinese style that he had grown accustomed to in Hong

Kong, and at other times, he experimented with a mixture of ensembles that included the latest in American vogue and styles from Hong Kong.

Bruce wanted to appear to be a person of independent means. To make such a distinctive statement, he had to spend almost all of the extra money that his mother sent him and a considerable portion from his earnings and tips to enhance his wardrobe. Though there never seemed to be enough cash to afford all the items he desired, the amount he could afford to spend, what remained from his first several paychecks and the extra tips earned as a busboy, afforded him a chance to begin assembling a frugal yet dapper wardrobe of select garments.

One night, after Bruce had seen another busboy, a Chinese teenager about his own age named Chinn Wah Min, leave the restaurant and drive away in a shiny blue Chrysler, Bruce realized there was more to Min than met the eye. He surmised that Min was either a young mahjong gambler who was pretty lucky or his parents were wealthy enough to afford such a luxury for their son. To have that kind of money and working at Ruby's restaurant as a busboy didn't add up.

The following evening, when Chinn Wah Min returned for his shift, Bruce approached him and asked how he could afford such a nice car working for Ruby. Min simply stated that he worked part time at the *Seattle Times* newspaper inserting supplements in the Sunday editions. He further explained that many Chinese people worked there to earn additional money. The newspaper had always hired Chinese to insert the advertisements, and there was always a job to be found there. Because the company had a daily circulation of over 150,000 subscribers, they needed additional workers to handle the extra work when advertisements were heavy.

To get more money, Bruce applied for a part-time position at the *Seattle Times*. Bruce relied on this predawn job from time-to-time, to earn extra money to add additional clothes to his wardrobe. Classy clothing like pinstriped sport coats, pleated and cuffed tapered dress trousers, long-sleeved custom dress shirts, thin ties, highly polished dress shoes, and other accessories were all part of his gradually expanding wardrobe. The dark-rimmed glasses and the pens and pencils tucked neatly into his shirt pockets gave the impression that Bruce was indeed a successful businessman or, at worse, a playboy with a discriminating taste for the finer things in life. More opted to perceive Bruce as the former than the latter.

The University of Washington admissions policy had two hurdles that Bruce would have to overcome before he could be accepted as a student there. First, he would need the necessary academic high school credits and aptitude, and second, foreign students who would be attending the university were required to have an adequate proficiency in the English language in both oral and written language skills. Ultimately, Bruce knew that this challenge was his and his alone. He realized that if he made sacrifices and a serious effort and gave attention to both of these requirements, he would have a favorable chance of being accepted at the university.

Since Bruce had not completed high school in Hong Kong, his highest priority was to achieve this goal first. After some exploratory research, Bruce learned that Edison Technical Vocational School was not too far from the restaurant. After speaking with one of the counselors there, he confirmed that this school had the curricula necessary for him to acquire a high school diploma and provide full eligibility for his admission to the University of Washington in the fall of the following year. However, it was going to be very difficult for him to accomplish this that quickly.

His initial trip to the high school left him with an impression that was quite different from what he had expected of an American school. It resembled a huge old four-story stone and brick citadel remotely reminiscent of a courthouse, with massive arched windows and doorways. In other respects, it looked like it could have been used as a military academy a hundred years ago.

To get to the school from the restaurant, all he had to do was turn left onto Broadway, take a bus up for a little over a half mile, and get off at East Pine Street. Then he walked a few blocks, until he reached the school. The building was located in the Capitol Hill district, an ominous structure that virtually took up the whole block from the corner of the Broadway Avenue and Pine Street intersection.

Having completed all of the necessary formalities for the admissions office to qualify him for enrollment at the Seattle Edison Technical Vocational School, Bruce was officially registered for the fall classes on September 3, 1959. Now with his assigned curriculum in place, he spent the next several weeks getting oriented to the Edison Tech academic environment. During this time, he was able to acquaint himself with the teachers, the school staff, and his classmates. He was finally able to settle into a study routine that utilized his time efficiently. This was something that he had not been able to do back in Hong Kong.

Return to Training

Ruby was beginning to assign Bruce duties as a waiter, and he now had more time off to pursue other interests. Bruce could now allot some of his free time to his martial arts training. Sometimes he practiced in his room and other times in the parking lot behind the restaurant. It seemed that his fighting spirit had never been far from his thoughts. Whenever he put his vitality and focused energy into use, he felt at one with his fighting spirit and could easily return to his training in Hong Kong.

Ruby's children and the other neighborhood kids curiously watched these impromptu workouts in the parking lot. Bruce seemed to undergo a personality transition during these workouts. In a period of several weeks Bruce's Wing Chun gung fu exercises and training routines felt almost as sharp as they did when he was working out at Grandmaster Yip Man's kwoon at the old Yao Ma Tei District kwoon on Lee Tat Street, in Kowloon. Just dropping into a Wing Chun stance and performing the Sil Lim Tao" form several dozen times seemed to have a calming effect on his psyche. The Taoist principles of yin and yang embodied in the form seemed to be tailored specifically to his situation. What was most noticeable by those that knew Bruce best was that, when he was working out with unrelenting passion, his academic studies seemed to improve. This unexplained channel between the spiritual and physical certainly would indicate that the ancient Chinese yin-yang phenomena had validity at a time when he needed it most. This control over his life appeared to justify his workouts, so with time and weather permitting, Bruce continued his training and often used the small, fenced back yard at Ruby Chow's restaurant to sharpen his Wing Chun gung fu skills.

Bruce had noticed a change in his attitude himself. Since he had resumed his workouts, he had become more personable and cheerful. Sometimes he thought he had to prove to himself what he was trying to prove to others. By overcoming adversities and hardships, by fighting through his woes, he felt better prepared for dealing with life. Furthermore, his academic test scores had improved at Edison Technical Vocational School. His early morning or afternoon workout sessions also seemed to charge him with a renewed vitality and sense of well being and, to some degree, put him in a jovial and joking mood while on the job performing his duties as a newly promoted waiter.

Because of these short solo practice sessions, he began renewing his interest in physical conditioning at a more serious level, perhaps more than any time previously. Daily walks to explore the nearby neighborhoods, and sometimes jogging to and from the vocational school, coupled with the impromptu Wing Chun parking lot workouts gave Bruce an opportunity to get into top physical condition. Besides, keeping his physique lean and trim made all of the clothes in his wardrobe look and fit a lot better. These excursions were responsible for him becoming acquainted with the Capital Hill district of the community. The "Hill" was a multiethnic neighborhood just northeast of downtown Seattle, where the city's diverse lifestyles and cultural ethnicity were integrated. Broadway, its main thoroughfare, was a lively entertainment hub both day and night. This quaint district contained a variety of neighborhood shops, galleries, cafes, and restaurants. everyone from students to senior citizens strolled and shopped there. Nearby was Volunteer Park, the forty-four-acre home for the Seattle Asian Art Museum, a beautiful Victorian conservatory, a regional water tower, and the famed Lakeview Cemetery, where many notable people were interred.

Unbeknownst to Bruce, his daily jaunts were noticed by the people who lived and worked in the Capitol Hill district. His carefree attitude and happy-go-lucky outlook combined with a broad, friendly smile made it easy for him to meet people. He also had a natural charisma and ability to attract attention to himself with his entertaining antics. Soon, many local shop owners and residents in and around Capitol Hill knew him on a first-name basis. Some knew him as the waiter at Ruby Chow's restaurant, others for his martial arts abilities, and some simply as the young Chinese kid that liked to joke, laugh and kid around a lot. When he saw some of the elderly Chinese practicing tai chi chuan in the park he would stop and chat with them.

By the end of the third school week, in September of 1959, the staff, faculty, and most of the students in his classes were aware of Bruce's presence. He was being described as the Chinese guy with the glasses who could do that ancient Asian self-defense stuff. Bruce's reputation had intrigued the staff at Edison, and he was asked if he would like to give a martial arts demonstration at the annual Asian Day celebration at Capitol Hill. This was set for the weekend. Bruce accepted the invitation and agreed to demonstrate Wing Chun and show some of the martial arts that originated in China.

The day of the fair, he appeared dressed in a dark suit and proceeded to the activities coordinator's booth. He was assigned a makeshift performing area, a designated time to begin his activity, and twenty minutes for his performance. With Bruce's performance scheduled concurrent with the hundred or so booths and assorted vendors promoting their services, products, and ethnic foods, his exhibition was considered just another folk demonstration that would broaden the array of Asian activities for the enjoyment of the fairgoers.

Bruce began his demonstration with the same flare and pomp as a barker at a county fair. Standing in a cleared space, nattily attired with thick horn-rimmed glasses and neatly combed hair, he resembled a certified public accountant or office worker rather than a martial arts expert. He began this extemporaneous performance by telling the small group of spectators that he was about to show them something that had always been kept secret in China. To the observers, this opening presentation was curiously amusing, since Bruce's distinctive Chinese accent had an obvious British inflection, and he delivered it with such authoritative audaciousness.

Then, without warning, Bruce swiftly executed a combination of movements that resembled those of a praying mantis. His wrists were flexed inward until his biceps were almost touching his forearm. His fingers were extended and positioned to resemble the claws of the mantis ready to attack its prey. This explosive display of speed and power was immediately followed up with a volatile sequence of artfully contrived arm and hand movements that were supposed to resemble the fighting gestures of various animals. Sensing that the spectators were losing interest rather quickly, Bruce described some of the fighting positions used to defend the attacks he had demonstrated.

But that, too, did little to satisfy or appease the dwindling spectator interest. Bruce stood motionless for several seconds, as he began focusing his gaze on a nearby front-row bystander. Then pointing at this sturdily built man, Bruce said, "You look like you can fight," as if to invite him to step forward and become a willing participant in this impromptu martial arts demonstration. As chance would have it, Bruce had singled out a person by the name of James DeMile. Bruce brashly exclaimed, "How about coming up here." DeMile, a brawny, street smart, twenty-year-old stepped out of the crowd and approached Bruce with an arrogant look on his face as he said, "Gee kid, that stuff looks good, but over here we're mean fighters." Bruce, not knowing he had just challenged someone recently discharged from the armed services who had been the air force's undefeated champion in 128 boxing matches, turned his head slightly to the side and made a gesture of invitation with his hands, retorting, "Come on. Try to hit me." To DeMile, this boastful challenge, coming from such a frail-looking Asian teenager, became even more annoying when Bruce smiled and confidently shifted his glasses higher up on his nose. Without warning, DeMile let go with a straight right-hand punch intended to teach this brazen Chinaman a lesson in humility and respect for what real fighting was all about. The moment James unleashed this punishing haymaker, Bruce swiftly blocked and redirected the punch and, almost simultaneously, counterattacked with a barrage of lightning fast punches of his own, all well controlled and skillfully directed to various areas of DeMile's head. Bruce appeared to have actually trapped both of James's hands during the interplay and prevented him from responding with further punching assaults. To add further insult to injury, Bruce confidently tapped on DeMile's head with his knuckles, as though knocking on a door to see if anyone was home. All of this had transpired in about five seconds, surprising James and astonishing all of the onlookers that were present to witness this impromptu self-defense demonstration.

Bruce Lee Becomes a Sifu

After Bruce had concluded his demonstration, the gathering now wanted to know more about this form of self-defense. Most everyone was astonished that someone so young could be so skillful in its application. With DeMile, an African American named Jesse Glover and several others expressed a keen interest in Bruce's martial arts technique, wanting to know more than had been shown in the demonstration. Jesse Glover told Bruce that he had studied judo but was actually interested in all forms of martial arts and would very much like to learn Wing Chun gung fu if Bruce was accepting students. As the conversation ensued, Bruce was pleasantly surprised to learn that Jesse was also attending Edison Technical Vocational School.

Bruce related how his sole purpose for attending Edison Tech was to attain the English and grammar credits needed for him to earn his high school diploma, which would then enable him to apply to the University of Washington. Jesse reciprocated by telling Bruce he was there to learn various technical skills for job placement in the workforce. He suggested that perhaps it might be possible for them to work out together. He could swap his judo techniques for lessons in Wing Chun. Bruce liked the idea. After this casual and serendipitous meeting, they would quickly form a friendship, founded upon their mutual interests. Over the next several weeks, Bruce's invigorating personality and friendly demeanor would play a pivotal role in creating a bond of friendship between Jesse and himself. Soon thereafter Bruce and Jesse began to share personal experiences about their dissimilar backgrounds and cultural diversities.

Sparks of awareness were beginning to ignite in Bruce, as he became conscious of the fact that he possessed something others wanted to learn. He had similar feelings when he taught cha-cha lessons aboard the ship coming across the Pacific, and in San Francisco. He began to feel that he had a natural gift for teaching, though he never had really thought about being a teacher in the academic sense. People were just interested in learning what he knew. He thought it ironic that he had to study classes that he did not particularly care about while being solicited to teach classes that he did. Ever since he had come to Seattle, his life had certainly become very paradoxical and complex. Bruce was quick to pick up on the West's thirst for the secret Eastern arts and its veiled philosophies. He recognized the possibilities that could develop if he were to introduce these little-known secrets to his new Western environment. Since his Wing Chun gung fu was a novelty to most Westerners, he could take this skill and capitalize on it. He laughed inside because, in America, even as highly advanced as it was technologically, the general populace had no knowledge, much less expertise, in this form of Asian self-defense. Except for a very few individuals, mostly military personnel that had spent time in China, Japan, Korea, or Okinawa, most of the western world had no knowledge of Wing Chun gung fu.

Bruce knew his short but extremely effective performance of Wing Chun was even more impressive when he could demonstrate it with someone possessing his level of skill. Bruce also knew he was a natural warrior, who had the ability to execute self-defense techniques so quickly and explosively that unskilled observers gawked with awe and disbelief. His self-defense technique impressed not only the persons he demonstrated on but also the spectators, who enjoyed a great new form of entertainment as well. He was inwardly thrilled to know that he could attract a crowd anywhere by performing in this manner.

Jesse confided that he had trained in Japanese judo long enough to earn his black belt and had been in competition on numerous occasions. He had won the title of Northwest Judo Champion in a recent tournament and had done a little boxing prior to that. He emphasized that he really liked the Asian martial arts and the philosophies behind them.

He also spoke of his good friend and roommate Ed Hart, who practiced judo with him. After Bruce mentioned that he was staying at a place above Ruby Chow's restaurant, Jesse stated that the restaurant was only seven blocks away from Ed's and his apartment. They were surprised to discover that they not only went to the same vocational school but lived pretty close to each other too.

Bruce was the first to suggest that perhaps they should form a martial arts group for informal workouts and the sharing of martial arts knowledge. Maybe they even could start a club that might meet at different locations and work out together. Jesse thought that this was an excellent idea and would begin putting something together as soon as possible, and he'd spread the word around to his friends. He thought they already had the start on an interested group of people, with James DeMile, who already had expressed an interest; himself; and possibly his roommate Ed Hart, who had boxing experience, and probably some of the guys from his judo classes who would also be interested.

Later that week Jesse contacted his friend Skip Ellsworth, who decided to join the group. This made him the third person to become a part of this embryonic club. Skip towered over Bruce by a good seven inches and outweighed him by about thirty pounds. When he was first introduced, Bruce asked him his name. Ellsworth replied, "De Welle F. Ellsworth, but you can call me Skip for short." Bruce looked up at him, smiling, and then commented, "I think I can remember that." Both laughed as they shook hands.

By the last week of the September in which they first met, the group began to meet at Jesse and Ed's apartment for informal classes and workout sessions. Jesse taught Bruce the techniques of judo and basic grappling, how to use an opponent's weight against himself, how to shift weight and make an adversary resisting the effort suddenly go flying in a direction that was totally unexpected, and many subtle ways in which the feet could be positioned to disrupt an attack.

Bruce amused himself and his friends by constantly playing with ideas as to how he could artfully integrate his Wing Chun into the judo techniques that were practiced during workouts. Jesse and the group also found it amusing how clever Bruce was when it came to playing around with a serious self-defense concept and modifying it until he could use it in a playful sparring engagement.

What was also hard for the older members of the club to fathom was how someone so young could be so skillful in fighting. Bruce could adapt something that Jesse had taught him so quickly that, after only ten or fifteen minutes of practice, he was doing it as if he had known it for years. Among the youngest in the group, he seemed to have a natural ability to take charge of a group of people and make his presence felt as an instructor of expert caliber. His age of nineteen did not seem to matter when he was teaching. Though most of these sessions were casual and relaxed, with lots of joking and kidding, it wasn't long after a session started that Bruce would assume command of the group and change his demeanor to that of a consummate professional. His slight stutter when trying to pronounce newly learned English words, combined with a distinctive British inflection, made him seem an underage Chinese professor. What he could not clearly explain verbally he made up for in his ability to demonstrate it with phenomenal expertise. To most, Bruce made a workout worth the effort, because they knew that they were going to learn something important. They also enjoyed just watching Bruce perform seemingly insignificant maneuvers with such panache and flare. Sometimes he would even dramatize a demonstrated technique on a willing participant by adding a little showmanship for extra measure, by punching or kicking so close that they thought he would hit them. These effects were magnified somewhat when one watched this slender Chinese lad, wearing thick glasses, dress slacks, and a short-sleeve shirt, demonstrate self-defense techniques against guys who stood six inches taller and outweighed him by sixty or seventy pounds.

As the class size increased, they decided to start holding their training sessions at the vacant area on the corner of Maynard Avenue South and South Lane Street. This was an area near the geographical center of Chinatown, about nine blocks south of Jesse and Ed's residence. Jesse and Ed rationalized that, by doing this, they would have more room to work out, without getting all of the traffic through their cramped apartment. Besides, Bruce figured, the exposure and visibility of practicing in these public places certainly could not hurt in attracting new students. It was through these close-knit associations with his first students that Bruce's notoriety began to blossom. James DeMile became convinced that Bruce was definitely more than he appeared to be when James had first tested him at the outdoor demonstration and decided to train under Bruce's guidance. Soon thereafter, the cadre of followers included LeRoy Garcia, Howard Hall, Tak Miyabe, Leroy Porter, Pat Hooks and Doug Palmer. Bruce's time away from the restaurant, and the close-knit fellowship he was enjoying with his friends that had a common interest in martial arts, gave him a sense of well being that he had not known in some time. Bruce Lee began to redefine himself again. A noticeable air of confidence and maturity was gradually melding with his already flamboyant personality, which gave those around him a sense of respect for one that was decidedly younger than they were.

Because Jesse attended Edison Tech with Bruce, their contact was a regular occurrence outside of their workouts. Over the next few months their friendship intensified. Jesse's interest in the Chinese martial arts, its history, tradition, and methodology, began to be the primary topic of many of their casual conversations. Bruce started educating Jesse and the rest of the group in this history. He said he wanted them to have a good basic understanding about

Wing Chun and would later teach them some of his own adaptations that he felt worked better against larger people like Americans than some of the typical Wing Chun maneuvers.

He then conveyed that Wing Chun is one of the world's youngest gung fu styles, and the only one founded by a woman. That woman was Ng Mei, a Buddhist nun of China's famous Shaolin Temple. As any responsible educator would do, Bruce simply relayed much of the historical information that Yip Man and his seniors had passed along to him from his times in classes in Kowloon. These lessons took place at training sessions at the parks, over lunch or dinner at restaurants or just hanging out at Jesse and Ed's apartment. Every time the gang was together, for whatever reasons, invariably the topic of martial arts dominated their conversations.

During the course of time, and throughout their many get-togethers, Jesse and the tight-knit group of devotees learned that Ng Mei was recognized as one of the top five martial artists in China during the early 1700s. Although she was reputed to be highly proficient in animal styles of gung fu, she felt it was possible to devise a more effective fighting method that did not rely so much on the emulation of animals as a defense mechanism. Movements mimicking clawing, ripping, tearing, biting, brute strength, and oddly contrived body postures were altogether eliminated. Unlike many of the animal-based styles of Chinese gung fu, she wanted to develop a style that was easier to learn and more natural for the human to use effectively for practical self-defense purposes.

Bruce further related that, according to the legend behind the creation of Wing Chun, inspiration struck Ng Mei one day while she was watching a fight between a stork and large rodent. She was impressed by the manner in which the stork used its wings and legs to deflect and counterattack at the same time. She adapted the technique to formulate a unique new martial art, which could be adapted to the natural way that the human anatomy functioned when assaulted by a more powerful and aggressive antagonist.

The gang learned that Ng Mei later named this new self-defense art after her student, Yim Wing Chun. *Wing Chun* translates as "everlasting springtime." Yim Wing Chun was a talented martial artist in her own right but wanted to learn this practical self-defense method. Bruce couldn't help adding some dramatics to his stories. He said that the legend went that Yim Wing Chun received an unwelcome proposal of marriage from a local warlord. She decided to train herself as a fighter to rid herself of his attentions. With Ng Mei's help, a challenge was made: If after one year the warlord could beat her in a fight, Wing Chun would consent to the marriage. If not, she was free to choose her own destiny. Bruce further elaborated by telling his students that, after training diligently under Ng Mei, Wing Chun challenged her would-be husband and easily defeated him. She later settled down with the partner of her choice, Leung Bok To, an exponent of the martial art Hung Kuen, and taught him her style.

Jesse, Ed, James, Skip, Doug Palmer, Pat Hooks, and the other students would listen attentively as Bruce recounted every nuance of the legendary history enshrouding this very secretive self-defense art. They sensed that they were pretty special in the first place to even be privy to learning a system with such a renowned past; the way Bruce drew them into the stories, with his solemn expressions and animated gestures to emphasize a point, only whetted their appetite for exploring this fascinating art to even greater depths.

Bruce also expounded on the fact that Wing Chun was completely different from most other martial arts, because it emphasizes economy of movement, which eliminates the need for brute strength. He also pointed out the basic differences between it and the arts of Praying Mantis and Hung Gar. He noted that they have similar qualities, but techniques were applied differently to similar situations. All of Wing chun's techniques are based on direct, practical, natural body movements that are easy to learn and can be applied to self-defense situations immediately. There was no need to spend countless years mastering a style before it could be put to practical use.

He further explained that, in Hong Kong, Wing Chun students develop skills in balance, speed, and positioning through specific exercises (known as "forms") to fine-tune movements and cultivate power, and they also develop skills in supervised combat that simulates real-life fighting situations. As in traditional boxing or street fighting, which the style closely represents, the focus is on protecting the body's centerline with short, sharp punches and kicks and following through with strikes to the opponent's vulnerable points.

Bruce stressed that there are no showy kicks, spins, or fancy leg maneuvers that glorified or sensationalized the effects, which are evident in many martial arts demonstrations of splintering cement blocks or wooden boards. The most impressive move, he said, the extremely close-range punch, is over in the blink of an eye, and usually the attacker never ever sees it coming until feeling its impact. James DeMile expressed a very serious interest when Bruce elaborated on the short-range punches. His training as a boxer had convinced him that the in-close knockout punches were some of the most valuable weapons that a fighter could have in his fighting arsenal. He hung on every word when Bruce spoke of instances he had witnessed in Hong Kong in which a Wing Chun expert could execute a single four- or five-inch punch and send a classmate flying up to three meters away. Upon inquiring more about this incredible feat, James and the others learned that this remarkable power found in Wing Chun's punches came from concentrated force, or the body's entire chi when released all in one explosive instant. It was like the compression of a coiled spring that had been suddenly released.

Bruce now knew that the gang was serious about learning the art of Wing Chun and some of the gung fu adaptations he had integrated. They were also curious to know more about his sifu, Yip Man. Bruce sensed that Jesse's curiosity would not be fully satisfied until Bruce had spelled out everything, right down to the very last detail. So, he began by saying that, during the Chinese Cultural Revolution, Wing Chun, like other martial arts, was banned in China and survived only through the persistence of practitioners like Yip Man. Sifu Yip Man first learned Wing Chun from Chan Wah Shun. At the age of fifteen, Yip Man traveled to Hong Kong to study at St Stephen's College. While there, he continued to learn Wing Chun under Leung Jan's son, Leung Bik. Through Chan Wah Shun and Leung Bik, Yip Man acquired complete mastery in Wing Chun.

After that, Yip Man returned to China after completion of his studies and became an army recruit. He was later involved in several bouts with other martial artists. In one volatile encounter with a policeman who challenged his skills, Yip Man grasped the man's revolver, removed the cartridges, and strewed them out on to the ground. By then Yip's skill was already well known in China, and he was regarded as the youngest and last remaining traditional Wing Chun master.

Bruce then revealed that, in 1949, after the Communist takeover in China, Yip Man returned to Hong Kong. Times were hard, but he found a friend in Lee Man, secretary of the Hong Kong Cafe Workers Union, who allowed him to use the union premises to train students. This union hall is where he accepted his first students in Kowloon on a professional basis. As time passed and his knack for teaching developed, Yip Man relocated his kwoon to other locations in Kowloon. Bruce was proud to also relate that his sifu was one of the best Wing Chun teachers in Hong Kong, and probably all over Asia.

Shortly thereafter, Bruce arranged for the group to train in the back yard area of Ruby's restaurant, as well as other locations, such as local parks he would select or at the Blue Cross Clinic parking lot across the street from Ruby's restaurant, when the groups were too big for Ruby's back yard. During the winter months or when it was raining, he would seek out other places, like recreation departments and local gymnasiums to train.

Bruce, always aware of his living conditions, was somewhat reluctant to invite people upstairs to his room above the restaurant, because of the embarrassment it caused him. However, on occasion, some of his students would follow him upstairs to pick up books or other related martial arts notes before setting out for a workout.

Bruce was finding the training at the adjacent parking lot very convenient since it was so close to the restaurant. On days when he had to report for waiter duty for the evenings, or for special banquets, he could work out with the gang a while and just jaunt across the street to his room, freshen up and report to work. Usually, this only took fifteen minutes or so.

Sometimes, depending on the weather and Bruce's propensity for varying the locales of where he wanted to work out, he would elect to train at playing fields and nearby parks. He figured that training with his friends in public places, where onlookers and the people that were curious about gung fu could see the sessions, would increase his exposure and help attract more seriously interested students to the club. Whenever Bruce was conducting these workouts outside, his attention was never far from those that stopped to watch the sessions. If someone was just mulling around watching and Bruce believed the person was not interested Bruce would simply ignore his or her presence. However, if Bruce's intuition told him that someone was a potential prospective student, he would make every effort to give him or her an impressive showing of his abilities.

For the benefit of these onlookers, he would arrange these impromptu staged demonstrations so that the people could see him execute flawless techniques against one of the guys. What was amusing to everyone that participated in the workouts was how Bruce, in order to make an impression, would usually call James out to be his demonstration partner. He did this to exhibit a noticeable contrast in size and reach between him and his demonstration partner.

James was also likely candidate because of his ominous tough guy appearance; he was big, stout, broad shouldered, and physically conditioned. He moved with the panache of a boxer and was versed enough in Wing Chun to know exactly what to expect from Bruce. This only added dramatic impact to the visually stimulating mock fight scenario.

With the experience of teaching in public places, Bruce had truly developed a keen eye for reading observers that happened by during a training session. Once they stopped to linger and observe, he would try to gauge their interest in the way they attentively studied him and his group. His intuition was uncanny at detecting if a spectator was seriously interested or was just curiously passing some time at his expense. If he detected someone was indeed sincere, he would saunter over and strike up a conversation just to see how serious he or she was. This worked well for breaking the ice when he sensed the observer was shy or did not know how to go about making their interest known.

Such was the case with his initial introduction to an older man by the name of Taky Kimura, who had stood by patiently watching one of Bruce's gung fu sessions at an athletic playing field. Near the end of a strenuous two-hour stint, Bruce approached this reticent middle-aged Japanese man and initiated a casual conversation by inquiring about his interest in martial arts. The gentleman responded that he knew Jesse Glover from the many times that he had been in his supermarket and that Jesse had spoken quite highly of Bruce and suggested that he should come down and check out the classes. Kimura also confided with unpretentious candor that he wanted to see for himself if what Jesse and these fellows were saying about Bruce were true, if he was as good as they described. Taky seemed impressed with the dexterity and speed with which Bruce had demonstrated his explosive self-defense techniques. After Bruce gave Taky a brief explanation of the purpose and history of Wing Chun, he used his standard situational demonstration to prove the effectiveness of this art. Bruce had Taky square off in a fighter's pose just outside of punching range. Then, in a burst of speed, Bruce delivered a flurry of rapid-fire punches to Taky's head and chest area—the dozen or so punches stopping just an inch or less from their intended targets. Taky was intimidated, fascinated, and convinced at the same time; and he was impressed enough that he then asked if he could join the club. As always, a proud, yet benevolent, smile appeared on Bruce's face when someone had witnessed his skills and bestowed a compliment by asking to train under his tutelage. Bruce then patted Taky on the shoulder and said, "Sure why not. After all it's free, and you got nothing to lose." Taky then followed up with a verbal compliment by saying, "Man that was fast." Bruce replied, "Man, you won't be sorry."

In further conversation, as the group was disbanding for the day, Taky casually shared that he had studied some judo when he was interned in a camp during World War II. He said his Asian heritage meant a lot to him, but here in the United States, after the internment that made him feel like a prisoner, he felt that he had lost a lot of confidence and self-esteem. Bruce assured him that he would not be sorry for training and regaining some of the lost pride from that experience. Just in the way Bruce expressed and represented himself (since he was also an Asian), Taky seemed somewhat self-assured that some good could possibly come from working out with Bruce. How much, he had no idea, but he was willing to give it a shot.

Word continued to spread among the gang's friends and their schoolmates at Edison Technical Vocational School. Even the faculty was now discovering that Bruce was exceptionally gifted in the martial arts, and he never missed a chance to impress them with his knowledge and talents. In response to the interest he was generating on campus, Bruce virtually had to reinvent himself as a sifu of martial arts. He had never taught before, so he was venturing into uncharted territory as far as he was concerned. He assumed he should teach in the manner of his teacher, Sifu Yip Man, and as his seniors taught in Hong Kong. Of course, his experiences with Yip Man, combined with the teaching experience he had gained from instructing the impromptu cha-cha classes in the San Francisco–Oakland area added validity to his role as a self-appointed Chinese gung fu sifu. Bruce, being so young compared to the venerated martial art teachers in Hong Kong and almost every part of Asia felt an elated sense of worth in assuming such a position. He actually basked in this glory and savored the notoriety that came with this newfound local fame. This feeling was something that he had not experienced since he was officially proclaimed the 1958 Hong Kong Crown Colony cha-cha champion. This, and the temporary notoriety he received in films that he had acted in when he was much younger, was about as close as he could imagine to the recognition he was getting in Seattle.

The subtle influx of new participants to his informal Wing Chun–based gung fu classes was beginning to fuel Bruce's enthusiasm more with each passing day. This, in turn, was the inspiration he needed to promote himself to an even greater degree. As a result, his classes expanded exponentially with his promotions and demonstrations. This growth, combined with his senior students' undaunted enthusiasm, was the impetus behind his own motivation to keep pursuing his promotional efforts.

Not long afterward his nucleus cadre of serious supporters increased to consist of Jesse Glover, Skip Ellsworth, James DeMile, Tak Miyabe, Charlie Woo, Ed Hart, Doug Palmer, Pat Hooks, Taky Kimura, LeRoy Garcia, Pat Strong, Fred Sato, Leroy Porter, Howard Hall, and Roy Hollingsworth. One disappointment that Bruce tried never to let show was that not all of the students ever showed up at the same time to workout. He was frustrated because he thought everyone would be as seriously interested in learning as he was in sharing his knowledge. Nevertheless, over time he realized that in America, people have so many different schedules and other obligations that it was probably impossible to get everyone to a work out together. Even the students had a difficult time in keeping track of the new guys that joined the group because of this.

On one of Taky's first workout sessions, after a brief stretching exercise, Bruce had them lined up in pairs and began practicing some single-hand sensitivity drills. Shortly thereafter, he shifted to the double-handed routines. Skip Ellsworth, arriving late for the class and feeling in a somewhat joking mood, ambled over to where the guys were practicing. Then, after seeing that his sifu had another newcomer that had joined the club, Skip decided to have a little fun. He pretended to be a stranger and, in a very loud and belligerent manner, angrily started shouting derogatory remarks toward the group, saying, "Gung fu is a bunch of hogwash, and any good street fighter could mop up the whole bunch of you guys."

Taky and the others in the group ceased their training and turned to see what all of the commotion was about. In a very serious and arrogant manner, Skip struck a boxer's pose, began making jabs and uppercuts, and challenged Bruce to a fight. Bruce and all of the regular students, caught on to what was happening right away. Taky, being the newest student, stood there dumbfounded at what was happening. He could not believe the brashness of this kid that wanted to start a fight for no reason except to prove that one form of fighting was better than another one. Bruce played along with the joke by angrily responding that if he wanted to fight he came to the right place. Bruce then assumed a fighter's stance and executed a few token animal-style movements that resembled a tiger ready to pounce on its prey. Taky could not help but think that this tall, crazy young white guy was going to be beaten up pretty badly. This derogatory banter continued for several minutes, as the students stood there reveling in the amusement that Skip and Bruce were providing in this mock challenge match. Then everyone suddenly burst out laughing while Taky stood there trying to figure what was going on. After it was over, Taky felt as if he had been the brunt of the joke, he realized that Bruce could be a joker as well as a martial arts teacher. He had been officially welcomed to the group and now was a member of the gang.

Bruce was delighted to discover that Taky Kimura's family business was only about eight blocks from Ruby Chow's restaurant. After making his first visit there, Bruce discovered that it was even bigger than he had originally imagined. The supermarket had a sizable area in the basement of the building and ample parking surrounding the two-entrance building. After Bruce kidded around about how the basement or rear parking areas would make excellent places to work out, Taky subtly offered his consent to hold some of their training sessions there if the gang needed a place to train when the weather got cold. Taky realized this was an amicable arrangement for him, and after giving it a bit more consideration, liked Bruce's idea even more. Should Bruce seriously want to conduct workouts at his store from time to time, it made good practical sense to him. He had to run his family's business and could not take off and attend all of the workouts when they were held at other places. Now he would be able to go to the basement or out back and train when the classes were held there. Then after the workouts, he could simply return to work. Bruce was learning that Taky was a very practical and down-to-earth man, who usually had good reasons for making the decisions he made. Bruce liked the fact that Taky was older and had a mature and responsible outlook on life. He felt certain that if Taky said he would do something or indicated he would do a favor for someone, it would happen.

Taky was almost twice Bruce's age. Bruce observed that Taky was slow in executing techniques that required fast footwork and body maneuvering as compared to the younger students, but what Tacky lacked in the nimbleness and stamina of his youthful classmates, he made up for with determination and perseverance. Taky, with his judo background, was used to the competitiveness of engaging a workout partner at close-range. This was something that stood out to Bruce as something that most of his beginning students did not possess. Bruce also liked Taky's organizational abilities, and that he was a no nonsense type of fellow. After classes, when the guys would hang around and tell jokes or talk about their dates and the girls they had met, Taky would excuse himself and return to his family's IGA Thrift Market to operate the business. If the classes continued after the market had closed, he would leave and go home to his family. Taky rarely stayed around to kid and joke with his fellow classmates, but this only reaffirmed Bruce's judgment of his character. Taky was a devoted person, with family priorities and commitments that he always honored first; everything else was secondary. In some ways, Bruce began sensing that Taky would make an excellent assistant instructor after he mastered the techniques of his art.

The continued signs of growth in the club had suddenly sparked Bruce's entrepreneurial aspirations. His new role as a teacher had real possibilities—financially and otherwise. Expanding this small club into a business was becoming a real possibility, but he would have to plan carefully. His classes could become bigger than he ever imagined. In any case, he felt that he had little to lose in pursuing a new challenge.

Using his time efficiently would need to become a priority, if he were to keep everything going and running smoothly, especially with the balancing act between the club and his other commitments and academic responsibilities. He would grow accustomed to this balancing act as the Wing Chun class student roll expanded. He began committing more time to his personal training and monitoring his students' progress with greater attentiveness than ever before. He also became more organized in the way he meted out Wing Chun gung fu knowledge. Shortly thereafter, he committed to paper a series of workout schedules and times that would best suit his students, based primarily on each person's skill level and physical attributes.

Taky's permission to train at the supermarket was turning into a good arrangement for everyone. The supermarket was centrally located and convenient for all of the students to attend. As a result, Bruce found himself getting there earlier on workout days and staying later after classes. On several occasions, while chatting with some of the early birds and waiting for other students to arrive for the sessions, Bruce had observed that people were pulling their automobiles onto the store property to park and then would do their shopping at other businesses down the street. After Bruce informed Taky of this, Taky became very distressed. They were taking advantage of the parking facility without patronizing the store that owned the property. Bruce patted Taky on the shoulder and told him that he would take care of the situation. He would become Taky's security guard when he was there at the store. Taky laughed and told his sifu not to beat the violators up too bad.

That evening after class, Bruce and several of the students were returning to the lot when Bruce noticed a rather large and burly man about thirty years of age exit his car and start walking toward the corner away from the store. It was obvious to all that he had not intended to shop in the Thrift Market but was simply using Taky's property as free parking while he shopped elsewhere. This infuriated Bruce, to see Taky being taken advantage of like that. He ran over to the man before he could get off the premises. Bruce yelled, "Hey Mister! You can't park here. This is private property for the supermarket!" Bruce had changed from the jokester that he had been several minutes earlier to a person in a fiery rage. The big, burly man turned and looked at the skinny Chinaman wearing thick eyeglasses and said, "Is that so?" In the most irate tone of voice they had ever heard, the students witnessed their sifu, with clenched fists, standing right in the man's face, forcefully reply, "Yes! That's so!" Bruce's serious expression and the angry spirit of his words were enough to make the man return to his car and drive it off the lot. Later, Taky mentioned to Bruce that he had heard that word was getting around that it was becoming unsafe for violators to park at the supermarket's lot if they were not shopping inside. Bruce laughed and said, "Those cats are finding out that there's a new Chinese security guard in town. One who knows gung fu." Shortly thereafter, very few people took advantage of Taky when Bruce was on the premises.

With his close cadre of students now starting to show real signs of improvement in physical conditioning from the intense regimen of calisthenics at thier informal workouts, Bruce began to intensify his own workouts. Mostly, in an effort to lead by example, he set up a schedule to increase the number of push-ups, sit-ups, and body strengthening drills he did, to add some bulk and definition to his slender frame. He also wanted to impress his students, and others, by showing just how physically fit he really was; he wanted to compensate for what he lacked in weight and height, especially when compared to guys like Skip Ellsworth, who outweighed him by thirty or so pounds and stood almost eight inches taller. Bruce referred to these big Americans as "trucks," and when he would demonstrate techniques against them, he would usually say, just before executing a swift and powerfully executed maneuver, "When a big truck rolls in you must react swiftly and precisely, otherwise it will roll over you."

During his younger days in Kowloon, Bruce had involved himself in various challenge exercises in which strength, or the lack of it, oftentimes determined who was best at any given type of exercise. It wasn't enough to just do push-ups, but to determine who could do the most under certain conditions. When someone could do fifty or more push-ups on their palms in a given time, the one that could do the same amount on their fingertips was considered even better. Naturally, these types of contests were escalated to new levels when one could take the exercise to even greater extremes like doing them with only one finger on each hand. Eventually, these challenges got to the point that the contestants would see who could do the most finger push-ups while using only one arm. Bruce drew from these types of friendly competitions when he wanted to demonstrate to his students just how strong he was in relation to his body size. Jesse, James, Taky, Doug, Charlie and most of the other students would try them and find them impossible to do. Naturally, Bruce had an advantage in these exercise contests, because he weighed less and thus had less mass to move. If anything, it proved quite convincingly that his sinew strength was nothing short of phenomenal.

With his strength, natural speed, and agility, Bruce was very impressive. When he got in the mood, it just seemed natural to flaunt his martial arts skills. Sometimes, at parties or other social gatherings, Bruce would find himself engaged in a stimulating conversation with someone and would direct the conversation into a discussion of gung fu. After several minutes of lively exchange, it was common to see Bruce doing one-handed push-ups on his fingertips, right there on the floor amid the guests. Naturally, these impromptu and unexpected displays of his physical prowess became the focal point of the party, and usually thereafter, the conversations eventually gravitated toward the topic of martial arts. Bruce would then demonstrate some of his specialty martial arts skills. Ultimately, Bruce knew that this was an ideal way of introducing people to Wing Chun, and he used it to his advantage in soliciting new students.

A Developing Romance

At one of these social gatherings Bruce met a Japanese American girl named Amy Sanbo. Bruce immediately felt an attraction for her and thought they had a lot in common. Amy was lively, creative, and articulate, and seemed to know exactly what she wanted. Bruce sensed that she was a compassionate person and not at all bitter, as he would have thought, after she mentioned living part of her childhood incarcerated with her parents in a United States internment camp at the outset of World War II. Her straightforward and pragmatic outlook on life combined with her stimulating intellectual conversations made Bruce feel slightly intimidated in her presence. He had never felt this way with other girls back in Kowloon. Amy found Bruce's claims of being in movies back in Hong Kong when he was younger a little farfetched, albeit titillating. She had seen and dated these types of guys before, guys who bragged or fabricated fantasies about their prowess. Bruce never tried to convince her that he was a child film star back in Hong Kong. He was just stating facts about his life in Asia. Unfortunately, most American women would find his stories hard to believe, unless they knew him intimately and were followers of Chinese cinema. When Amy and Bruce were together, he even flirted with other women in her presence, and Taky or Jesse couldn't tell if he was trying to make her jealous or just kidding around in his childish sort of way.

Amy was infatuated with the fact that he was skilled in self-defense, but she did not like him to flaunt it in public. Bruce, being somewhat artistic, appreciated that Amy had aspirations of becoming a writer and dancer. After he revealed that he had been a cha-

cha dancing champion in Hong Kong, she became even more skeptical about his stories, unsure if Bruce was lying or simply trying to impress her in hopes of sexual favors.

The fact that Bruce was the dancer he said he was, and that he had showed her some of the clever steps he had created when they were at social events on Sunday evenings, started to give Amy reason to believe that he had more substance and character than she had originally assumed.

Amy could not quite figure out why Bruce, having so much natural talent, did not pursue dancing as a professional career. He laughed when he heard Amy say that and thought she was joking, but Amy was emphatic. She had seen a natural talent that she felt Bruce was not utilizing to his fullest ability. Bruce tried to explain that dancing was a career with a short and not-too-profitable future. From his own experience, other than the short-lived exhilaration of being crowned a cha-cha champion a couple of years earlier, it had done very little to enhance his professional career. The only exception was the small amount of money he earned teaching cha-cha in San Francisco, thanks to his father's friend and sponsor Mr. Quan Ging Ho.

When she tried to proffer her opinions about his career, Bruce would turn the tables on her and invariably try to convince her to support his aspirations to open gung fu schools and become famous as a martial artist. When they were together, this was always a topic of contention.

She was also smitten when he spoke so proudly of his Chinese heritage and mentioned that he was born in the United States but raised in China. He shared with her that, by birthright, he was an American citizen from China and wanted to make a start in the land of opportunity. What Amy could not fully understand was that Bruce very rarely spoke of his parents. He never bragged about his father being a famous actor in the Chinese opera or his mother being associated with royalty. Amy found more often than not that she was the listener and Bruce was the talker in most of their conversations. She'd even laugh at some of his off-color jokes and chastise him for being vulgar at times. Bruce's students who came to the parties sensed that there was the possibility of a relationship here that could blossom beyond the platonic rapport Bruce and Amy had when they were together. The students would kid Bruce about this, and he would shrug it off with an insincere laugh.

Experimentation

During this time, Bruce began training individually with his students at their homes or apartments, when time and circumstances permitted. During this experimental period, Bruce discovered that no two of his students had the same abilities. Some were extremely coordinated at simultaneous blocking and counterattacking but lacked quick footwork. Others were more aggressive and, at times, would let sheer brute force dictate their actions. Some were smooth and fluid in their movements, and others were somewhat awkward at gauging distance and spatial positioning from their attacker, and since almost all of Bruce's students were larger and physically stronger then him, he had to use every clever ruse at his disposal to neutralize their attacks when they trained together.

Bruce also wondered how effective his teaching should be when it came to fighting. He wrestled with the idea of just how much he could reveal to a student before the student would become competent enough to threaten his own ability. Bruce felt this was a double-edged sword that could result in bad consequences if it were not addressed in a very cautious manner. This perplexing dilemma was one of the primary reasons that Bruce began considering rank levels for his students. He earnestly wanted them to be the very best fighters they could be, yet he did not want them to be skillful enough to defeat him. This situation was made even more complex when he considered the bonds of friendship that were forming between himself and his students. Bruce ultimately came to the realization that there was more comradeship developing between his students than he would have ever anticipated. They were genuinely sincere, helpful, sharing, and accommodating any time he needed their help. He tried to convince himself that he need not be concerned. "Why would friends want to use knowledge you had taught them to defeat a friend?" he thought.

Living as a student by day, a waiter and busboy by night, and then cavorting as a sought-after instructor in his spare hours posed several dilemmas to Bruce's once simple existence. Bruce realized that, some time in the future, he would need to adjust his priorities. It was conceivable that, in order to get a clear perspective on his real goals, he would need to eliminate the least favorable of the three. But, for the time being, he was content to flow with the situation and let destiny take its own course.

Not long after classes resumed at Edison, all of Bruce's students had made remarkable progress in their Wing Chun gung fu skills. Their interest in the martial art's philosophical truths was beginning to match their insatiable appetites for achieving physical mastery. As a result, their questions were becoming much more complex. Their incessant curiosity was gradually veering away from the physical precepts of Wing Chun and more toward the technical and philosophical interpretations of the style's subtle movements. From Bruce's perspective, this gave a new meaning to the title sifu. Their thought-provoking questions required thoughtful responses. Bruce could provide reasonably satisfactory answers most of the time, but in some instances, when one of the students sought elucidation pertaining to the theoretical applications or ventured beyond the ordinarily expected inquiries, Bruce was placed in the uncomfortable position of providing shallow answers to appease his students. When this happened, Bruce was confronted with his own need to seek the answers to these deeper philosophical questions. He was not pleased at these times and could only wish that he had the answers or his old teacher Yip Man's ability to speak at length on philosophy. Moreover, Bruce's English vocabulary was not broad enough to explain things that he would like with the completeness he needed to insure that his students understood the depth of his explanation.

James or Jesse were the students that usually posed the seriously perplexing questions. Bruce discovered that Caucasian Americans seemed to want easy or short answers to difficult subject matter from their teachers; in the Eastern cultures, however, it was believed to be academically more beneficial for the student to seek the answers within themselves. Regardless of the differences between Eastern and Western cultures regarding the student-teacher relationships, Bruce tried to appease his pupils in the best way that he knew under those awkward circumstances. He personally confided in James and Jesse on several occasions that he was as much a student as a teacher of the Wing Chun style and philosophy, let alone the vast subject of martial arts. He also mentioned, as his sifu had often said during Bruce's study at the kwoon in Kowloon, that martial arts were often dualistic in purpose. Martial arts were as deep as the person studying their complexities wanted them to be. They could be used to heal or kill. Esoterically speaking, Bruce used the Taoist concept of yin and yang, which represent dual aspects in nature that needed each other to form completeness. Bruce used the concept of yin and yang to explain the least difficult type of philosophic questions that evoked his students' curiosity. From yin and yang, he could, in a rough fashion, provide explanations for his reasoning on the subject of Wing Chun and teach how to perceive its interacting components. Fast and slow, rigid and yielding, hard and soft, were some of the basic concepts he suggested using to analyze the techniques found in Wing Chun.

Because of his students' questions, Bruce realized he needed to pursue philosophical matters more thoroughly. He began to spend additional time at the local library, earnestly searching out texts on ancient Chinese philosophy.

Also Bruce's students were beginning to notice that their sifu was beginning to make minor adaptations to the techniques they had previously learned. Even the basic Wing Chun stance was modified to suit Bruce's particular needs when Jesse another senior student posed hypothetical conditions based on realistic situations. Though Bruce liked to create self-defense scenarios and find a solution for them within the Sil Lim Tao form, his students were now getting well enough into their Wing Chun training that they could see that some situations could not be realistically addressed with the knowledge they had had.

Bruce then started to modify his Wing Chun teaching, by gradually introducing and mixing in the subtleties that he had learned from Sifu Gin Foon Mark's Praying Mantis style and techniques Bruce created that seemed to him most logical for attacking a particular situation. Jesse and Jim were quick to see that Bruce was changing or adding to the foundation of his traditional Wing Chun. Not that they objected or complained, but they thought it interesting that, with all that Bruce had said about Wing Chun and its effectiveness, he was adding things that were obviously not in the form. Bruce justified this by explaining that some of these techniques, or variations of them, were found in the other two Wing Chun forms.

He also started experimenting with various types and styles of kicks. Although Wing Chun was rather limited in kicks, due to the short straddle-legged stance, Bruce found that, by shifting his posture to one that closely resembled a boxer's crouch, he could use the rear leg for straight-line kickand a variety of low-level circular kicks. Even the slightly bent front leg could be readily adapted for kicking and extremely close-range knee strikes to the opponent's groin area. He began to incorporate close-range self-defense solutions into his teachings, using some of the leg reaps and leverage throws that Jesse had taught him. While blocking or interacting with a training partner who had learned his chi sao routines, Bruce would almost instinctively slip in a controlled leg throw behind their leg, and with the aid of a shoulder or extended arm grab, his partner would find himself on the floor.

When Bruce discovered that some of his students had 8 mm movie cameras, he would have them film his workouts as he applied these newly contrived techniques. After the film was developed, the group would get together, set up the movie projector and screen, and watch these techniques. They would spend hours rewinding these brief three-minute reels, laughing and bantering about their techniques. All the while, Bruce was studying the film closely to see if the techniques could be improved upon. This helped Bruce evaluate his own performance and point out mistakes and weaknesses in his senior students' performances. One thing Bruce learned was that, when he inserted different kicks into his Wing Chun techniques, his timing remained pretty constant when he kept the kicks below belt level. If he kicked any higher than that, he had momentary lapses in his timing that made it difficult to follow up as quickly as he was used to doing. During these sessions, Jesse, Ed, Skip, Taky, and most of the gang then started looking at Bruce's teachings in an entirely different light. They could see by the way that Bruce was adding things to his art that there was virtually an unlimited supply of techniques that could be developed from the integration or fusion of styles and methods of maneuvering in a fight situation.

Bruce Sets Up Formal Lessons

More of a fraternal relationship began to emerge in the group during this time. They had reached such a point in their relationship personal matters, problems, and needs were discussed openly. Bruce was noticeably more forthright and less embarrassed about divulging his poor financial situation. This was something that was rather rare for Chinese in American society. He confided that he was very unhappy with his employment relationship with Ruby and Ping. He openly expressed that he was satisfied with her gracious hospitality but was dissatisfied with his job as a waiter and busboy. He candidly revealed that he felt it was far below his station in life, considering his background, to be tolerating this type of treatment in exchange for such little pay. Bruce could not ignore the fact that he had played in seventeen Hong Kong motion pictures in his youth, had enjoyed a rather cloistered and more than modest lifestyle that his family wealth had made possible, and to some degree, had come to enjoy and expect the finer things in life. From that perspective, he felt uncomfortable and unhappy when he was ordered around or assigned the tasks at the restaurant that made him appear to be a peon in others' eyes.

After hearing Bruce's predicament, Jesse made the off-the-cuff remark that Bruce should begin charging for his services as a martial arts instructor. Bruce listened attentively as Jesse explained American professional business practices. Anyone that possessed certifiable professional skills, he said, charged premium fees for their services, advice and knowledge. Lawyers, doctors, accountants, specialists, and the like earned their living by attracting new clients while maintaining accounts with their older clients. "After all, these types of business professionals had specialized knowledge in a given field or expert training that came with years of schooling," he said. Because Bruce had unique skills and knowledge acquired over years, he should take a professional approach to teaching. Bruce's mind raced as he tried to figure out how to apply this information to his situation, given the nature of something as new as gung fu to Western society.

Jesse mentioned several different types of people who might seek instruction—people who wanted to overcome low self-esteem or inferiority complexes, people who felt powerless or threatened by larger and more physically empowered individuals, curiosity seekers who had boxed or wrestled and wanted to learn gung fu to make comparisons, women who wanted some form of self-defense against overzealous suitors and predators, and law enforcement personnel who wanted something extra in self-defense to use in the line of duty. Jesse pragmatically pointed out that there was no guarantee that the American public would come rushing to Bruce seeking instruction, because gung fu was something that they did not know, much less understand. Nevertheless, Jesse figured a percentage of the American population would undoubtedly seek out Bruce's services as a gung fu instructor simply to learn self-defense. But Jesse also pointed out that, like any other business enterprise, Bruce would have to advertise and let people know who he was and what skills he taught. He could not just sit back and wait for people to stumble accidentally upon his Asian self-defense classes. In essence, if a good plan was successfully implemented, his present and future students would actually become his longtime clients.

Jesse's words seemed to make a lot of sense. Bruce realized that, if he did indeed charge a teaching fee for his professional service, it could possibly be the beginning of a different and more prosperous existence. In a relatively short time he could quit his job as a waiter-busboy at the restaurant and embrace a livelihood that was more in harmony with the way that he had envisioned himself. His new life would be independenct, and he would have personal freedom and sufficient funds to afford what he liked when he liked. Bruce had envisioned owning a prestigious automobile such as a Rolls Royce or a sporty Lamborghini some time in the future, and a wardrobe that made the ultimate fashion statement at any occasion.

Now, the big question was if it was actually possible to recruit enough seriously dedicated students to offset the paltry salary and tips that Bruce earned at the restaurant. He did not wish to merely supplement or replace those meager sums that he was forced to subsist on since his arrival in Seattle but to exceed the stipend significantly. Jesse had opened his eyes to a whole new world of possibilities, if Bruce pursued this plan seriously. Regardless of what Bruce imagined, any doubt was soon dispelled as Jesse, Taky, LeRoy, James, and Charlie began to spread the word that gung fu lessons would soon be available in the area. It was as if a five-man publicity team had been unleashed to spread the gospel according to Saint Bruce. In a matter of weeks, Bruce's intentions were common knowledge around Chinatown and the school campuses. People began coming up to Bruce and asking to join his club. The Tai Tung restaurant in Chinatown had become a favorite of the gang. It was centrally located, not far from Hing Hay Park, and well within walking distance of everything in the Chinatown district. This, old world–style Chinese eating establishment was the longest continuously operating restaurant in the area. Owned by a popular figure in Chinatown named Quan Lee, it had been in operation since 1935. The fact that it stayed open on the weekends until around three o'clock in the morning made it a convenient place to hang out after Bruce had completed his work shift at Ruby's restaurant. In many ways, the restaurant was like many of the eateries that Bruce remembered back in Hong Kong. It had subtle details reminiscent of traditional Asian ambiance, charm and friendliness. A plethora of colorful characters frequented the place, which gave this quaint dining facility a distinction that could not be found any other place on South King Street. Not long after first visiting the Tai Tung, the gang started meeting there on a regular basis. Sometimes it was just a place to meet, and other times it was a place to socialize and talk about martial arts. Soon, everyone in the area knew who Bruce was. His unusually spirited behavior, combined with his propensity for kidding and joking with the elderly locals, was something that one could not forget very quickly. After they had gotten a taste of Bruce's humor and raucousness, or had been the recipient of one of his harmless pranks, all of the regulars knew him on a first-name basis. And through Bruce's antics, all his close friends and students became known at the restaurant as well.

After they began frequenting Chinatown regularly, the students soon discovered that Bruce was definitely a creature of habit when it came to selecting items from the menu. Invariably, when they visited the Tai Tung or other Chinese restaurants, Bruce would order the oyster beef over rice and a root beer soda. When Bruce ended up at the Tai Tung after a movie or date with Amy, the waiters and waitresses would just assume what he would order and bring one menu to the table, usually for Bruce's guest. They were celebrating Bruce's twentieth birthday on Sunday night, November 27, 1960, at the Tai Tung restaurant when Jesse Glover initially suggested to Bruce that, in order to get things rolling, he, Skip, Ed, Taky, James, and Charlie would agree to pay four dollars a week for instruction. Their instruction fees, combined with the lesson fees of several dozen new prospects, would become enough to offset the salary and tips Bruce earned at the restaurant. This gratuitous offer seemed immeasurable in alleviating Bruce's sense of insecurity, and certainly stimulated his ambition and determination to succeed even more.

Bruce realized that, in order to attract more students, he would have to generate his own publicity. Lacking the resources of a company or corporation, he would have to resort to methods that did not require a major outlay of funds for advertisement. This usually meant giving demonstrations and conducting his classes in locations where people could witness him teaching and see his students training. Public parks, gymnasiums, recreation centers, parking lots, and even the his students' yards were typical locations where he promoted himself and his art. He was attracting a following of spectators that simply wanted to watch these workouts. Some even followed the gang from one location to another to observe his teaching and demonstrations, in hopes of learning some of his self-defense techniques and possibly glean some martial wisdom without actually participating. It was obvious to his students that Bruce resented and disdained these people, who thought they could get something for nothing. He even mentioned to his class on numerous occasions that you cannot learn the martial arts by watching. You must get in there and train as if your life depended on it to gain the valuable knowledge.

Relationship Troubles

While formulating all of these plans, Bruce found it difficult to get around town with the speed and punctuality that he would have liked. Lacking an automobile, he always felt somewhat embarrassed when he had to go somewhere to promote himself and his classes. Even his ability to date in the evenings when he was off work was very limited without a viable form of transportation other than the bus. He was totally dependent on his friends for getting around Seattle. Taky Kimura, sensing that Bruce needed transportation from time to time, offered to drive him places he needed to go. When Bruce and Amy would go on a date to a movie, restaurant, or party, Taky usually picked them up and returned them home after an evening out on the town. Sometimes it was early in the evening when Bruce called Taky and asked for a ride to take Amy out on a date. Then it was usually after two o'clock in the morning when Taky would later return to chauffeur his sifu and his date back home. Taky always readily obliged, even though the awkward hours inconvenienced the Kimura family. He never complained or claimed to be too busy when Bruce asked for help. Taky just saw it as an honor to help his sifu, which was a very old custom in Asia.

Sometimes when Taky arrived at a party to pick up Bruce and Amy, Bruce would be demonstrating some of his Wing Chun techniques or his specialty calisthenics, such as one-finger push-ups. Amy became very embarrassed when Bruce would show off by doing some of these feats in public. She believed this type of behavior was a sign of immaturity. When she mentioned this to Bruce, he would shrug it off and tell her that he just wanted to see how people would react when he did things like that.

Deep inside Amy knew that Bruce was trying to impress people with his physical skills. But she also knew that his ulterior motive was to recruit new students for his classes. Sometimes, on dates, Amy would become disenchanted with Bruce when he became the center of attention at a party. He would speak in philosophical terms about martial arts, and usually, these one-sided conversations were too deep for his listeners to grasp. And Amy would become upset when he ignored her while he talked about martial arts for the better portion of their evening outings. She recognized his many good qualities, but they were always overshadowed by his lack of concern for her happiness when they were together. She felt his pretentious behavior stood in the way of his feelings toward her. When they were alone together, she wanted to share her compassionate side with him and wished Bruce would open up to her about how he really felt about life and what it meant to him. Rather than share what he felt about love, family, and mutually enjoyable interests, Bruce only revealed his ambitions for a future in which martial arts played a major role. Though Amy wanted to be a dancer, and possibly a writer, as she became closer Bruce, all he wanted her to do was support his dreams and ambitions. Bruce told her that he wanted to be wealthy and independent, and in order to do that, he needed someone by his side that he could love, trust, and expect to be present to support him and share in his success.

They had begun to develop problems in their relationship. Sometimes it was cordial and platonic, and other times it was romantic and passionate. Neither Bruce nor Amy seemed to be able to find a middle ground where they were more compatible, at least during this period of their lives.

On occasion, Bruce would take Amy with him to Hing Hay Park, which was located in Chinatown. He tried to impress her with his familiarity and associations with many of the local business owners there. They had become familiar with Bruce's reputation as a gung fu teacher and jokester of sorts; he was always kidding with the locals. Amy often felt that she was just along to keep him company. When he felt like the situation warranted it, Bruce would flaunt his youthful enthusiasm by showing off and doing coin tricks for the shop owners. Amy felt embarrassed when Bruce displayed this side of his personality.

Bruce usually only spent Sundays with Amy and was almost never available on Saturday, when she liked to go out. She began to fear that, because he was only available on Sundays, perhaps he was seeing other young women and trying to keep his dates isolated from one another by assigning them certain nights. When she called Bruce on this, he simply shrugged his shoulders and said, "That's the only night that I get off from work when we can spend some time together." This only made Amy more suspicious, because she felt he never fully explained his answers. He just told it the way it was and hoped she would believe it, because he knew it to be true. Bruce, in an attempt to clarify himself, explained that when he was not seeing her on Sundays, he usually spent the time with his students, going to movies or to Chinatown for dinner. At the heart of Hing Hay Park was a rather modest red brick gazebo that formed the centerpiece of an ornate Asian-style sanctuary. It had a copper-colored cable roof structure trimmed with dragon heads, red lacquered supports, and a low fence that resembled typical shrines in Hong Kong or other countries in the Far East. The gazebo was a regular lunch location for people in the community and tourists. Bruce felt at home and relaxed there. In fact, he and Amy spent Sunday afternoons having lunch there on many occasions, but not without some strings attached. While she simply wanted to spend the time together enjoying a nice lunch and watching the tourists, Bruce always seemed to have another agenda. He saw the park as an ideal location for handing out flyers to attract new students. Besides that, the area had many restaurants, wholesale seafood companies, and import/export businesses, and Bruce often dropped in to the businesses to visit. Amy would have much preferred him to spend this time solely with her.

Bruce Lee Gets a Driver's License and His High School Diploma

The problem of finances was never too far from Bruce's thoughts. He was constantly contemplating and searching for ways in which he could break the bonds of what he considered indentured servitude at the restaurant. Since he didn't have any overhead expenses, such as rent or bills, that normally were associated with operating a commercial establishment, he believed that if he continued to recruit students and budgeted carefully, the additional money earned from teaching could possibly be spent on some of the finer things that, until now, had been beyond his budgetary means. Under other conditions, he would have opted to purchase another business suit, a sport coat, and possibly a fashionable doeskin blazer to expand his wardrobe. However, logic dictated that practicality should prevail under the circumstances. Bruce was finding that traveling in and around Seattle was becoming more of a necessity than before. He rationalized that, since school was almost over, a Corvair would be an excellent graduation present to himself. And once he enrolled for his first semester at the university, it would be much more convenient traveling the usual ten to fifteen minutes to the University of Washington campus. Also having a vehicle to go places without having to take a bus or constantly request rides from friends would definitely make life a little easier for everyone concerned.

Over the course of several weeks LeRoy had the formidable task of teaching Bruce the rudiments of driving. At times, LeRoy feared that he and his sifu were destined to die together in Seattle traffic. He found it amusing that Bruce, who was skilled and coordinated in the martial arts, was having such a difficulty in managing something as simple as steering a car and regulating the gas or even sensing the right time to apply the brakes. At first, Bruce's timing and coordination seemed altogether out of sync. If he had to estimate the distance before he started breaking the automobile, it never happened in a gradual and smooth fashion. Sudden stops would send LeRoy lunging toward the dash on the passenger side. Wearing thick glasses and having what LeRoy discovered was pretty poor vision didn't help matters either. LeRoy also found that Bruce would spend an inordinate amount of time focusing on one task at a time rather than try to orchestrate the tasks into one nice well-planned driving maneuver. Bruce was trying to watch the speedometer to insure that he was not going to fast, gauge the proximity before negotiating a stop, keep an eye on where he was going, and follow LeRoy's driving instructions.

This was not an easy task by any stretch of the imagination, but Bruce learned exceedingly well, as his performance got better. With practice driving became natural enough that Bruce could manage without LeRoy in the car. Still, when it came to parallel parking and backing up, Bruce had more difficulty than most people with impaired vision. To LeRoy, it seemed that when Bruce turned his head to look behind him, as he steered the automobile backward to park, there was a moment when Bruce seemed blind. He momentarily saw out the side of his glasses and not through the thick lenses. During these moments, LeRoy thought he had definitely sealed his own fate. But with practice, over several sessions, Bruce got the hang of parallel parking and could do it pretty well. LeRoy also tutored Bruce on the possible written questions on the driving examination.

A week later, Bruce applied for his driver's license at the Seattle Department of Motor Vehicles. He fared rather well on the written test, but he had some difficulty with the actual driving portion of the examination. The driving instructor's commands were a bit different than the simple, familiar commands that LeRoy had tutored Bruce in. When the instructor would say "make a left at the corner, get in your right lane and prepare to stop," he spoke in such abbreviated terms that Bruce did not seem to grasp the instruction. Nevertheless, after returning to the Department of Motor Vehicles office and getting out of the car, the examiner gave Bruce a passing mark and recommended that he learn to smoothly negotiate corners and to be a bit more relaxed when he was behind the wheel. The instructor also emphasized that Bruce should practice parallel parking maneuvers, so he could do it naturally without having to worry about hitting the bumpers of other cars.

On Friday, December 2, 1960, just five days after Bruce turned twenty, he graduated from Edison Technical Vocational School with a certified high school diploma. With this honor, he had faithfully fulfilled the necessary academic requirements to enter the university in March. With almost three months before the University of Washington's spring term would begin, Bruce had the better portion of each working day to pursue his martial arts recruitment activities. The gang sometimes helped out, by passing out the advertisement flyers. Taky did this mostly by passing them out to potentially interested customers that came into his supermarket. The mornings would provide Bruce with ample time to work out on his own. He was slowly disciplining himself to return to the training routine he had when he was studying under Wing Chun master Yip Man, in Kowloon. With renewed inspiration, he pursued training with more sincerity than any time earlier, since he felt that his martial arts had been somewhat neglected because of his hectic school and work schedule and the time he spent trying to teach his students. He felt that in order to stay ahead of his students' development and also be patient enough to teach them without expending all of his physical energy he needed to work out longer and harder than his students did. This was the first time that Bruce was confronted with the real meaning of his responsibility and how he would handle his obligations. He understood that if he gave away all his energy teaching, working for others, and applying himself at school, he would have no energy left for himself. Then he would become a victim of circumstances, and he did not want that to happen.

Bruce's Wing Chun Classes Continue to Develop

In January of 1961, after watching local programming on KCTS Channel 9 public television, Bruce decided that he should contact them about possibly demonstrating gung fu on their station. He figured that if television could feature shows that taught people how to cook, paint landscapes and portraits, and other types of self-improvement skills at home, the station might be interested in featuring him teaching a self-defense course. Jesse and Skip thought this was a fantastic idea and one that should be followed up on. So Bruce wasted no time in calling up the program director and setting up an appointment to visit the station and discuss his idea. The following week he put together a basic instructional study course outline on a notebook pad and prepared for a meeting with the station manager. He figured that a nice, concise, professional demonstration should be easy enough for the people at the station to understand and should also be interesting and exciting enough that anyone that would possibly catch it on television would be enthralled enough to want to learn more. His plan would be to demonstrate the Sil Lim Tao Wing Chun form and then break it down into simplified self-defense techniques. Perhaps he would have his students perform some of the basic form, and then he would follow up by demonstrating the specific techniques with each of them, using variations that he had developed. Then, he would add some chi sao sticking hand sensitivity drills to highlight the high-speed precision that one could achieve if one became skillful in Wing Chun. He would emphasize explaining to the viewers what was happening as the techniques were performed. After Bruce discussed the plan with Jesse, he agreed that it seemed logical that KCTS Channel 9 would like something like this. Jesse suggested he could even add a little spontaneous free-style sparring to show the audience just how effective the techniques are against even someone that's skilled in the art of fighting. The next step was for Bruce to make a presentation and pitch his idea to the television station management.

After researching the yellow pages of the Seattle telephone directory, Bruce found out that Channel 9 was located right there in town. The following afternoon, Bruce confirmed his appointment for the next day to discuss his proposal with the manager. After hanging up the telephone, Bruce had a good feeling about the prospects of getting them to accept his idea. He thought television would be an excellent way to reach vast numbers of people and give him the exposure he needed, which could ultimately generate more students.

When Bruce arrived at the station, he introduced himself to the receptionist in the lobby. She directed him down the hall to a programming office. After Bruce had explained his idea for a show and described what he thought would be the best way to present self-defense for a viewing audience, the management informed Bruce that there was a Chinese man named Fook Young who had had an idea very similar and that he taught a style known as Sil Lum. The program director suggested that, in the best interest of the viewing public and to insure that the air time was properly utilized without being redundant, perhaps Bruce should contact Mr. Fook Young and discuss an arrangement in which they could organize a demo show together. Though Bruce did not anticipate this situation, he surmised that a collaborative program was better than no show at all. Bruce left the Channel 9 station with Mr. Fook Young's phone number.

By the first week in February, 1961, Bruce had contacted Sifu Fook Young and worked out a plan to share the show for their proposed demonstrations. Bruce would present the Wing Chun style and Sifu Fook would present the Sil Lum style. Bruce had also spent a lot of additional time rehearsing with Jesse Glover, Skip Ellsworth, Tak Miyabe, Jim DeMile, LeRoy Garcia, and Taky Kimura on the various parts of their demonstration.

During the same week, Bruce had been very busy with other projects as well. It occurred to him that Mrs. Mei Wong, a seamstress that he had met one night when she was dining at Ruby's restaurant, owned a laundry and alteration shop on South King Street in Chinatown and would be the ideal person to sew some Chinese gung fu uniforms, or jing mos, for him.

After retrieving her business card from his cardboard filing box, Bruce telephoned her and explained what he needed. Mei Wong immediately remembered him and told him to come down to her shop and discuss the style and type of design he required. That same day, Bruce paid Mrs. Wong a visit and detailed every item he wanted sewn. He wanted her to use shiny black rayon and traditional frog button design to create a Mandarin-collared uniform that would make him and his students look first-class when they were filmed for the television show. Mei Wong agreed that she would make the uniforms as authentic as possible, to insure that their Chinese culture was properly represented for Bruce's television appearance.

When Bruce received the call at Ruby's restaurant that the jing mo gung fu uniforms were ready, he could hardly wait to get down to South King Street to see them and bring them home. The following morning his first priority was to travel down to Chinatown and inspect the uniforms. They were perfect and exactly what Bruce had designed on the tablet paper he had left with her. As Bruce left with his newly sewn uniforms, he promised that he would definitely be back to get more uniforms and patches sewn from her. She smiled an acknowledgment as Bruce left her small shop.

Through contacts he had made at the Yesler Terrace Community Recreation Center Gymnasium, Bruce had made in-roads in starting a formally sponsored gung fu class there. Basically, the administrative staff wanted to keep the facility constantly active, by offering a variety of educational programs and physical activities. Rather than have periods of the day and evenings when the facility was not being utilized, the community center's plan was to integrate programs such as Bruce's class as a recreation activity for the youth and adults. At this point the proposed arrangement was a perfect fit, ideally suited for both the recreation center and Bruce's allotted time for teaching. Bruce believed this would be an excellent opportunity for him to expand his club's visibility in the Broadway and Yesler Way area of Seattle and at the same time provide him a steady base for teaching on a commercial level, possibly generating the income that he needed.

After Bruce had determined a time that accommodated the recreation center, he designed and drew a fairly artistic handbill and had several hundred of them mimeographed at the center. The flyer stated that a martial arts demonstration was scheduled for Tuesday, February 14, 1961 at 8:30 P.M. at the Yesler Terrace Community Recreation Center Gymnasium. Bruce hosted a judo and gung fu demonstration featuring some of his advanced students, Charlie Woo, Tak Miyabe, Pat Hooks, Jesse Glover, Roy Garcia, Skip Ellsworth, Jim Demile, Taky Kimura, Jon Jackson, and George Mac-Namara. He had assigned Jesse to head the judo portion of the demonstration, and several of the gang would be his throwing partners. Bruce elected to perform all of the more advanced gung fu techniques, using each of the students to assist in various aspects of the forms and practical self-defense maneuvers. This demonstration gave Bruce opportunity to practice and refine portions of the routines that he planned to do when he returned to the television station and shared the limelight with Sifu Fook. As part of this demonstration at the Yesler Community Recreation Center, he decided to include each of his featured students doing some of the Wing Chun Sil Lim Tao and the breakdown of the self-defense techniques found therein. Bruce thought this would add professionalism and polish to their routines, in preparation for when they went before the cameras at KCTS Channel 9 public television. From his early childhood days in the motion picture industry in Hong Kong, he knew how important it was to rehearse as much as possible before going before the camera, and this small gymnasium exhibition was an excellent forum to provide his students experience in public performances.

The day before the demo Bruce gave his students the gung fu jing mo uniforms that Mrs. Mei Wong had made for them; as he had instructed, she had fashioned and sewn a crimson red silk sash to signify his rank as the sifu of the club on his jing mo. For his senior students, Jesse Glover, Charlie Woo, Tak Miyabe, and Pat Hooks, he had had her fashion black silk sashes indicating their advanced ranks. The other club members—Jim Demile, Skip Ellsworth, Taky Kimura, Roy Garcia, Jon Jackson, and George MacNamara—had outfits without a sash, connoting their status as either novice or semiadvanced students. The gang was pretty impressed that these uniforms fitted them so nicely. Bruce explained that these uniforms were for demonstration purposes only. He said, "Consider them tuxedos to be worn only for special occasions like demonstrations and television performances and not for everyday training."

At 8:30 P.M., Bruce and his students arrived at the gymnasium in their uniforms and gave an excellent performance. The seventy-odd spectators that had shown up for the demonstration were impressed with the gung fu and judo demonstration. This pleased Bruce very much, and it was the clincher for establishing a place to teach and train his classes. Only one person in the crowd seemed unimpressed with Bruce's performance. He was a martial arts practitioner named Uechi who had openly flaunted that he was a certified black belt in Japanese karate. Uechi had begun to show up regularly whenever the students would train or when Bruce was teaching his classes.

Now Uechi was making his presence felt at this anxiously awaited demonstration. As Bruce explained some technical points pertaining to tactics, strategy, or fighting techniques, Uechi would disrupt Bruce's demonstration with his own opinions of how the art of fighting should be applied. Bruce restrained himself and tried to keep focused on the demonstration, and when he narrated portions of the demo that his students performed in, he directed most of his commentary away from where Uechi was standing. Bruce seemed to be ignoring Uechi, which irritated the spectator even more. As the well-planned and executed gung fu–judo demonstration concluded, Bruce and his students basked in the glow of the applause. The acclamation gave them reason to be quite proud of themselves. After a few rounds of applause and multitude of handshakes from the spectators, Bruce and his team members exited the floor and made their way to the locker room in the basement level of the gymnasium. Unbeknownst to the gang, an excited crowd of well-wishers was already forming a line leading into the downstairs locker room. They were waiting for Bruce and his students to come back up after changing back into their street attire, so the crowd could congratulate Bruce and his students on such a fine performance.

A fellow by the name of Joe Cowles and a friend were among the spectators that had watched the demonstration and were waiting patiently in line to meet and congratulate the performers. Uechi, who was among those loitering near the exit, conceitedly exclaimed to everyone within earshot that the demonstration was a farce and that anyone with knowledge of Japanese karate could take Bruce apart in several seconds. He added that he was a fifth degree black belt in karate and that guys like Bruce gave fighting a bad name. Then, as suddenly as he had appeared in the corridor leading to the downstairs locker room Uechi made his departure. Joe Cowles thought to himself that this fellow had some gall to act so insolent and antagonistic. He sensed that someone that was this arrogant was trying to start a fight, or at least trying to be a troublemaker.

In the meantime, the gang in the locker room was jubilant. As they changed into their street clothes, they kidded one another and laughed about several minor goof ups during their impressive performance. While they were chatting and recalling the highlights of the demonstration, it was obvious to everyone that their sifu was abnormally quiet and reserved during what they thought should be a time for celebration. They instinctively knew that the obnoxious remarks made by the spectator while they were performing had had a profound impact on him.

While the students simply cast off their irritation as they were changing clothes, Bruce tried to conceal his resentment by forcing a smile and interjecting a little of his wry humor. However, everyone could see that his actions were forced and not at all spontaneous, as they were accustomed to seeing their sifu at times like this. Finally, Bruce quietly put on his shoes, collected his jing mo and stuck it in his bag, and then turned and somberly walked up the stairs of the locker room. A moment later, his students followed closely behind, still basking in the glow of their successful event. As they reached the top of the stairs and saw the awaiting crowd, Bruce's mood suddenly changed and he appeared boldly confident. His composure, though somewhat reserved, was perceived by those that greeted him at the doorway as one of a true master of gung fu. Their respectful yet anxious behavior also gave the members of the demonstration troupe reason to feel proud of the performance they had provided. They felt like rock stars that had just finished their last set on stage and now had a moment to mingle with the fans backstage. After shaking hands with over two-dozen people that had observed the demonstration, and as Bruce handed out his mimeographed business cards, Bruce suddenly spied Uechi standing off to the side smirking, his arms held across his chest and his feet spread wide. He stood there leering at the gang as they thanked the spectators for coming to the demonstration.

Bruce decided it was best to ignore this character and give his full attention to the interested spectators that had waited after the performance to get more information about Chinese gung fu and judo. After about thirty minutes of additional comments on the philosophical and esoteric tenets of his art, Bruce nodded to the gang that it was time to leave. As they picked up their gym bags and walked toward the front entrance, Bruce realized that this Uechi fellow was no longer present. Some time while Bruce was handing out business cards and chatting with the crowd, this troublemaker had simply vanished. Bruce put it out of his mind as he walked to the parking lot and prepared to leave the recreation center with his students.

About a week after witnessing the Yesler Terrace Gymnasium demonstration, Joe Cowles called Bruce and asked him if he would accept him as a gung fu student. Over the telephone, Bruce told Cowles he could meet him in front of the Tai Tung restaurant in Chinatown and take him to that evening's class, after explaining the class program. Bruce reminded Joe to bring a pad and pencil so he would be able to take notes. When Joe arrived at the designated location in Chinatown, he spotted a young Chinese man walking around as if looking for someone. Joe remembered Bruce in a gung fu uniform, without his glasses. This fellow was wearing a sports coat and sharply tailored dress slacks. With the thick, dark-rimmed glasses and hair neatly combed, it was very difficult to determine if, in fact, he was the same person Joe had seen performing the awe-inspiring gung fu techniques. Then Bruce somberly walked up to him and said, "Are you Joe Cowles?" Joe Cowles said, "Yes I am. It's a pleasure to meet you."

Bruce returned the salutation and then explained that he was on his way to teach at the home of a student, LeRoy Garcia, located on the other side of Lake Washington, and if Joe wished he was welcome to come along and get started training. After hearing Bruce briefly describe the gung fu training regimen, Joe affirmed that he really wanted to learn this Chinese art. They walked for about half a block, to where Bruce had parked his car, and immediately departed for Garcia's home.

Once there, Bruce introduced Joe to the students that were present and then joined the workout session outside. In that particular class, Bruce had the students paired off and working on a *sam sing* arm-conditioning drill. Watching Jon Jackson bang arms with another student, Joe thought, "I'd like to try that." Next, Bruce paired Joe with Jon and showed him the routine. After about ten minutes of this forearm bashing, Jon Jackson's arms were almost raw, and he was obviously in pain. Bruce had been observing as he tutored other pupils in the group and walked over to Joe and said, "Let's see how long you can go with me." Bruce suddenly realized that Joe had naturally tough arms and a very high tolerance to pain. He did not seem fazed as Bruce began slamming harder and harder against his inner forearms.

Although this was Joe's first lesson, he sensed that his sifu was signaling in an indirect way that he should pound even harder still. Suddenly, Bruce, somewhat irritated, executed an explosive and unexpected back-knuckle fist technique that struck Joseph just above the right temple. Joe suddenly stopped, and appearing somewhat stunned. As Joe stared in bewilderment, Bruce smiled and said in a pleasant tone of voice, "You didn't get your hand up in time." Still a little confused as to what he should do, Joe followed Bruce's lead and continued to slam arms even harder than before. Bruce then became sternly serious, looking at Joe coldly, and said, "Don't be a hero. If it hurts, stop, or I'll break your damn arm!" Joe then acquiesced and curtly replied, "That's enough." The impact from the sam sing drill hadn't really hurt or causeed Joe discomfort; he certainly wasn't trying to be a hero, but he sure was not going to tell Bruce that.

After class was over and everyone stood around chatting and joking around, Bruce told Joe he would drive him back to Seattle. The trip gave Joe and his sifu a chance to be better acquainted at a personal level. Bruce learned that Joe was a letter carrier for the postal service in the city and had always been interested in the martial arts. Bruce jokingly, although in a quite serious vein, complimented Joe on the tenacity he had displayed in class and commented on the toughness of his arms. Joe casually stated that he assumed that his arms had gotten that way from the exercise they received from a few years of handling and carrying heavy mail sacks all day.

Bruce chuckled at that and stated that tough and highly conditioned arms were an asset to a close-range fighter, and by what he had observed in the class, Bruce felt that Joe already had a head start on some of the other beginners. Bruce sensed that Joe Cowles was a tough-minded and no-nonsense guy, and told him that if he stuck with the training he would be a pretty incredible fighter. Joe responded, "I'm going to try to be the best I can be." As they arrived in Chinatown close to the place where Bruce had first picked Joe up, Bruce asked Joe where exactly he lived. Joe said that he lived in the Holly Park district in southeast Seattle, but he would not have any problem making the classes as long as he knew where they were held. They exchanged telephone numbers, and then Bruce told Joe that he would keep him informed as to where they would be training, since it would change from place to place every now and then.

As they turned onto South King Street, Bruce asked Joe if he would like to join him for dinner at the Tai Tung restaurant. They could discuss Chinese gung fu in more detail. Joe immediately accepted the invitation and felt privileged that his new sifu would take personal time to share his knowledge of this little-known self-defense system. As Bruce drove the car up to the curb so Joe could exit, he told Joe to bring his pad and pen and that he would meet him inside the restaurant after parking the car. Joe nodded in agreement, and as he turned in the direction of the eatery, as an afterthought he mentioned that he would reserve a table.

As they enjoyed their fried rice, oyster sauce beef, and Chinese green vegetables dinner, Bruce began categorically diagramming some of the class training routines. He sketched some related illustrations, showing the stances and fighting positions. Joe was mesmerized with how eloquently Bruce spoke and the detail with which his new sifu drew the stance postures and the fighting positions. Joe was also enthralled at how easily and effortlessly Bruce committed his illustrations to paper, without hesitating to think about how he wanted to draw the images. They literally flowed from mind to hand to paper in one easy stroke of the pen. He wondered, but never really inquired, if Bruce had been an artist before he got into Chinese gung fu. If he was not an artist, he certainly possessed a keen sense of perspective and attention to detail when it came to illustrating his training methodology and what he intended to teach a student. These simple line drawings even depicted motions, with little ink lines that indicated action and animated positions in the movements. Bruce also wrote a complete training schedule that indicated what Joe could expect to learn as he progressed in the classes with the club. From time to time, when Joe would ask questions on points he did not fully comprehend, Bruce would put down his chopsticks and become very serious. Exactly like a college professor conducting a lecture for a technical class, Bruce precisely and carefully explained the finer points pertaining to Joe's questions. Joe learned that his sifu had a very scientific and organized mind.

Then, just as suddenly, Bruce changed his disposition, showing a less serious demeanor. At the class earlier that evening, he had noticed that Joe had extremely strong arms and was oblivious to pain. Not discounting the ruggedness and toughness of his extremities, Bruce could not help wondering if, in fact, Joe's arms were as strong as they looked. Kidding around a bit, Bruce jokingly coerced Joe into engaging in a friendly arm wrestling match at the table. As they put their arms in position and clasped hands, Bruce prepared for what he thought would be a real struggle to flatten Joe's arm against the table. He applied an unexpected jolt of sheer force, and the table and all of the dishes were almost overturned. The patrons in the Tai Tung turned to see what caused the disturbance. Unaffected by the sudden silence in the restaurant, Joe continued resisting with tremendous effort until Bruce initiated a second explosive effort. Because of the overwhelming strength that Bruce had applied against his student's wrist and forearm, Joe had to relent. That moment definitely made a believer out of Joe regarding Bruce's wiry sinew strength.

Bruce then explained the secret behind his strength. He had learned a long time ago that the secret of techniques that require a lot of power for short duration was to apply the "focus" principle found in martial arts. He elaborated, for Joe's benefit. To achieve incredible feats of strength, one had to use isolated muscle groups, center one's energy by harnessing the body's chi, and focus it to a specific place in time.

As they left the restaurant that night, Joe knew that the sum of his sifu's parts added up to a lot more than anyone who did not know him would ever suspect from his slender frame and wiry musculature. When they parted company, Joe said, "How long does it take to learn gung fu?" Bruce replied, "You never quit learning until they close the lid on your coffin." Then he sauntered down the darkened street in the direction of his parked car to go home.

On the third week of February, Bruce's club entered the television station and performed their demonstration for the studio crew. Although they recognized a few minor mistakes and misjudgments in their exhibition of the prearranged portion of their self-defense exhibition, Bruce and his students did not appear to make many errors. The studio cameramen, producers, engineers, and lighting technicians stood watching in amazement as Bruce exhibited his explosive speed and power, as he demonstrated his techniques with the students. Even Sifu Fook and his group were duly impressed with Bruce's agility and impeccable timing.

The following week in March, the KCTS television manager informed Bruce that the station wanted to do a short yet complete series of segments for public television broadcasts. All of the students were elated that their self-defense demonstrations was so well received by the station, and it was even more exciting when they saw themselves on television for the first time. They met at the station on three separate occasions and filmed the entire series. The station even interviewed Bruce so that they could use portions as segues into and out of the various instructional programs. About three weeks from the initial airing of the self-defense demonstration, Bruce became very busy at the recreation center enrolling new students and instructing them in a fundamental regimen of exercises and basic martial arts training. The enrollment fees of the first ten new students had insured him the additional income of one hundred dollars per month; it was roughly equivalent to what he was making at Ruby's restaurant. Bruce was somewhat chagrined by this and knew that he had to be patient, at least until the notoriety of his services could spread and he could fully establish himself.

He also knew that it would be necessary to retain his waiter position at least until he had acquired more students. Nevertheless, for the time being, he was OK with the earnings from teaching Wing Chun and working at the eatery. What was certain, however, was that his fraternal relationship with his students was strengthening with the passing of each week. Even his newest students were becoming staunchly devoted students and good friends. They enjoyed each other's company and, after classes, would often spend hours at a time at a restaurant or at a student's home talking about Wing Chun and gung fu in general.

As he prepared to embark upon his academic curriculum at the university, Bruce took a little time from his rushed schedule to write to Yip Man in Hong Kong and report on the progress that he had made in America spreading the word about Wing Chun gung fu. At the same time, he was hoping to reestablish communications with some of the seniors of the Hong Kong kwoon and try to acquire a traditional training dummy known as a mook yan jong. The mook yan jong is constructed of hard wood, such as teak, and is a simple upright post about five feet in height with three protruding arms positioned in a relative angle comparable to the arms of the human torso. Bruce felt the apparatus would be a great training tool for his students and would enhance and hone his own blocking and counterattacking skills.

The conditioning that one's wrist and forearms received from continuous impact with the hard wooden arms of the mook yan jong was sufficient to harden the bones and toughen the skin, so when actual contact was made with an aggressive opponent, the mook yan jong practitioner was not in for any surprises. The training routines, numbering one hundred and eight sequential defensive and countermaneuvers, would also instill a real sense of rhythm and continuity in the students' punching and blocking skills. The purchase of such a piece of equipment would be money well spent, since it would benefit both Bruce and his students, plus buying it directly from Hong Kong would be much cheaper than hiring someone with carpentry skills in Seattle to try and build one.

Bruce Registers at the University of Washington

The time had rapidly arrived for the ritual of registration to begin at the university. Bruce, like thousands of other students, began the arduous process of enrollment. He was required to select his own courses but found that, for the most part, he really had little choice in what courses he could take. To his surprise and frustration, he discovered that the upperclassmen had already enrolled and filled most of the classes. He also learned that some of the professors had reputations of being easy and hard. Being a freshman his choices were very limited and reduced to the compulsory courses. Nevertheless, he found it interesting meeting the counselors and going through all of the rigors of the enrollment processes.

Two weeks later Bruce was notified by mail that he was officially enrolled at the University of Washington. Between numerous trips to the university bookstore, going to his classes and doing the assignments, teaching his gung fu classes, working at the restaurant, and trying to get enough rest, Bruce somehow managed to balance this agenda well enough to keep himself physically and emotionally charged. His new ambitions to improve himself were becoming obvious to all of his students. Even Ruby and Ping Chow noticed a change in the way Bruce carried himself around the restaurant. He had regained his cajoling sense of humor. Kids in the housing across the street from the restaurant had noticed Bruce's jovial and high-spirited good nature and would wander over to play with him whenever he was around and didn't seem too busy. And even Ruby's children found his antics and playfulness exhilarating, when he would play hide-and-seek in the restaurant before it was open for business. It was hard, sometimes, for Ruby to chide Bruce for shirking his station setup duties when she saw her children having so much fun. Bruce interpreted her reticence as a sign of permission to play with the children whenever they were around. Even Ping Chow enjoyed seeing his children having so much fun at the restaurant, and Bruce's antics were usually ignored.

Bruce's schedule at school included English, American history, mathematics, and an elective in humanities. He had perused the university curriculum several times and had underscored some of the courses that looked interesting. There were several physical education courses, such as gymnastics and Greco-Roman wrestling, that appealed to him. However, he initially planned to structure his course of study around the required subjects. He would have ample time over the course of the next few years to fit in the elective subjects that he desired. The electives that attracted him the most were the classes in the areas of social dance, speech development, theatrical performance, speaking techniques, art and freehand drawing, and several courses in Chinese language.

Even though Bruce was uncertain of his major, he was discovering that the university's academic curriculum was literally a smorgasbord of scholarship that covered almost every conceivable study in the world. Interestingly, this American university had a diverse array of subject matter dealing with Asian studies. In addition to the language classes, one could earn units learning to write in Chinese and other foreign languages. There were a few courses in Far

Eastern economics and another one dealing with how ethnic Asians could learn to fit into the modern world outside of their own country. Other subjects that interested him to some degree, and which he would probably take in his junior or senior years, were classes in psychology, health, business, and management.

It was becoming very clear why his mother and father thought it was so important for him to get a good education. One could never tell what a person really knew by simply judging their appearance alone. He felt pretty fortunate to be able to study at an educational institution where so much knowledge and opportunity to improve one's life was there for the taking, if one was willing to study and take their educational studies seriously. Bruce knew that, over the next four years, he would have a lot of different courses to take and a lot of knowledge to acquire, which he was preparing himself mentally to undertake.

Bruce Opens His First Kwoon in Seattle's Chinatown

By June of 1961, Bruce's agenda was focused on one aspect of martial arts or another, and not a day went by that he was not in contact with the gang or some of his students. He was making plans for possibly opening a commercial gung fu school, if a good location could be found within the immediate area. Everything had to be planned correctly, if he was to become successful in expanding his enrollment and creating an image of professionalism. The dependability of his original students was a must and their support could be counted on when these plans unfolded before the general public. His senior students had agreed to help him search various areas in and around Chinatown where they would look for a vacant building that might be suitable as a gung fu kwoon. Bruce emphasized that the location should reflect the cultural essence of the art. It made sense to him that the best possible area would be in the Chinatown district of Seattle.

Bruce felt that it was imperative that the kwoon should be as close to his room above the restaurant as possible, so he would not have to travel a great distance to get there and back on a regular basis. His intuition also told him that anything that embodied Chinese teaching and philosophy, including Chinese herbal shops and acupuncturists, should be located in an area where the people of that culture were located. Thus, he believed that the closer one got into the center of the culture the truer the essence, and the further you went away from the center the more watered down the art would become. In essence, this was how he viewed his gung fu, as he believed that it epitomized the true spirit of the ancient Chinese cultural self-defense arts.

Bruce's dream of the growth and expansion of his martial arts business seemed to occupy much of his thoughts. Just seeing the huge number of potential gung fu students walking around at the university made him realize the tremendous opportunities that lay before him. He knew that opportunity did not knock on the door every day, and when a situation presented itself, one had to move swiftly to take advantage of good fortune. He remembered his father telling him that on numerous occasions back in Kowloon, however, although not in reference to martial arts or any such related enterprises. Bruce thought it was of paramount importance to get the word out and let the university students know of his plans for a kwoon.

After Bruce was certain to his own satisfaction that Chinatown would be the ideal location for a gung fu school, he and his students embarked on a mission of finding a suitable location in Chinatown.

This task seemed to be fraught with disappointment. Several real estate brokers failed to show up for appointments to show the interiors of their vacant buildings; others quoted costs that were well outside the range of what Bruce could afford for rent. Well-maintained buildings with ideal locations and nice facades were clearly out of the question. The only site that seemed affordable was in the basement of a laundry in an old three-story turn-of-the-century building in Chinatown. After inspecting the dingy downstairs vacancy, Bruce decided the only workable solution was to accept this affordable yet dilapidated basement as is and, with the help of his students and some ingenuity, decorate it to make it look acceptable as a gung fu school. Fresh paint, a variety of martial arts posters and photographs, a yin-yang sign, and simple furnishings like a desk and chairs and some basic office equipment would certainly give the basement facility a more professional ambiance. Most of these improvements, he thought, would be inexpensive and, with the help of the gang, could be done rather easily. To try to enhance the entry to the basement at the bottom of the narrow staircase, he designed a colorful red and gold yin-yang logo on poster board and affixed it to the wall just outside of the entrance.

Bruce knew that this attempt at opening a commercial school could be the key to gaining independence from the drudgery he had endured as a waiter and busboy. He geared himself up to the fact that he would have to use every bit of his creativity in making the place look acceptable and reflect the professional excellence he hoped to convey to potential students that dropped by the school to inquire about his lessons.

Before he could open for business, Bruce needed to obtain a business license at Seattle's downtown city hall. This required him to provide a name for his business. An adequate name for his school had to be selected, one that would reflect the essence of his art and yet still be generally acceptable and easily identifiable. Bruce realized that the name had to represent the art and still retain a uniqueness that showed that it was distinctly his own operation as well. He felt that, since his Chinese name was Jun Fan, it made sense that when his commercial school was finally opened it should be expressly known as the Jun Fan Gung Fu Institute. Besides, he figured the word *institute* would give prestige and credibility to the name, much more than just calling it a school or gym. The following week, for the cost of thirty-five dollars, Bruce had procured a business license for the Jun Fan Gung Fu Institute; he was now officially recognized as a merchant in the Chinatown district. The next week, after completing the renovation and decoration of the basement facility, he was finally teaching classes there.

A Challenge

In less than two weeks after starting his studies at the university, Bruce had a chance encounter with the karate man Uechi. As Bruce was walking toward the stairs of the university library, Uechi approached him and attempted to block his path. With a brash air of cockiness, he smiled at Bruce, pushed him hard, and scornfully said, "Man, you are a fraud. These people think you are a fighter. You're not a fighter, you're a showoff."

Bruce looked at him with a cold and steely gaze as he searched for the right words to express himself. After looking down and back again into Uechi's face, Bruce calmly said, "You want to fight me, man?"

The moment had come that Uechi had been longing for. "Yeah! You need a lesson! How about we go over to the main gym and do it there. Everybody over there can see you get your ass kicked."

Bruce, still displaying a steely glare, then said, "No. How about over at the handball court at the YMCA on 4th Street this Sunday night, say around six o'clock."

Uechi, pondering Bruce's rebut to his challenge for a moment, arrogantly said, "What's the matter? You don't want all the people on campus to see how phony you are?"

Bruce began to fume and forcefully said, "You want to fight me, man. We'll fight under my terms."

Uechi, eager to prove his skills, relented and said, "OK, man. It's the YMCA handball court at six o'clock in the evening." Then, stepping to the side and letting Bruce pass, he snorted, "You be there, OK!"

"I'll be there!" Bruce said and walked up the stairs into the campus library.

That night at the Chinatown kwoon, after the workout was completed, Bruce told Jesse Glover, Ed Hart, and Howard Hall that he had encountered that fellow Uechi who had caused so much grief at their demonstration. He told them that he accepted Uechi's challenge. Bruce wanted them to be there to insure that nobody jumped in when he was fighting. The gang said they would be there to back him up in case Uechi brought along some cronies that wanted to interfere with the contest. Bruce then told them that they would meet at the kwoon earlier that evening and go over to the YMCA together.

Sunday night at 5:40 P.M., Bruce arrived at the 4th Street YMCA with a half-dozen of his students. Among them were Jesse Glover, Ed Hart, and Howard Hall. As they entered the handball court, the anticipation for the fight was high. Several minutes later, Uechi boldly and arrogantly walked into the handball court and approached the group. With minimal pomp, he abruptly said, "You ready?" Bruce said, "You challenged me. Is that right?" In a confident and threatening voice, Uechi smiled and said, "Yes!" Bruce said, "That's all I wanted to know."

They decided the ground rules before the contest began. There would be three rounds of two minutes each. Ed Hart would be the timekeeper, and Jesse would assume the role of referee. With his gym bag in hand, Uechi said, "You wait here. I'm going to the locker room and get in my gi." Everyone stood around and waited for Uechi to return from the locker room in his uniform. Bruce had decided to dispense with the notion of wearing his traditional jing mo. He would fight in his regular street clothes, since he was not there to make a fashion statement. He was not there to represent a style of fighting but simply to prove the point that his fighting techniques would work just as effectively on Uechi as they did when he taught them to his students in practice.

Ten minutes later, black belt Uechi returned to the handball court where everyone was waiting. He was attired in his gi and wearing an old worn and frayed black belt. Bruce stared at him coldly as Uechi approached the center of the floor. Uechi reinforced his cocky and impudent attitude as he executed a few crisp punches. The sleeves of the karate gi snapped, and the sound echoed throughout the enclosed room, as he tried to make a spectacle out of this basic warm-up ritual. Then Uechi said, "You ready?" Bruce tersely said, as he vigorously shook out his arms, "Just a minute." Ed stood to the side and gazed at the secondhand of his watch as he waited for Jesse to give the command to commence the bout.

When Bruce and Uechi appeared ready for action, Jesse broke the silence with the order to begin. For five seconds or so, neither Bruce or Uechi moved from their upright stance. Uechi cautiously edged forward, and as his hands were brought into a defensive fighting pose, he artfully lowered himself into a karate forward stance. Bruce, undaunted, gazed through him and suddenly assumed a Wing Chun stance, positioning himself squarely in alignment with Uechi's deeply rooted battle stance. Bruce remained poised with his arms partially positioned in a fighting pose in front of his upper torso and waited for a sign of aggression from his adversary. Uechi, seeing that Bruce looked somewhat ill-prepared to deal with a powerful attack, detected an obvious opening at the lower groin area. Then with a forceful *kiai* (a guttural yell), he unleashed a rear-leg forward kick to this open and exposed area. Bruce, with his finely honed reflexes, detected the kick before it had reached the halfway point and effortlessly deflected it. Before anyone could determine exactly what happened, Bruce swiftly followed up with a barrage of punches to Uechi's face and upper torso. Bruce continued to pummel Uechi until he was backed against the handball court wall. Uechi's face was bloody from a broken nose. Blood was all over his white karate uniform and in splatters all over the wooden floor. Uechi tried to get away from the unrelenting attack, but Bruce kept right on top of him until he started to drop. When Bruce's opponent collapsed, Bruce unmercifully kicked him in the face, just as his knees hit the floor. Bruce then swiftly flipped Uechi onto his back, as though to continue bombarding him with punches and kicks. Jesse, afraid that Bruce was going to kill Uechi, yelled, "No!" Uechi was flat on his back, unconscious. The encounter had lasted only eleven seconds. Bruce regained his composure, as he looked down at Uechi, who was lying in his own blood. Because of the action and focused attention on the fight, neither Bruce nor any of his students had noticed a tall blond fellow who had been standing nearby. As Bruce glanced around the room, he caught a glimpse of the man, who Bruce thought might be a friend of Uechi's. After gazing at the man for several seconds, Bruce said, "Do you want to fight me too?" The fellow nervously replied, "No man. I don't want any of this." Then Bruce said, in an angry and commanding voice, "Good. Now clean up that blood." Without another word, Bruce turned and walked toward the entrance of the handball court with his students.

Life Goes On

Between doing his freshman university coursework and trying to keep his grade point average to at least a B level, his job, and his teaching at the Jun Fan Gung Fu Institute, Bruce was busier now than he had ever been since arriving in Seattle. and now it felt more like his own doing rather than a burden cast upon him by his family and Ruby Chow. At least, he felt there were beginning to be moments when he had more control over his life and had the authority to call his own shots. Especially, now that his promotional endeavors and the word-of-mouth publicity that his students provided were finally paying off.

Whenever Bruce made progress in one area another troublesome issue seemed to always pop up. One experience that gave Bruce reason for concern happened with respect to several of his original students. Since he had to structure classes to accommodate the new beginners as well as the seniors, a few of his original students felt like they were not getting all of the attention and training that they thought they deserved. They also had noticed that Bruce was teaching the beginners in a much different way than they had initially been taught. Among themselves they had seen changes in the way their sifu taught the Wing Chun techniques of Sil Lim Tao and how he was integrating more and more actions that resembled basic karate and Praying Mantis movements. To the seniors it also appeared that Bruce was trying to manage and make definite distinctions in the skill levels of the students more than he had done any time previously. The incoming beginning students were not getting anywhere near the amount of technical training or the deeper philosophical explanations that the older students had received when they were being taught privately and personally as a small cadre of select students. The techniques that Bruce was teaching were definitely different from the techniques that the students had learned when they were working out in parks and back yards. Bruce was now mixing back-knuckle strikes with longer-range fighting ploys, and the beginners' training curriculum now had kicks and more calisthenics. Jesse and Jim tried to justify this by assuming that Bruce was trying to get a structure in place that would systemize his teachings in a way that everyone got an equal amount of his time and knowledge at the skill level they possessed. After discussing this with their sifu, they began to understand when Bruce assured them that he was only trying to organize his classes so that he could provide all of his new beginning students with the knowledge and services they expected for the money they were paying for classes. He further explained that otherwise it would turn into a vicious cycle, with many people starting and then quitting if they did not get the thoroughness they expected from their martial arts training. Then he would be right back where he started, before he began the Jun Fan Gung Fu Institute.

Remarkably, Bruce completed his first term at the University of Washington with very good results. When he averaged his grades, he came out with a high B average. This pleased him very much. Bruce spent most of the summer months of 1961 improving the skills of his advanced students and teaching the newly interested converts at the Chinatown basement kwoon.

Bruce conducted the sparring sessions in such a manner that he was required to work twice as hard as did the most dedicated student. Since he actually participated in sparring with the students, he needed extra stamina. Bruce realized that his eating habits would have to change if they were to supply him with the necessary energy to keep up his endurance to both teach and continue to progress with his own training. He reasoned that a well-balanced meal that was high in energy was the answer, and thus began his thorough research on nutrition. As his dietary habits changed for the better, so did his ability to withstand long workout sessions with the students without becoming fatigued, when they normally ran out of energy. This was perhaps the greatest discovery that Bruce made during the summer break of 1961.

Although the summer recess passed by rather quickly, the members of the Jun Fan Gung Fu Institute had many opportunities to travel to different outside locations for extensive and advanced training, perhaps helping to increase enrollment at the kwoon, since gung fu was totally foreign to many people. Curious onlookers were compelled to inquire as to the nature of this training, and some had a spark of desire to learn this art for their own personal benefit. Bruce, with his many hours of introducing new students to the gung fu program at the kwoon, was adequately prepared to give firsthand demonstrations to believers and nonbelievers alike. Anyone that had any doubt when a demonstration began was a true believer after the spontaneous exhibition was completed. This method of presenting and introducing gung fu and self-defense to the populace worked extremely well, and Bruce often gave demonstrations when he felt that it was time to recruit more students.

As the fall term of 1961 commenced at the University of Washington, the Jun Fan Gung Fu Institute was sustaining a moderate enrollment and affording Bruce the necessary income to supply his needs—necessities such as schoolbooks, new clothing, gas for the old Corvair, food and occasional spending money. He could maintain this lifestyle as long as students kept current with their fifteen-dollar-per-month lesson fees. He used some of that money to send home to his mother, to purchase various traditional Chinese items that he could use to embellish his sparse kwoon. He had picked up a few adornments in Seattle's Chinatown, but they had cost over five times more than items that his mother could purchase in Kowloon. Moreover, at this time any way to save money was a dire necessity.

After several weeks of serious devotion to his academic studies, Bruce found the required reading and writing assignments to be a bit more difficult to handle than he had previously experienced. He decided to drop a humanities course and concentrate on the remaining required subjects that would, in all likelihood, be more beneficial to him in the long run. Dropping the course meant that he could devote more time to studying for the remaining classes, and possibly he could maintain the grade average that he had enjoyed during his first term. Not having this additional self-imposed pressure also meant that he could concentrate the greater portion of his out of school hours pursuing his first love, the expansion of his Jun Fan Gung Fu Institute.

Romantically, Bruce was still at an impasse with Amy. Their on-again, off-again courtship was going nowhere fast. Bruce had mentioned to Taky that he was thinking of proposing to her, but he was not too sure if she would accept or not. She was sometimes very warm and expressed feeling for Bruce, but when he called her the next week she acted as if he were just another friend calling to chat. Taky simply told Bruce, "If it was meant to be it will happen naturally." Though Bruce was headstrong on matters of the heart, inwardly he knew Taky was right. After almost three months of trying incessantly to make their relationship work, Bruce decided to let it take its own course. When Bruce would call Amy and ask if she was interested in going to a movie, on a drive, or on a trip to Chinatown for lunch or dinner, he did it in a delicate and casual manner. He would just throw it into the conversation as if it was not that important and he only thought she might like to get out of the house and go somewhere to have fun. More often than not, when he took that approach, she accepted the offer and did not feel pressured as she would going out on a date. When she did decline, Bruce would casually mention that it was probably a good idea that they did not go out since he had homework assignments to complete, though he did not like resorting to those types of dating tactics.

Bruce's grade point average picked up considerably during the months from September until the middle of November. Several of his teachers commented on how much he had improved over the past two terms. This gave Bruce a reason to feel that all of the times Amy had declined to date him were actually turning out to be blessings in disguise, since they had actually produced such positive results. Furthermore, when he talked to his mother in Kowloon and told her about his grades she was very pleased. Even Bruce's father was happy that he was doing so well at the university.

On Monday night, November 27, 1961, Bruce celebrated his birthday at the Bush Garden Chinese restaurant with a small group of senior students. Bruce was now twenty-one years old and delighted with the prospect of being legally at the age of adulthood. He could now represent himself legally in any fashion that suited his liking. Under Washington state law, twenty-one was the legal drinking age, but since Bruce did not drink alcohol, achieving this milestone did not concern him in the least; the strongest drink that he ever drank was root beer. Nevertheless, the fact that he could now legally enter a nightclub or cocktail lounge had its merits. His students joked and kidded with him about his new status. They also educated him on the new possibilities that now presented themselves. He could enter dance clubs and lounges and meet women that liked to meet college men. This had a certain appeal to Bruce's sense of adventure. The sense that he was legally an adult and totally accountable and responsible for his actions gave him a certain feeling of independence. This feeling was another of those firsts that Bruce remembered as only having experienced since returning to the United States.

Bruce Lee Discovers His Niche in Philosophy

The campus bookstore and library were quickly becoming two of Bruce's favorite haunts. He often went to the library between classes or after his classes were over for the day. He knew all of the librarians by their names, as they did his. Bruce used the Chinese philosophy section more than anyone else on campus, and he could literally spend hours in quiet solitude delving into the lives and philosophies of the great Chinese scholars. He extracted many of his early influences in Chinese philosophy from the available volumes on the bookshelves in the university library.

Bruce extracted thick sets of notes regarding the teachings and prophecies of Confucius, Sun-tzu, Mencius, Lao-tzu, Chuang-tzu, Yang Chu, K'ang-hsi, Kuan-yi-wu, Yu-tzu, Ho-tse-chan, and Ts'en-ts'an from the many volumes. Many of the sources were reference books, and Bruce could only have access to them while in the library. This interest nearly became an obsession with Bruce, and at one time or another he checked out almost every book that was available at the campus library on the subject. Bruce often only returned a book after the library sent notice that the book was overdue. He would get involved with the contents and completely overlook that he had to return the book. On more than one occasion, two or three such books would be in his possession at any given time. This caused concern for the librarians, but since they knew Bruce was readily available, they gave him a little leeway and were rather lax in enforcing the library's book return policy often, just extending the return period for him.

Although Bruce had attended Catholic schools during his childhood in Kowloon, he was not very religious. He was well versed in the teachings and practices of Christianity, but he never cared to profess his knowledge of the subject. The Eastern philosophical religions, such as Taoism and Zen, were more in tune with his psyche. In his free time at the university library, he would spend many hours reading about Taoism and Zen to gain a fuller understanding of the role they played in the philosophies of the great Chinese sages. As his knowledge expanded in these two interrelated studies, it began to manifest in his gung fu teachings at the kwoon.

Maxims, aphorisms, and ancient Chinese proverbs held a curiously strong fascination for him. Phrases of simple significance began to take on deeper meanings when Bruce examined the Asian philosophical interpretations. Until he was convinced that he knew the true essence of their deeper esoteric meaning, he would continue to go over them repeatedly in his mind. If these maxims had relevance to the art of gung fu, Bruce would incorporate them into his teaching as the situation or opportunity presented itself.

As Bruce's thoughts were committed to paper, seemingly simple yet complex analogies became apparent to him. When he was explaining or equating the interaction that is present in the symbolism of the yin and yang to his students, specific questions would be asked and answered in the simplest of terms. When a student asked, "What is gentleness?" Bruce emphatically replied with a metaphor: "It is a pliable reed in the wind. It neither opposes nor gives way." To the question, "What is the highest state of yielding?" The answer came, "It is like clutching water." Bruce revealed the depth of his inner being with the question he posed on the subject of movement as it applied to the art of gung fu. He asked, "What is true stillness?" His gung fu pupils were mystified with his seemingly illogical answer: "Stillness is movement."

The application of Zen principles and precepts played an important role in revealing the explanation for his answers. He would often demonstrate an exacting Wing Chun gung fu movement for a specific fighting application to clarify a particular meaning. Soon the students understood the real purposes behind the specific and often pointed questions that Bruce directed at them. When asked, "What is adaptation?" Again the students were puzzled when the answer "It is like the immediacy of the shadow adjusting itself to the moving body" was revealed. This did not seem like the kind of answer they could immediately understand without clarification and an appropriate self-defense demonstration. Bruce became extremely proficient at presenting these questions and following them with the necessary physical applications that proved his points. Most of the senior Wing Chun students began to realize that their instructor was indeed quite unique, and they demonstrated their appreciation by becoming more involved with the philosophy behind their gung fu training. To give the advanced students a finer essence of his teachings, Bruce began using the exact Chinese phrases for concepts and techniques, as he had learned them in Hong Kong. The students considered it a mini lesson in the Chinese language, but Bruce taught these terms to them so that the students would get a real feel for the spirit of their training.

New Equipment

At the end of the week before Christmas, the mook yan jong and some new Chinese jing mo gung fu uniforms that Bruce had ordered from Hong Kong arrived at Ruby's restaurant. It was as if Christmas had arrived early, and his euphoria was obvious to all of the restaurant employees. Even Ruby Chow and her husband Ping detected more enthusiasm in Bruce's behavior than they had seen in some time. Immediately after the equipment's arrival, Bruce wasted no time in unpacking the large wooden box and inspecting its contents. With the aid of a hand truck, Bruce transported the training dummy out into the small back yard below his upstairs apartment, and he began assembling the component parts. He mounted the base stand, bolting the leg attachment, and finally inserted the three round, tapered teak arms into the square holes on the cylindrical upright wooden trunk. Shortly thereafter, he started working out on this odd-looking contraption. It was the first time in several years that he had actually practiced his mook yan jong pattern on actual equipment, and it began to evoke memories of his time training in Kowloon. As Sifu Yip Man had stated many times, "The mook yan jong is much different than trying to ply the prearranged defense-offense sequence against air. Air does not offer the resistance and therefore is less realistic." Bruce was literally making up for lost time away from training at Yip Man's kwoon in Kowloon.

It felt good to make contact with something as hard as the arms of the device. He could block, counter harder, and inflict greater impact on it than against most of his students' arms, and without the choppiness that was usually associated with these types of combinational maneuvers. Getting his arms in better condition while fine-tuning his sensitivity drills for chi sao training was important to him, since he was now working with Americans who had bigger and brawnier physiques. After some reflection, he decided to keep this little secret to himself for a while, at least until he thought the time was right to introduce his students to this piece of equipment. Bruce felt that the mook yan jong would give him an edge and keep his students guessing as to how he could possibly have such strong and well-conditioned wrists and arms.

Bruce decided to nickname the mook yan jong Bodhidharma after working with it for a while. Several of the employees reporting for work heard what sounded like rhythmic bongo drums emanating from the side of the building and decided to investigate. Once they rounded the corner, they witnessed Bruce standing under the stairs in front of the mook yan jong, pounding it so viciously that they thought he had gone insane. As they walked closer, Bruce detected their presence and suddenly stopped the drill. He smiled and said, "Meet my new training partner, Bodhidharma." As they touched and inspected the wooden dummy, Bruce proudly said, "Now I'm really going to get my arms conditioned." The restaurant kitchen workers shook their heads then turned and began walking toward to the rear restaurant entrance.

After a vigorous arm workout and satisfying himself that he had finally situated the mook yan jong to his liking, he turned his attention to the other box. Upon a closer inspection of its contents, he was pleased that the jing mos he had ordered arrived in good shape. His jing mo fitted nicely, but the uniforms he had ordered for his students seemed to be a bit on the small side for Americans. Even the extra large sizes that he ordered would be too small. His first thought was to have Mei Wong do whatever modifications she felt necessary to make the uniforms fit his students. He was sure she could do it.

That week Bruce delivered the recently imported jing mo gung fu uniforms to Mei Wong at her laundry and gave specific instructions on the alterations and sizes for each of his advanced students. He asked her to embroider red and gold yin-yang emblem patches and have them sewn onto the uniforms. These symbols of the Chinese harmony seemed like the ideal way to embellish these silky, black frog-buttoned gung fu uniforms. As before, Mei was impressed with Bruce's attention to the details. Mei informed Bruce that she did not do embroidery work, but she would have her friend that owned an embroidery shop make the patches, and once the emblems were made she would then stitch them on the uniforms. Bruce told her that it was important that the uniforms signified the pure essence of traditional Chinese culture. Bruce returned two weeks later and picked up the uniforms. Mei Wong had done an admirable job of altering and resizing the jing mo uniforms and attaching the patches. Bruce was so pleased with her work that he promised that, in the future, when he needed more uniforms made, he would have her do the work. Over the next several days, he personally presented each student with another, albeit much nicer, formal workout uniform for gung fu demonstrations and performances.

With the opening of the 1962 Seattle World's Fair on April 21, the world's tourist economy had suddenly converged on Seattle. By Sunday, October 21, of that year, the day the fair closed, ten million visitors had passed through the fair's turnstiles. This unrelenting tourist influx had bordered on becoming a frenzy. Downtown Seattle and all of the local areas had discovered the meaning of long lines and continual congestion that accompanies such a grand event.

Bruce Lee Meets Wally Jay

On a warm and humid evening in May, while Bruce was busy conducting an informal class at the basement kwoon, a quiet gathering of curious onlookers formed at the entranceway to the teaching area. Heading the group was a dignified gentleman of Chinese Hawaiian decent. He and his entourage waited patiently for Bruce to conclude his class. This was the first time Bruce had seen a group of men like this enter his school at one time and was not sure if this was a social call or a gang that would like to test out his martial arts skill. In either case, Bruce studied the group closely before approaching the men. As he walked in their direction, the Asian gentleman that seemed to represent them politely bowed in the traditional Chinese manner. Bruce relaxed as he got closer but was uncertain of the purpose of this impromptu visit. The tall rugged-looking Asian extended his hand and politely introduced himself as Wally Jay, the chief nstructor of the Island Judo and Jujitsu Club from Alameda, California. Bruce reciprocated and extended a cordial handshake as he introduced himself as Sifu Bruce Lee, instructor of the Jun Fan Gung Fu Institute. He then shook hands with each of the men in Wally's party.

After all members of the Wally Jay troupe had been formally introduced, Bruce asked what the group was doing in the Seattle area. Wally explained that his judo team was on a goodwill tour to several judo schools in the Northwest, to compete in the yearly matches between the associated schools in that area. These judo and jujitsu students prided themselves on their camaraderie and their collective ability to exhibit their martial arts acumen against competitors of world-class caliber. This was always obvious at such important competitive events as the preliminaries for national and world championships. As a coach, Wally was noted for producing some of the top judo and jujitsu champions in the world. He was very proud of his students' talents, so it was important that he travel with them when they competed at these interschool events.

Bruce's inquisitive nature compelled him to ask Wally how he had heard about him and his Jun Fan Gung Fu Institute. Wally replied, "By coincidence, a parent of one of my judo students in Alameda, Dr. Jane Lee, had taken cha-cha lessons a few years ago from you in Oakland, California. She had mentioned that you were also an expert at Chinese gung fu and presently teaching in the Seattle area. Shortly thereafter, when I was preparing for our trip up north, she had requested that, if perchance, I happened to make contact with you while in Seattle, to convey her regards for your success and continued good health. Dr. Jane expressed this for herself and your other former cha-cha students." Wally also jokingly said, "I had done a little research, and by asking around in Seattle's Chinatown, it hadn't taken too long to find you." Bruce smiled when Wally added, "Your reputation is growing here in Seattle, because everyone we asked seems to know who you are." A broad crossed Bruce's face. The attention and recollections of some of Bruce's past cha-cha students brought back fond memories of his time in San Francisco and Oakland. It had only been three years since he had taught the dance classes, but it seemed so long ago. It made Bruce very happy to know that those nice people cared for his welfare and health, and he was inwardly impressed with how popular he still was with people who he had not seen in so long; he had made a lasting impression.

Bruce gave Wally a short but detailed account of the events of his life that had transpired over the past few years, with special emphasis placed on his serious study and teaching of Wing Chun, which he had first learned in Hong Kong. It wasn't very long before he was espousing his personal beliefs about martial arts philosophy and how he was enhancing some of the Wing Chun techniques to make them more effective for fighting against adversaries that would fight just for the sake of fighting. He emphasized that, since he had came to America, it was really his first time experiencing so many very large individuals who were not only big but strong. In addition, Bruce pointed out that he was devising techniques—using Wing Chun, Praying Mantis, Hung Gar and other styles of Chinese gung fu—that would work against these burly types of fighters. These adaptations were mostly what he was now teaching to his students in Seattle.

These impromptu conversations usually turned quite serious for Bruce when he engaged someone that was well versed in another respected style of martial arts. Wally Jay was certainly one of those distinguished individuals, with whom Bruce felt he could be totally candid and forthright. Wally noticed that Bruce could banter, play devil's advocate, concur, or absolutely disagree with somebody all in the same conversation. More than just merely discussing punching and kicking ideologies, Bruce would relish analyzing the traditional martial arts moves and contrasting them with those that he felt were of a real practicality. He was speaking to a like mind when engaging Wally Jay in this very spirited conversation. Wally Jay possessed martial arts wisdom and could understand Bruce on all levels, when it came to judo, jujitsu, or the other martial arts of Asian origin.

Bruce had an uncanny and keen sense for detecting when someone knew what he or she were talking about when it came to martial arts. He instinctively could read a person's earnestness and body language, and along with evaluating their technical vocabulary, could determine how versed a person was in the subject matter.

Bruce would immediately know when someone was talking for the sake of impressing someone or when he or she was just trying to spread some bullshit around. Wally, likewise, from his many years as an experienced *sensei* (teacher), could also invariably tell when someone spoke factually about the intricacies and technical dynamics of martial arts. Even taking Bruce's young age into account, Wally knew that Bruce was a real expert and sincere exponent of the Chinese martial arts. This is what kept Sensei Jay interested in what Bruce said. As the conversation veered more and more toward the art of gung fu and stylized self-defense, Bruce inquisitively asked Wally and his students if they would be interested in a demonstration of his art. Since virtually all of his judo devotees were unfamiliar with the Chinese art of Wing Chun, they all responded enthusiastically. Their eagerness brought a smile to Bruce's face as he began to explain, in a rather eloquent and philosophical manner, the directness and practical applications of the Chinese Wing Chun gung fu techniques and how superfluous movement had been eliminated, retaining only effective fighting elements. The way that he verbalized words with *R*s in them and enunciated them with the sound of *W*s gave his brief yet concise dissertations a distinguished professorial quality, a trait that Wally Jay and his students found amusingly mesmerizing. The first maneuver that Bruce demonstrated stressed the dynamics of explosive, close-range centerline self-defense fighting. Essentially these were integrated hand and arm tactics that were useful for blocking and counterattacking simultaneously. Except for Wally, his visitors found it difficult to evaluate and comprehend the significance of the techniques they were witnessing. Wally had always felt, being a devout advocate of the judo principle that emphasized using leverage and an opponent's weight and balance against them, that judo could produce favorable results for the skilled practitioner. As Bruce performed his maneuvers in the air, Wally could appreciate Bruce's lightning swift techniques and was astute enough to know that, in order for his group to better visualize what was happening as it applied to self-defense, it would be necessary to demonstrate the techniques on a willing partner.

Wally had learned years ago, from the many demonstrations he had performed and the thousands of classes he had taught, that using another teacher's students to demonstrate a point was a touchy area. He was fully cognizant of the adverse repercussions that could result from damaged egos that usually occurred from this type of impromptu mock fighting and self-defense demonstration. However, he reasoned his students were good sports and always ready to learn something new, and they were disciplined enough to take directions from someone that had more skill than they did. Wally suddenly spoke up and volunteered one of the students to participate in the demonstration. Wally had purposely selected one of the larger and taller students from the group. Using the largest student would reinforce and validate the point that a bigger physical specimen always made a self-defense demonstration much more effective. Bruce could appreciate the validity of the logic as well. It made perfect sense for him to use a larger and stronger opponent so that the contrast made a greater impact on any spectators or observers, especially if he was trying to make a specific point in practical self-defense. Having a larger opponent would also illustrate the reason of why Wing Chun was developed as an effective style of self-defense in the first place. The Wing Chun style had originally been created by a woman monk several centuries back, and it had often proven that size was not a determining factor should Wing Chun be used in a life-threatening confrontation.

Bruce stood in front of the student and beckoned him to throw several strong punches at either his face or chest. Both opponent's stood in a boxer's crouch, and Bruce's request was almost instantaneously satisfied. As fast as the volatile barrage of punches came, Bruce instinctively and simultaneously reacted with a tight combination of multiple blocking and followup counterattacks. To the astonished dismay of the onlookers, it was obvious that this unrehearsed performance was for real. They were utterly amazed that the *judoka*'s (judo practitioner's) punches barely traveled halfway to their target's on Bruce's upper body and face before Bruce had swiftly intercepted and effortlessly thwarted them. Bruce's Wing Chun defense tactics had worked exactly as he had foretold.

The student, feeling somewhat intimidated by the thought that he had possibly let down his coach, was impelled to give a much more forceful showing in his next few attempts. Encouraged to continue by Bruce's subtly coercive hand gestures and his verbal refrain, "again, again, again," the frustrated judoka resumed his attacks with renewed tenacity and determination. After what seemed like several dozen attempts, the student's energy and stamina began to wane, signifying that his efforts were, at best, altogether futile, not to mention that his ego had been slightly bruised by the size difference of the two mock combatants. Wally, with his many years of experience in dealing with pugilistic demonstrations, realized that, although his student was an exceptionally skilled judo practitioner, this youthful and assuredly gifted Chinese gung fu artist obviously outclassed him. Wally also knew that Bruce had set the criteria and established the setting to prove his point; and unfortunately, the practice partner was unwittingly being used as a proverbial guinea pig. However, this was necessary if anyone was to fully validate a point or demonstrate the effectiveness of his or her style of self-defense.

Wally was duly impressed with Bruce's skills and fully recognized that Bruce was really just toying with his student and, if he had wanted to, in the blink of an eye could have seriously injured the young judoka. The other students were equally impressed with the mock demonstration and were convinced that this dynamic Chinese martial artist of only twenty-one years of age was extremely proficient and thoroughly understood the principles of real fighting and self-defense.

Wally knew that diplomacy was as important as physical skill, so rather than chance ill feelings, Wally alleviated any tension created by the situation by intervening. He shifted the subject and began elaborating on other topics of martial arts that were common knowledge to both Bruce and the students. Wally began by telling Bruce that the students were doing extremely well on the judo circuit and that they had won many awards and trophies all over the United States. He then mentioned that the students who were there with him had recently competed against the Obukan Judo Club in Portland, where they trounced their rival judo practitioners. This brought a grin to Bruce's face, knowing he was in the company of such a renowned judo expert. It pleased him immensely to know that Wally was such a well-respected emissary in the world of judo and one that had produced some of the country's top champions. Bruce accepted the obvious shift in the theme of the discussion. Everyone present sensed a change in his attitude. He casually interrupted Wally's proud account of his students' heralded achievements to inquire as to his nationality. Bruce had detected some Chinese traits in Wally's facial features. Wally was quick to declare that he was of Chinese ancestry. Another smile suddenly appeared on Bruce's face as he said, "I knew it! Man, I thought you were all along." He then patted Wally lightly on the shoulder several times to express his solidarity with a martial arts comrade.

The conversation took a new direction as both started talking candidly about the mutual pride they had in their Chinese ancestry. Most noteworthy, from Bruce's perspective, was how proud he felt that the Chinese were getting the recognition and were receiving the justly deserved credit for their efforts and contributions in promoting martial arts outside of the Far East. He said he felt that a majority of Westerners believed that the Chinese people who were active in sports were only proficient in Ping-Pong or tennis and were not recognized, or given full credit, for their athletic skills in other fields. He thought the world's recent awareness of the martial arts, especially judo, was doing a lot to change all of those unfounded stereotypical misconceptions. Bruce was quick to compliment the sensei after learning that he was one of the true pioneers in this development in the United States. As the students stood quietly watching the men converse about their common ancestral roots and how martial arts played a vital role in life, a newer and closer camaraderie seemed to be forming between these two men. Wally Jay and Bruce Lee shared similar feelings on other closely related subjects as well. That Wally was Chinese, at least partially, and had lived in Hawaii before coming to the U.S. mainland, had trained with a Japanese judo and jujitsu instructor, and was well respected by his students and martial arts peers was perceived by Bruce as positive qualities that only a few Asians in the United States possessed.

As quick as the conversation and the gung fu demonstration had changed to one of a more cordial nature, it shifted back to one that was more physically oriented. Without wanting to provoke any animosity, and also realizing that he would become the focal point of the group's attention, Bruce asked Wally if he had ever played around with chi sao sticking hand techniques. Wally said that he had intermittently dabbled with the techniques over the years, but he was not an expert at this type of two-man training. He elaborated that he usually did chi sao when a few of his Chinese gung fu friends skilled in it dropped by to visit his dojo in Alameda, California. Bruce unpretentiously followed up by asking if he would care to try out his technique. Naturally, Wally, being the natural competitor that he was, readily accepted.

After a momentary pause to position facing each other, the two men began to maneuver in and out of the intricately circular and linear patterns; Wally's familiarity with these interactive drills and the intrinsic feel associated with this practice, signaled to him that Bruce was not a rank amateur at employing these close-range sticking hand trapping maneuvers. Moreover, Wally was just as impressed with the speed and power that Bruce applied to these ruselike manipulations. The students stood silently as they witnessed this brilliant exchange of swiftly executed arm play. This was both amusing and enlightening to the students, since they had never known of their sensei's skill in this type of mock combat. In fact, most people that did not know him well thought that Sensei Jay's forte consisted only of judo and jujitsu. After a short yet intense bout of strategic wrangling, Bruce's gained a fond respect for Wally's skills in chi sao. Each knew and inherently felt a newfound mutual respect for each other that comes from engaging in this playful but very serious form of pugilistic jousting, one that's primary purpose is to read the other's sensitivity to attack and instinctively route a path for counterattacking.

When their brief session ended, Wally complimented Bruce on his exceptional chi sao technique. A smile appeared on Bruce's face when Wally stated that his springlike footwork was incredibly agile and added more explosiveness to the techniques than he had expected. It was as if each of Bruce's techniques were charged with the additional force generated from the body rather than from the arms, wrists, and shoulders. Wally, impressed with Bruce's artful manipulations, still found it very difficult to believe that a man of his relatively small stature could possess so much dynamic physical capability. Even the larger student who had participated in the previous self-defense demonstration was in total dismay after witnessing how a person of only about five feet six inches in height and weighing about 135 pounds could use techniques so effectively against someone of his own six-foot and 180-pound stature. Bruce seemed to defy the laws of physics in the way he used opposing force and redirected it so easily. Perhaps what impressed the students most, however, was the uncanny quickness that Bruce used in his techniques. In addition, he was very unpredictable, even to the highly trained eyes of Wally Jay. Wally was quick to realize that Bruce possessed exceptional skills for anyone, regardless of their size or weight, and he openly complimented Bruce on this exhibition of natural skill.

Wally's most curious judo protégés had the opportunity to direct several questions to Bruce regarding his particular style and methodology. Bruce obliged their request with a stark change of attitude. He suddenly smiled, relaxed, and became more personable, as he began asserting emphatically that he was constantly in search of martial arts knowledge, regardless of style or method. He shared that it was his belief that many martial artists became so entrenched in their own style that it became difficult for them to see other styles in a true light. He felt that most styles have something valid to offer if the practitioners did not close their eyes to them. Wally wholeheartedly agreed and interjected that he had been working on innovative developments in the art of judo and jujitsu for some years and was constantly discovering new techniques that better suited his particular needs. Bruce was very glad to know that he was not the only martial artist who had altered techniques to better suit the needs of a specific individual.

Bruce then became very specific, as he emphatically verbalized his dislike for the rigidity found in most classical styles of martial arts. He felt that it limited the full potential of the serious practitioner. Uninterrupted, he continued his critique by stating his views of the yin and yang. He purposefully expressed this in a rather simplified manner so that the onlookers could grasp just how important the delicate balance between power and speed was to fighting and how it applied to combative situations in general. They were drawn to the charismatic way in which Bruce eloquently and articulately painted a simple picture of such a seemingly complex subject as fighting and self-defense. Bruce's physical actions were clear, concise, and yet somewhat florid. This, with artfully punctuated with verbiage, was very persuasive indeed. It was also quite evident to Wally's protégés that Bruce and their sensei shared views on most of his points, even though they were practitioners of two entirely different styles of martial arts. Their sensei would give a nod of approval every time Bruce said something that he knew to be factual.

With midnight quickly approaching, both Bruce and Wally realized they had completely lost all track of time. They sensed a kinship developing from this engrossing sharing their common interests in the Asian fighting and self-defense disciplines. It furthermore had given both men a chance to know one another on a personal level. Before parting company, Wally explained to Bruce that his group was on its way to the Vancouver, B.C., Judo Club to enter a competition. Afterward, they would return to the Portland, Oregon, area to compete against the Randori School of Judo. Before the evening ended, they exchanged addresses and phone numbers. Bruce asked Wally to call him after the judo matches to let him know how his students did against the competitors. Wally promised he would do this as soon as the competition concluded and he was home at his dojo in Alameda, California. As they parted company, it was clear that they had begun to develop a strong bond of mutual respect and friendship for each other. That Sunday Bruce called Amy and told her what had happened that week. As usual, she was not overly impressed with such things. Judo, jujitsu, gung fu, fighting, and other related matters did not appeal to her in the least. When Bruce ask her if she'd like to take a ride over to the world's fair and see if they could go on the Space Needle she declined outright. She kept bringing up the subject of automobiles and asking Bruce, in a condescending way, "Don't you think you should get a newer car?" To which Bruce responded, "What's wrong with my car? It runs good. You never disliked my car before." Amy tried, in an unusually polite way, to infer that Bruce's old car was not the type of vehicle she wished to be seen riding in. Rather than come right out and say it, she simply said that she thought Bruce should not be seen riding in a car with dents and a faded paint job when he was traveling around town or going to his gung fu kwoon. After hearing this, Bruce began to ponder her words. After hanging up, he thought long and hard about what she had said and knew that she was correct on every count. He was trying to promote an image of success and conduct himself in a businesslike manner while driving around in an old, beat up automobile. This was definitely a matter he was going to have to look into more thoroughly. Naturally, the subject of finances was going to have to be factored into the equation, so

Bruce made an oath to himself to try as hard as he could to make saving some extra money from teaching and his job at the restaurant a number one priority. That would take some doing, because a fairly new used car could run upward of a thousand dollars. And at this time, he mused, a thousand or a million seemed like about the same amount. These astronomical amounts were so far out of the question that is was not even worth thinking about.

Bruce Lee Meets Allen Joe

With the month of June drawing to a close, most of the downtown Seattle business district was still in a state financial prosperity and economic boom due to the continuing influx of vacationing tourists flocking to this beautiful Northwestern American city and spending huge sums of money patronizing the various shops, restaurants, and hotels.

Among the nearly four million midsummer arrivals who had taken the excursion to holiday and enjoy the experience of the Seattle World's Fair pageantry was a Chinese gentleman named Allen Joe, who was accompanied by his immediate family. Allen was the proprietor of a small grocery store and meat market in the suburbs of Oakland, California. He felt that a trip to the world's fair would be an ideal way to conclude his family's vacation before returning to the Bay Area and resuming work at his grocery store. He had been overwhelmed by the experience of being a part of this gigantic historical happening. Two of the most popular exhibitions, and the ones they enjoyed the most, had been the U.S. Science Pavilion, which was dedicated to the country's advances in science and space exploration, and the Century 21 Exposition. These two pavilions gave the world a glimpse of the future and of what life would be like when it arrived.

Allen was a very close friend of James Yimm Lee and had studied the Chinese gung fu art of Sil Lum under him for several years in the Oakland area. In a sense, the vacation was a dual-purpose pilgrimage, and if all went well, Allen and his family would get the opportunity to meet Bruce Lee, whom they had heard about from James. Prior to Allen's vacation, James had asked him, time and situation permitting, to check out a fellow who was teaching gung fu in the Seattle area. The casual introduction between James and Bruce in 1959 had been less than significant at the time, but James, being the martial artist that he was, always tried to stay updated on the whereabouts of individuals who had knowledge pertaining to the arts that he loved. James informed Allen Joe that the address of Bruce Lee was at the Ruby Chow restaurant in Seattle's Chinatown. He instructed Allen, in the event that he was able to locate him there, to give his regards to Bruce Lee and to convey sentiments of goodwill. Allen knew that this search could prove fruitless, but the respect that he had for his gung fu instructor was such that he would make every possible effort to find Bruce Lee.

It was after eight o'clock in the evening when the Joe family pulled into the crowded parking lot at Ruby Chow's restaurant. Even though the facility was quite busy, Ruby took time out from her reception duties to exchange pleasantries and inform Allen that although Bruce was not there at that time, he would return later in the evening. Allen congenially conveyed to her that he and his family would return later that evening after he had secured hotel reservations. Ruby was happy to recommend a nearby motel and promised to leave a message the moment Bruce returned. Ruby told Allen Joe that if Bruce were his normal self he would probably be returning around midnight.

After settling into their motel, the Joe family returned to Ruby's and enjoyed a delicious Chinese dinner while awaiting Bruce Lee's return. As dessert was served, Allen ordered a scotch as he continued perusing the dimly lit entrance, looking for anyone that entered the restaurant that fitted Bruce's description. At about eleven o'clock that evening, Bruce sauntered into the restaurant, feeling pretty good after having received $150 from his mother in Kowloon. He was almost immediately informed by Ruby that there was a family from Oakland who wished to meet him. After she pointed Allen Joe and his family out, Bruce approached the table where the Joe family was sitting.

His introduction was graciously formal, and Allen was impressed with the way in which Bruce carried himself. After a bit of social discourse, Allen mentioned that he was a Sil Lum student under the tutelage of James Yimm Lee in Oakland, California. This at first seemed to manifest a defensive psychological posture in Bruce's attitude, as he apparently felt that a challenge might be in store for him. Allen quickly dispelled any such notion and respectfully complimented Bruce on his martial acumen, and as the conversation continued, Bruce realized there was no cause for alarm and began to relax. The other members of the Joe family were content to sit quietly and listen unobtrusively as Bruce and Allen became totally enthralled in their martial arts conversation. It was obvious to his wife that Allen was duly impressed with this young man of about twenty-one years of age. Just by the captivated look on his face, she could tell that her husband was trying to figure out how one so relatively young could be so knowledgeable about the art of gung fu.

At about midnight as the restaurant was closing, Bruce invited Allen and his family into the back yard of the restaurant. They promptly accepted, and in what seemed like an instant, they were all in the small backyard. Here Bruce demonstrated some of the intricacies of his Wing Chun gung fu. Bruce then positioned himself in front of the mook yan jong, which was planted securely in the ground, and he began executing a rapid sequences of offensive and defensive combinations that were randomly extracted from the one hundred and eight sequenced routines of the Wing Chun mook yan jong drill. The wooden arms of the training dummy vibrated incessantly as Bruce pounded out a steady rhythm against the sturdy protrusions. Allen jokingly commented that Bruce's rhythm was such that it sounded like a calypso drummer playing a bongo drum. It was also so loud that he thought Bruce was going to wake up everyone in the vicinity.

Personally, Allen still had a few reservations about Bruce's gung fu skills, particularly as they applied to realistic situations in actual anything-goes street fighting applications. Bruce simply did not appear to be one who possessed too much of that kind of practical experience. Dressed in a business suit and wearing glasses, Bruce appeared to be someone who had led a rather cloistered young life in an upper income family well removed from any environment where fighting would ever occur. Bruce Lee, just by his general appearance seemed more suited as an office worker or a clerical employee than a skilled gung fu practitioner. However, any of Allen's initial remnants of doubt were swiftly erased when the base of the mook yan jong started to rock violently. Then he knew that this young Chinese gung fu artist undoubtedly possessed some functional fighting skills. After the display of dynamic power and explosive speed that he had just witnessed on the wooden training dummy, Allen was convinced that Bruce was not only well versed in the theoretical aspects but could adequately protect himself against assaults as well.

Allen, not one to be completely outdone, decided to show Bruce some of his techniques. Bruce stood aside as Allen struck a fighting pose and began performing a Sil Lum set. Afterward he explained that he had learned from his Sifu James Lee that the best way to take on an attacker was to tuck the arms in close and lunge out with powerful attacks and then rapidly recover. Bruce watched and listened until Allen finished his demonstration and then curtly and authoritatively said, "That will not work against an inside fighter." Then Bruce set up in a position in front of Allen and told him to throw some punches as if in a mock street fight. Allen lunged in and delivered five explosive, rapid-fire punches at Bruce's head and upper torso. Bruce swiftly intercepted the volleys and instantaneously counterattacked every punch, each return punch and strike only missing Allen Joe's head by mere fractions of an inch. Allen was very surprised by the swift retaliatory counterattacks. Not only was this person fast, he thought, he is powerful as well.

Allen's immediate thoughts were that James would be overwhelmingly impressed with this young man's martial arts skills. It was going to be a real pleasure to report to James that this privileged encounter with Bruce Lee had actually taken place. Allen would certainly have to convey that he and his family had personally witnessed Bruce exhibit an incredible display of dynamic body power and coordinated hand speed while demonstrating his artful technical fighting prowess on the mook yan jong. This was something that Allen felt was virtually impossible to do for such a slight-framed individual of maybe only 130 pounds or so, who only stood about five and a half feet tall.

Afterward, for the better portion of another hour, while standing around in back of the restaurant, Bruce and Allen exchanged philosophical opinions and discussed how those ideas applied to their respective styles. Bruce seemed to have all of the answers, not only as they related to his own style, but for other styles as well. Allen was especially impressed with Bruce's detailed explanations of the animal styles of Chinese gung fu. As he gave an explanation, Bruce would strike a pose and emulate the movement form of the tiger while rapidly executing a series of powerful circular hand techniques. Then he would just as suddenly change his body style and hand manipulations to resemble those of a graceful crane. Then, while continuing to reveal the purposes behind each movement, he would gracefully change his torso and arms to resemble the smooth flowing antics of a snake. Bruce artfully displayed the dragon, with its forceful energy release, by exhaling roughly and making multiple punching attacks with the opened hands, making each finger of his hand appear to be that of a dragon's claw. Then, as if nothing had happened, Bruce would recoil his forearms, clench his fist while extending the first two fingers of his hand, and swiftly execute explosive eye-blurring combinational blocking and punching attacks into the air resembling the praying mantis. These mock simulations of China's most traditional gung fu styles were very impressive to watch, and Allen was fully convinced that Bruce could apply them to fighting situations if the need ever arose. After these violent appearing outbursts of physical energy, Bruce regained his calm and relaxed composure in a few seconds, as if nothing had happened. Allen complimented Bruce on his power and explosive techniques.

As Bruce and Allen Joe parted company, at just shy of four o'clock in the morning, a feeling of mutual respect and friendship had been established, and they agreed to remain in contact with one another in the future. Bruce felt good to have met another Chinese gentleman who valued the cultural heritage of their common ancestry and sought to retain these values through practice of the art of gung fu.

His Sundays off were providing Bruce the special time he needed to be with Amy Sanbo. He was now feeling like she was his girl-friend, though there were times he doubted this feeling. During a Sunday dinner at the Bush Garden, Bruce was thoroughly con-vinced that this was perhaps the right time to propose marriage to Amy. After holding her hands across the table and telling her how much she meant to him and how she could be the person behind him to insure his success, he asked her if she would marry him. Amy was aghast that Bruce had proposed. It was the last thing imag-inable that she could think of that Bruce would ask of her. She tried to find the right words to decline the proposal as they had dinner. Bruce was trying so hard to convince her that his plans for the future were going to be really big. He could see himself as the head of a large chain of gung fu schools and being independently wealthy, and she would be right there by his side to enjoy it all. Amy, on the other hand, tried to explain, in a calm and soothing manner, that she thought that they were too much alike to be married to each other. After all, she had her own dreams to chase and did not want to be supporting anyone's ambitious desires when hers were just as important. She told Bruce she did not want anything, or any-body, to get in the way of her becoming a writer. Bruce took this rebuff personally but finally had to yield and recognize that Amy was sincere in her position. They agreed to remain friends and try to help the other in any way they could. They kidded each other about marriage as Bruce drove her home that evening.

On Tuesday, November 27, 1962, Bruce turned twenty-two years old. That night he and some of his students went to the Hong Kong Cafe in Chinatown and had a family-style dinner. Amy was noticeably absent, and Bruce's spirits were not dampened in the least. Between the gang's kidding, laughing, and telling off-colored jokes, Bruce announced that they were going to share in a different kind of Chinese dining experience. Each person at the table was to make a different selection from the menu and then everyone at the table would be sharing in the food from the various selections. Bruce told the gang that this was Chinese-style and the way eating out was generally done in Hong Kong and Kowloon. He further explained that each person would order one or two different varieties of meats and vegetables from the menu, and when the dishes arrived at the table, everyone could select anything they desired from any of the platters.

Shortly thereafter, all of the student guests celebrating his birthday got a taste of what oyster beef and rice tasted like. He insisted that all of the gang get a taste of his favorite food. Bruce in jest also poured them all a teacup of root beer so they would know exactly how his favorite food tasted as they washed it down with his favorite drink. Raising their cups, everybody laughed and toasted this mock commemoration. After the sumptuous nine-course meal, Bruce rejoiced with the announcement that, as a birthday present to himself, he decided to sell the old beat up white Chevrolet Corvair and purchase a newer and definitely better-looking car. This time the students raised their cups and made a congratulatory gesture that was more serious than in fun. After dinner, as a close to the birthday celebration, they had all planned on taking Bruce to the Varsity Theatre located on University Way in the heart of Seattle's University District. It was featuring famed Japanese director Akira Kurosawa's newly released film *Yojinbo* (The Bodyguard) double-featured with his famous 1952 hit titled *Shichi No Samurai* (The Seven Samurai).

By Saturday, after having placed an advertisement in the Seattle Times to sell his old car, he found a buyer that had seen his evening edition advertisement in the newspaper. The man was willing to pay $50 for the car. With this money, plus an additional $575, Bruce bought a shiny, black 1957 Ford sedan from a seller listed in the newspaper too. At the time, it seemed to be a relatively good buy, and the ideal choice for what his budget could handle. Ever since he had learned how to drive and to appreciate the value of a quality automobile, he had longed for the day when he could actually afford a finer looking car. This one seemed to be the all-around best choice of the lot that he had inquired about from the used car ads in the newspaper. The car ran extremely well when he gave it a test drive. It appeared in good condition, with nice shiny hubcaps; unsoiled upholstery, good tires, no dents, and reasonably low-mileage. The previous owner had even shinned up the engine and installed a new battery and air filter cover, to give it a newer and less used appearance. Bruce felt his new, albeit used, Ford Fairlane 500 undoubtedly had a certain air of mystique. It would surely be alluring enough to arouse the interest of the beautiful campus coeds at the university to date him, even if Amy decided she did not want to see him when he called. Bruce also fancied how much this black car, with its white and chrome trim, resembled a Seattle police car. It tickled him to think how much fun he could have referring to his Ford Fairlane as a police car to his students and friends on campus. He also imagined that, by wearing stylish suits while driving this sleek sporty Fairlane, he could make such an impressive statement about his refined taste that it would cause those that he met to overlook the trivial fact that he was working as a waiter in a restaurant. That was something he chose not to make known to people he met unless it was necessary.

During the Christmas break, Bruce initiated plans to establish an organized structure in his gung fu ranking system. After careful consideration, he decided to be more specific and apply a title system that categorically defined students by their status within the club. He realized that, with the different levels now evident in his pupil's skills, he needed a way to organize and arrange the class sessions more effectively. He had separated them into categories for beginner, semiadvanced, and senior student classes, so he could more effectively plan his teaching responsibilities and utilize his time more efficiently. The ranking system would also give the beginners goals to work toward and provide the semiadvanced and seniors with a curriculum that was comparable, with their elevated skill levels. Chinese rank titles appealed to Bruce, and he decided to structure his ranks in much the same way as Yip Man had.

He penned a neatly written Chinese ranking title system on lined, loose-leaf notebook paper. It read:

	Male	Female
Senior Student	Sihing	Sijei
Junior Student	Sidi	Simui
Disciple	Sisuk	Sigoo mui

Later that week Bruce typed the ranking structure and mimeographed copies for distribution among his students. Because of Taky's sincerity and unwavering dedication, Bruce promoted him to assistant instructor and gave him the title of *si hing,* meaning, "senior or older brother," which is symbolic of the close family structure that is common in China and other Eastern countries. With Taky as his assistant, Bruce could divide the teaching authority and responsibility between them. This would ease some of the pressure and demands placed upon him. Since Bruce had devoted much of his free time promoting his school and trying to build a reputation as a professional, it would be some relief that he could now spend time elevating the quality of his training and improving his own skills. It would also mean that in a lengthy absence he would have a truly qualified representative to carry out his instructions. Now he could even take a vacation and visit his family and friends in Hong Kong and Kowloon if he desired. The deep respect that Bruce held for Taky was obvious to all of the juniors and seniors alike. Most of them felt that Taky exemplified the same professional quality and attitude that Bruce reflected in his training and teachings.

The Jun Fan Gung Fu Institute was receiving much more notoriety than ever before, and it was nice that all of the hard work and preparatory planning was beginning to pay off. Bruce was getting more popular in and around Chinatown and, to a limited extent, on the college campus. However, he knew that in the following year he would have to improve and expand his promotional efforts so that he could recruit more students from college if his overall plans were to pan out the way he envisioned them.

As he had expected, the kwoon's enrollment increased to around fifty students, and more than ever his spare time was committed to teaching. Some students were regulars, but others only showed up on an intermittent basis. Nevertheless, all were considered paying customers and, much to Bruce's relief, had helped in keeping the kwoon financially in the black. In addition, the notoriety of his gung fu expertise was steadily spreading throughout the immediate community and even outside into the districts surrounding his geographical location. Bruce, Taky, Jesse, and Charlie were beginning to get offers to perform self-defense demonstrations for local groups and various associations that wanted to learn more about this relatively unknown Wing Chun style. Bruce and his pupils readily obliged, and after several of these successful demos, he began feeling like a martial arts goodwill ambassador of sorts. There was an obvious pride reflected in the way he authoritatively conducted these terse but very well planned exhibitions.

What was amusing for Bruce was how Americans would perceive him prior to and immediately after his performances. What irked Bruce the most was the fact that some American spectators who witnessed these eloquently performed and usually flamboyantly executed, self-defense exhibitions chose to continue to look at him in the same old stereotypical light. This prejudicial assessment was typical of that reserved for Asians in general, but now these faulty assessments included the Asian self-defense arts too. These people normally had preconceived notions that anyone of Japanese ancestry must know judo or some other form of jujitsu. Though it was far from true that all Asians knew some form of Asian self-defense, Bruce had hoped that, through his demonstrations, the spectators would gain some sort of deeper understanding about these old Asian cultural arts. In another way, he almost wished people would continue to believe all Asians practiced martial arts, especially if this belief forced naive Americans to develop a greater respect for people of Asian extraction.

In another sense, Bruce felt like a pioneer of sorts, by introducing Wing Chun to the Seattle area. Although he was not the first to teach Chinese gung fu in King County, he took pride in knowing he was among the few Asians that took an active role in promoting and propagating the martial arts in hope of waking up the general public. And Bruce was aware that by spreading the word of Asian arts and philosophy, it would certainly bolster his reputation as a sifu and undoubtedly serve the useful purpose of expanding his student base.

During the daytime hours, Bruce generally allotted time for his own personal development. He was beginning to relish these special morning and early afternoon workouts. He could challenge himself in the privacy of the kwoon and be out of the presence of his students as he continued to explore and improve his fighting skills. Since workouts varied, depending on what he was trying to accomplish in a given session, Bruce always tried to go into a training session already knowing what he wanted to work on. Some sessions were basically repetitive drills that he had contrived and that he had intended to refine and develop to integrate into his own fighting style. Swiftly executed mock combinational scenarios using lead-hand back fist strikes followed up by explosive rear-hand punches and single rear-leg kicks was a usual routine. He found that using three or four simple combinations of low-level kicks and straight-line punches, when mixed in different sequences, created some surprising results. To set up an opponent using one basic routine and then instantaneously change to another variation in the theme worked really well. The techniques in these original creations never got boring when he customized his private workout sessions in this manner.

By also experimenting with the basic blocks, straight-line punches, and upper torso centerline block-counter patterns that he extrapolated from the Sil Lim Tao Wing Chun set, Bruce devised his own select mini patterns. Again, he would change the order of the maneuvers, and by altering the speed or rhythm of these self-defense vignettes, he figured he could literally create hundreds of defensive or offensive techniques. At this point, Bruce began figure out just how many self-defense and fighting maneuvers could be devised by adding just a few more moves to these various patterns, all stressing the constantly evolving philosophical principles that were gradually becoming an integral part of his teaching protocol. His aim was to become faster and stronger with each passing day, never letting anything get in the way of his being the best that was humanly possible. To become faster, he simply executed the self-defense techniques and combinational maneuvers extracted from chi sao until a rhythm and a sense of timing materialized. His naturalness in executing smooth, fast, and highly explosive techniques came from hours and hours of rigorous attention, practicing a single maneuver. To feel, look, and express this naturalness is what he felt distinguished a skilled martial artist from the novice. He surmised correctly that the way great fighters could recognize flaws and inferior skills in other professed martial artists was in how naturally and automatically they could respond to a nonprearranged self-defense situation without looking awkward.

Bruce and James Make Telephone Contact

It was during a busy evening training session when Bruce's assistant instructor, Taky Kimura, interrupted Bruce to inform him of a long-distance telephone call from Oakland, California. Taky said, "It is a Mr. Lee." Taky immediately took over the instructor's duties and Bruce retired to the small office to receive the call.

Bruce was puzzled about who would be calling him from Oakland, California. Bruce listened intensely for several moments as the caller on the other end of the line inquired if he was the gung fu man Bruce Lee, who taught the cha-cha in San Francisco. Bruce affirmed that he had taught dancing in San Francisco and Oakland some time back and then coyly divulged that he did know a little Chinese gung fu. After listening for a moment as the caller identified himself, Bruce was surprised to hear that it was James Yimm Lee. Bruce remembered hearing about James from Allen Joe at Ruby's restaurant. The instant that James reminded Bruce that they had informally met through his brother Robert, who had been in Bruce's cha-cha class in Oakland, Bruce was able to recall him and the exact time and place that the meeting had occurred. James explained that his friend Allen Joe had reported that he had met Bruce Lee at Ruby Chow's restaurant in Chinatown during his vacation to the world's fair in Seattle. Allen Joe had been very impressed with Bruce's gung fu abilities, and it was because of this that James had decided to make the call and chat with Bruce a bit about martial arts.

Bruce immediately sensed that James was a serious practitioner of the art of gung fu and that he was noticeably interested in possibly meeting him and sharing martial arts knowledge. As their conversation progressed, Bruce mentioned that, just the week before, he had met Wally Jay while his team was in the Northwest competing in some judo events. James indicated that Wally Jay was a very close friend, as well as an avid martial arts practitioner. Having the mutual acquaintances opened the conversation further, and James stressed his sincerity in wanting to learn more about the Wing Chun art that Bruce taught. Bruce was glad to hear that martial artists from places other than Seattle were also beginning to recognize his talents.

James asked Bruce, rather directly, if Bruce could come to the Oakland area and perhaps teach him some of his Chinese art. Knowing he was still popular in the Bay Area and had family there, Bruce deemed this an opportunity to expand his teaching and pay respects to friends and relatives that he had not seen since he had left for Seattle in the fall of 1959.

While Bruce was still conversing with James, his mind was working at what seemed like a hundred miles an hour. Bruce consented to make the trip to the Bay Area the following week. Bruce said he would be happy to discuss martial arts and possibly teach, if there was a sincere interest. James quickly reassured him by saying, "I am as serious as they come, and while you are in Oakland, you can stay at my home." James's cordial invitation made the teaching and social aspects more appealing and gave Bruce the chance to expand the art he now professed as his style. James was ecstatic that Bruce had accepted his offer. The conversation concluded with Bruce stating that he would begin making plans for driving to the Bay Area.

The entire following week was a time of serious anticipation for Bruce. He was looking forward to the opportunity to visit his sister and revive some old friendships by seeing Mr. Quan Ging Ho and perhaps some of his former cha-cha students. He looked forward to visiting Wally Jay, Allen Joe, and of course, James Lee, and he was excited about the chance to expand his reputation in the Bay Area by teaching Wing Chun instead of cha-cha. Bruce was delighted that his martial arts labors were taking priority over everything else in his life at the moment. Plus, it felt like the right time to actually take a small vacation, since he had not had one since he had come to the United States.

Bruce Lee Drives to Oakland

This was the first long-distance drive that Bruce had ever attempted, and it would be a real challenge. Driving his "police car" on a trip of this magnitude was going to be an adventure in his car like none he had ever had before; even the episodes of his learning to drive or taking his driver's license test could not compare. Driving through the states of Washington and Oregon and into California would be a challenge in which Bruce would ultimately prove to himself that he was indeed independent and self-reliant behind the wheel of a car. He had never used American road maps to any extent before, and his unfamiliarity with the highway road signs showed whenever he suddenly found himself lost in a small, out-of-the-way town along the coast. His biggest challenge was trying to reorient his sense of direction after becoming lost for the second or third time. Every gasoline stop became a stop for instructions and a lesson in map reading. One consolation, at least, was that the service station attendants along the way were quite helpful in aiding him on the 810-mile journey that would take him into Oakland. Despite the challenges, the fifteen hours, thirty-one minutes that it took to make the trip in his black 1957 Ford seemed to have passed rather quickly, since he had been preoccupied with thinking about all of the things that he had to do while in the San Francisco Bay Area.

As Bruce entered the Bay Area, the heavy traffic, road construction, and complex collection of freeways and interstates disoriented him. He concluded, correctly, that the afterwork commuters were partially to blame for this incredible tangle of traffic. He recalled that James had said that there would be a lot of freeway connections in the San Francisco and Oakland areas, but he had not realized there would be so many. The interstates and freeway systems in the Seattle area were nothing compared to this mess of convoluted twists and turns down in the Bay Area.

Bruce thought he remembered James saying that when he arrived in San Francisco he would have to drive over the Bay Bridge and take a connector road that flowed into what was known as the MacArthur, and then turn off MacArthur at High Street. James had told him that the Henry J. Kaiser Center, a large building near the middle of downtown Oakland, would be a landmark indicating that he was nearing the MacArthur. Unfortunately, after crossing the Bay Bridge, Bruce found himself in a construction detour and unknowingly made the wrong junction and continued on Highway 17. As he neared the Oakland airport cutoff, he noticed a rather large structure on his left that he thought might be the Kaiser landmark. However, after traveling about fifteen miles, he realized that he was no longer in the Oakland area but a town called Hayward.

After that mistake, he decided to stop at another gas station to get new directions. To his dismay, after Bruce explained his predicament to the station attendant, the manager laughed and then informed him that the large structure that he had thought was the Kaiser structure was actually the Oakland water tower. The manager then wrote out a detailed hand-drawn map on an empty page of Bruce's spiral-bound notebook. As Bruce turned around and backtracked on Highway 17, he had time to think about the possibility that he may need a prescription change in his glasses. Although his black-rimmed glasses had served him well over the past several years, he surmised that his vision, which was 20/400, might be getting worse. If that were the case, it would soon be time to have a new set of lenses made. His thoughts quickly shifted as he spotted a sign reading "High Street Exit" and was finally driving up High Street heading toward the Oakland hills. Shortly thereafter, he was pulling into the driveway of the James Lee residence at 3039 Monticello Avenue.

Bruce Lee Meets James Yimm Lee

Bruce felt an uncertain air of anticipation as he walked up the stairs and knocked on the door. An affable James Lee immediately opened it and cheerfully welcomed him into the home. Bruce had barely seated himself on the large sofa when James's two children greeted him; Greglon and Karena were immediately attracted to the warm and friendly smile. Katherine, James's lovely wife, entered from the kitchen and was graciously introduced to Bruce. In a matter of minutes, it felt as though they had know one another for years.

Bruce began to relax and feel comfortable in the warm environment of the James Lee home. The happy family environment reminded Bruce of his childhood in Kowloon, when all of the family members would gather in the evening after everyone had completed their daily routines. The social receptiveness of James and his family had certainly made the trip worthwhile, and Bruce felt like a natural part of the James Yimm Lee family.

After Katherine had served Bruce and James a cup of hot Chinese green tea, James immediately steered the conversation in the direction of the martial arts. Their first topic involved the meeting between Bruce and Wally Jay in the Seattle Chinatown kwoon. Wally had contacted James after his return to Alameda, so James was already aware of the introduction and well acquainted with Wally's assessment of Bruce's exceptional gung fu. Bruce mentioned that Wally had called him in Seattle to tell him that the judo troupe that had traveled with him to the Northwest had won all of their matches. James suggested that they call Wally and inform him that Bruce was in Oakland. Bruce was pleasantly surprised at the attention he was receiving from someone whom he had only met briefly at a cha-cha class over three years ago. As James picked up the telephone to call Wally Jay, Bruce sat quietly taking in the decor of the living room. He was attracted to the unique and orderly way the home was arranged; it had a flavor of both Chinese and Western cultures. He sensed that James was a man of many talents and that the family had a close and harmonious relationship.

It had only been two short weeks since Bruce had met Wally Jay, and now he was over nine hundred miles and fifteen hours from home visiting martial arts practitioners whom he barely knew. His intuition told him the men were both friendly and knowledgeable in the art of gung fu. A warm feeling of comradeship began to come over Bruce as he listened to James speaking to Wally Jay on the telephone. "Remember the gung fu man that you met by the name of Bruce Lee in Seattle? Well, he's here at my home," James said. There was a long silence as James listened intently; then James resumed the conversation. "We plan on sharing some gung fu knowledge and getting to know one another better." After another brief silence James said, "Just a minute, here he is now." He handed the telephone to Bruce. "Wally would like very much to speak with you," James said.

Bruce's conversation with Wally seemed like a reunion of long lost friends. Wally was glad that Bruce had traveled to the Bay Area and wanted to see him if time permitted. Bruce assured him that there was plenty of time, and they would get together before he returned to Seattle.

As James resumed the conversation with Wally, the excitement of Bruce's visit became more obvious, and even the children were happy that Bruce was visiting them. James concluded the conversation with Wally by telling him that they would pay him a visit later that evening. James, being the congenial host that he was, offered to show Bruce many of his martial arts–related projects. After a tour of the Lee home and a visit to the lower level garage where James taught his own Sil Lum gung fu classes, Bruce was beginning to feel that his decision to come to Oakland was one of the better choices that he had made in some time. Bruce was dumbstruck by the creative innovations that James had developed in martial arts training equipment. The garage was filled with all sorts of steel punching and kicking devices that James had welded. Although many were still in the design stages, Bruce could sense that James Lee was years ahead of his time. An assortment of every spring-loaded apparatus imaginable was securely mounted to the wooden studs and beams of the garage. Bruce could not help becoming distracted from the tour of the training area because of the many innovations that he had never seen before. Even in Kowloon, when Bruce had been immersed in a classical martial arts environment, he had never seen such clever types of training equipment, and his mind whirled as he desperately tried to absorb all of the creations that James had constructed. By technical standards, James's unique creations were on a whole other level than those that Bruce had been exposed to at Sifu Gin Foon Mark's Praying Mantis kwoon in New York.

James could sense Bruce's intense interest and realized that he would have to demonstrate and explain the functions of each of these devices if Bruce's curiosity was to be fully satisfied. James was happy to oblige and gave Bruce a full demonstration on each and every piece of the equipment. After each display, Bruce was inclined to try his skills; despite the long drive from Seattle, Bruce still displayed an abundance of energy and each time he struck the devices, the entire frame structure of the house would shake. James smiled enthusiastically, as Bruce became acclimated to the tempo and rhythm of the equipment and attempted different variations, and good-naturedly offered suggestions that had worked well for him. James was tremendously impressed with the way that Bruce adapted to the devices and could see that, with the power and speed of his punches and kicks, the equipment would be an asset to his already adequate gung fu skills. For his part, Bruce was amazed by James's vast knowledge of physics, mechanics, leverage, and his ability to foresee equipment needs that would ultimately enhance the overall ability of anyone who seriously undertook training in the martial arts.

After leaving the garage area, James offered to show Bruce some of the books that he had written on the subject of martial arts. Bruce was particularly impressed with James's first book, *Fighting Arts of the Orient, Elemental Karate, and Kung Fu,* and he tried to glean every bit of knowledge that he could in the short time. One of the first things that he noticed was the way in which James had spelled the words *kung fu,* and he asked why James had chosen to spell it that way, rather than the more traditional *gung fu.* James casually replied that, since most Americans were not familiar with the Chinese pronunciation, he had felt the alternate spelling would have more market value in the United States. Bruce was impressed with the foresight that James had shown in his projects. Bruce also noticed that the contents of each of James's books were outlined simply and directly, so that anyone who was interested in martial arts could learn in a relatively quick fashion. The book *Modern Kung Fu, Iron Poison Hand Training* especially interested Bruce; it clearly explained methods for developing strong hands that could break bricks and boards in 100 days. His own knowledge of hand conditioning, as he had learned it in Kowloon and from Sifu Gin Foon Mark in New York, concurred totally with the way that James had presented it in the book.

James went on to explain that he had started his own company for marketing and selling his books. He believed it was better for him to sell his valuable and unique information himself, since no one else was going to take his product as seriously. He explained that his company, Oriental Book Sales, was also selling previously published books by other noted authors. If other people had something to offer the public, he thought he could help them achieve their objectives through his company. James was not only devoted to the martial arts but was something of an entrepreneur as well.

On the way to visit Wally Jay at his judo and jujitsu school in Alameda, Bruce and James continued to discuss the similarities and differences between their two styles. James explained how he had taken a somewhat creative approach to his martial arts and was continuously looking for further knowledge that he thought would be more practical in a self-defense sense. He confessed that he did not see the importance of *kata* or traditional martial arts forms, and he felt that he had wasted much time in learning them from his instructor in San Francisco. Bruce explained that some styles of gung fu were more elaborate than others and that the art of Wing Chun, even though it contained three forms, had only the necessary essentials of true self-defense. Bruce reinforced his explanations by commenting that simplicity and directness were the most effective means of self-defense. By the time they had reached Wally's school on Eagle Avenue in Alameda, they had discussed many concepts of fighting and self-defense; James was deeply impressed with the philosophic wisdom that Bruce possessed.

The visit at Wally's dojo was cordial and hospitable, and Wally proved to be the host that Bruce had anticipated. Wally's sincere friendliness was as meaningful as it had been when he had visited in Seattle, and he was genuinely happy to see both Bruce and James. The entire evening was spent discussing the deeper meanings of true martial arts. Many of the practical applications that Bruce taught in his Seattle kwoon were demonstrated in Wally's dojo training area. James enthusiastically participated as Bruce's practice partner as he showed the different applications that exemplified the art of Wing Chun. Both Wally and James were extremely impressed with the shocking power and speed that Bruce injected into the straight and direct attacks and counterattacks, and it seemed to Wally that Bruce's skills had progressed in the two short weeks since their meeting in Seattle.

After about an hour of comparing styles and evaluating practical applications, the three men retired to the office area of Wally's school. There they shared a pot of hot Chinese tea. They continued to discuss the philosophical aspects of the martial arts and the way they had derived from the basic philosophy of the Asian countries. James could not believe that Bruce was so knowledgeable on the subjects of Zen, Taoism, and the classical wisdom of the great sages of ancient China. This left an indelible impression on both he and Wally. As the visit concluded, they all agreed to stay in touch and continue to share knowledge and ideas. They seemed to be forming the base of a strong and lasting friendship, and Bruce couldn't help but feel that destiny must have brought them together.

On the return trip to James's home, Bruce expressed interest in writing a book on his beliefs and teachings in the art of Chinese Wing Chun. James could sense that Bruce had some very innovative ideas and encouraged him to pursue them to the fullest. James felt that there were very few knowledgeable martial artists in the United States, and one who possessed such knowledge should share it with serious martial artists everywhere. However, he iterated that this was not the belief of many gung fu teachers, who commonly felt that the Chinese art of gung fu should only be made available to pure Chinese and no one else should have access to this ancient knowledge. James said he didn't agree with this belief, and thought that everyone should have access to this knowledge. Bruce was thrilled that James felt the exact same way that he did on the subject, and this shared belief in the accessibility of martial arts wisdom prompted James to encourage Bruce to write a book on his unique art.

The following day was Saturday, and it proved to be quite an experience for both men. Most of the day was spent discussing specifics of the Sil Lum and Wing Chun styles. James was constantly comparing movements and making evaluations on which he felt was more effective. Bruce's reasoning proved to be a determining factor in James's opinion of many of the concepts, and James decided that there were going to be changes in the way he taught his students in the future.

During that day, Bruce discovered that James was deeply committed to physical fitness and, more specifically, to bodybuilding. He had noticed the weights and barbells in the garage the day before but had not mentioned them because of his intense fascination with the other training equipment. Although James was somewhat reserved when it came to touting his knowledge or discussing, at length, his lifelong interest in bodybuilding, he did mention that he had won several awards in that sport; and by the casual off-the-cuff manner in which he mentioned it, Bruce could detect that James wasn't a braggart. Bruce could tell just by seeing James's physique that bodybuilding was a subject in which he was an expert, and Bruce imagined he could learn a lot from him about it.

Bruce told James that he was impressed that a Chinese American of his stature was so physically developed. He confided that he had never seen an Asian that was so well developed. In Kowloon and Hong Kong, most Chinese, with such slender frames and so little muscle mass or bulk to work with, could never really achieve those kinds of results. James shifted his head sideways, laughed, and said that bodybuilding was only half of the training. The other half was in diet and proper nutrition. Then Bruce mentioned that

James, being almost twice his own age, was definitely a unique specimen and certainly must know what he was talking about.

James said that the muscles, when exercised to the point of where the muscle tissues actually tore or shredded, needed an abundance of protein to help in the rebuilding process. Naturally, the isolated muscle group that had been worked also needed appropriate time to rest as the healing process occurred. The result, he stated, would be muscle with more bulk and mass. He also pointed out that the body needed fuel foods in the form of carbohydrates to provide energy to sustain the workouts. All the while, James indicated, the bodybuilder had to use good judgment and proper training techniques in working each muscle group in the body at regular intervals. James concluded by saying it was a constant process, and the person that undertook such a stringent regimen had to be truly dedicated to it for a lifetime. Otherwise, if the person quit, the muscles would retain their mass but the bulk had a tendency to turn to soft flabby tissue, leaving the person carrying around a lot of weight that would be hard for the skeletal system to support.

Bruce absorbed every word. After James had finished his short explanation, Bruce asked him for some tips and pointers on bodybuilding so that he could possibly increase his own body development when he returned to Seattle. James offered to help him and noted that, with consistent training, given his frame size and slender musculature, he could probably increase his 135 pounds to maybe 150 or 160 pounds. The added muscle would increase Bruce's power and strength while still maintaining the flexibility to keep his incredible speed and quickness. Bruce, partly out of curiosity, but mostly in jest, asked James if he thought it was possible for him to put on sixty or seventy more pounds and have it be all toned muscle with lots of deep-cut definition. James looked at him as if he were crazy. Then he became very serious and confided that there were people that got into that mindset with bodybuilding. They didn't want to stop getting bigger and stronger. Unfortunately, these fellows started resorting to steroids and chemicals to increase their body size. Then they began having trouble with testosterone imbalances, liver ailments, kidney failure, and the like. James warned Bruce never to get into that stuff. "It will kill you with a very slow and agonizing death," he said. They spent the latter part of the day developing a program that Bruce could continue when he returned to Seattle. In exchange for the bodybuilding information, Bruce was happy to share his knowledge of chi sao sticking hands training and some of the fundamental skills of the art of Wing Chun. Bruce was impressed with James's progress, and James was equally impressed with Bruce's talents. Their friendly and unselfish exchange of wisdom and knowledge and their serious commitment to the same disciplines were also very obvious to Katherine, Greglon, and Karena. Katherine had not seen James as enthusiastic about anything since he started his earlier training with Professor T. Y. Wong in San Francisco. She was happy that James had discovered someone who shared many of the same hobbies and sports. Bruce seemed to be a very compatible individual, and she could sense that they were forming a very swift and solid friendship.

As they ate lunch that day at the Monticello home, James thought it would be a good idea to call Al Novak, his senior student in the Sil Lum style. Al quickly responded to honor his sifu's urgent request to come visit. While waiting for Al to arrive, Bruce and James conversed at length about Al's unique gung fu skills and physique. Al tipped the scales at about 300 pounds and was as solid as granite. He had been in law enforcement for many years and, as a police officer, felt he needed to know as much as possible about the various forms of self-defense. He had been James's only student for more than two years and had learned a tremendous amount about the Asian art of Chinese Sil Lum gung fu. Al was not only James's student, but also his friend, confidant, and business partner. He had assisted James in producing the *Modern Kung Fu Karate, Iron Poison Hand Training* book. As the perfect example of what 100 days of serious iron-hand training could do, Al even appeared on the book cover. Al, noted for his incredible breaking feats of strength, could easily demolish bricks, boards, or any other breakable material with his fists. In fact, Al had begun his Sil Lum gung fu training after witnessing James perform incredible breaking feats during a demonstration at one of Wally Jay's famous martial arts luaus. Bruce was very curious about this huge man, and as he paged through the iron-hand training book, kept asking James for more detail about Al's experience in gung fu. He looked forward to meeting Al Novak and was a bit impatient for his arrival.

James informed Bruce that Al was one of the very first Caucasians to gain entrance into the mysterious and secret world of the gung fu kwoons of San Francisco's Chinatown. He was proud of the fact that he had helped Al gain acceptance into this restricted inner circle of traditional and culturally ancient martial arts. Bruce was impressed with the confidence and trustworthiness James placed in Al and realized that both he and James had the same ideas concerning serious students. Race and creed were not important to them when considering students, only the reality that a person was truly serious about learning the art of Chinese gung fu. Bruce appreciated that James was open about his views and did not adhere to the restrictive practices that many of the senior gung fu masters followed. This only made their bond of friendship stronger.

About twenty minutes after the telephone call, there was a knock at the door. James welcomed Al into his home and immediately introduced him to Bruce, who quickly rose and extended his hand in friendship to this giant of a man. Bruce could not believe the size of Al's huge hand as it wrapped around his own. He could tell that Al was an extremely strong and capable individual and was everything that James had alleged.

After the introductory formalities were finished, Bruce and Al were quick to seize the opportunity to get to know one another. Al was very interested in seeing for himself what his sifu had said about Bruce being exceptionally skilled in the art of Chinese gung fu. The three of them spent the rest of the afternoon absorbed in conversation and in studying each other's various displays of martial arts. As Bruce shared his knowledge about his Wing Chun gung fu style, James and Al reciprocated by demonstrating their breaking techniques and fighting styles. As the evening progressed, their sharing of martial arts skills and technical wisdom inspired harmony among the three, and through this impromptu meeting, an indelible impression of mutual respect and unity had developed.

As the weekend drew to a close, Bruce reflected on this auspicious experience. It had definitely been more exciting than he had anticipated. The new friends that he had made and the martial arts acquaintances that he had the pleasure to meet were a sure sign that his trip had not been purposeless. He felt that the impression he had made with his views on Chinese gung fu had been well received by his hospitable host and James's close martial arts associates.

Monday morning came all too soon. Bruce was not looking forward to the long drive back to Seattle but knew that he had to do it. Although the car had run fairly well on the trip to the Bay Area, he thought he should at least have it looked at to be on the safe side before driving back. He felt that the precautionary measures would be well worth the cost rather than take a chance and have unexpected car trouble somewhere between Oakland and Seattle. Bruce asked James if there was a garage nearby where he could get a quick tune-up on the car without spending a great deal of money. Although Bruce was not overly concerned with the prospect that the car would possibly malfunction on the return trip, James was quite concerned. He had been stranded at one time or another in a strange place without ready assistance and did not want Bruce to have that experience. Fortunately, James's brother, Robert, ran a Gulf service station in the Oakland's Chinatown district and could readily tune up Bruce's car. Out of curiosity, Bruce asked if he was the same Robert Lee who had been in the cha-cha class in Oakland that he had taught several years ago. James confirmed that he was and was surprised that Bruce remembered him from so long ago. Bruce also found it somewhat ironic that both he and James had brothers named Robert, and they shared a few laughs over that common point.

James gave Robert a call at the station and arranged for Bruce to drive his Ford in for a tune-up before he began his return trip to Seattle. After receiving driving directions from James and bidding his farewells to Katherine, Greglon, and Karena, Bruce embarked on the short drive to Oakland's Chinatown district, where Robert's service station was located. Encountering only a small amount of local traffic congestion, Bruce soon arrived at the Gulf station where Robert greeted him. They were both very happy to see one another again, and Robert was glad that he could assist Bruce by getting his car ready for the return trip to Seattle.

While Robert worked on the automobile, they reminisced about the cha-cha classes that Bruce had taught. Bruce gave a short dance demonstration, to show that he could still perform with the same flair. Between laughing, working on the car, and joking about Robert's need for another dance instructor, the work on the car was finally completed and Bruce was on his way back to Seattle. It had been a delightful and productive trip, to say the least, and Bruce seemed to exude confident exhilaration throughout the long journey home. Even the tiring driving did not seem to have any effect on his jovial mood.

∞

For More Information Contact:

Sid Campbell

2019 Mac Arthur Blvd.

Oakland, California

(510) 530-0241

e-mail: DRAGUN3@aol.com

Web sites

www.SIDCAMPBELL.net

http://members.aol.com/dragun3